4.00

1. Maturing the Spirit

MATURING THE SPIRIT

MATURING
THE
SPIRIT

a continuation of spiritual growth
for contemporary men and women

DOMINIC M. HOFFMAN O.P.

The author of "Beginnings in Spiritual Life"
and "The Life Within"

ST. PAUL EDITIONS

248
HoM

Imprimi potest:
H. F. Ward, OP
PROVINCIAL

Nihil Obstat:
Rev. Msgr. Maurice O'Connor
CENSOR DEPUTATUS

Imprimatur:
Most Rev. Alden J. Bell, D.D.
BISHOP OF SACRAMENTO
January 17, 1973

Library of Congress Catalog Card Number: 73-77628

Copyright, 1973, by the Daughters of St. Paul
Printed in U.S.A. by the Daughters of St. Paul
50 St. Paul's Ave., Boston, Ma. 02130

The Daughters of St. Paul are an international
religious congregation serving the Church
with the communications media.

To
St. Dominic
and to
my Dominican brothers and sisters
in heaven and on earth

In gratitude
for my vocation

CONTENTS

11

Part III: The Life of the Spirit

Part IV: The Gifts of Nature

Part V: Gifts of Grace

Part VI: Advancing in Prayer

INTRODUCTION

The spiritual life, like life itself, presents a distinctive appearance at different stages of growth, while maintaining the essential elements, and much else, of the previous stages. It is life and not a series of airtight containers. Again, like life the most important lessons are those which were learned first, or should have been learned first. The question thus arises as to what this book proposes to explain, a book which intends to lead the whole man farther along the way toward spiritual maturity.

One major reason for this book is the fact that the prayer of the former beginner may be undergoing a basic and perhaps puzzling change. He may need instruction on this if he is not to become confused and discouraged. So this instruction will be given in its proper place in the broader framework of the second general reason for the book, the relationship between nature and grace.

An examination of this relationship is indicated by the name usually given to this intermediate state in the spiritual life, *the illuminative way.* The soul is illumined in the sense that it begins to understand more about itself and the way it is going to God. And, especially after what is called the Dark Night of the Senses, the now-enlightened man no longer has the illusion of being ready for canonization.

The spiritual man takes another look at the mountain which he is climbing. He sees that he has not only to reckon with the unwillingness and rebellion of fallen nature, but that he must deal with nature itself. Perhaps in the first fervor to reach the top of the mountain in one day's journey, he thought to crush nature after the manner of some of the lives of the saints. But now, forced to climb more slowly, he sees that nature is not only a companion for every step of the journey, but also that he can use it instead of futilely trying to eliminate it in the arduous ascent. This is indeed a great light, and one which will principally illuminate his soul during the reading of these pages.

Human nature has been variously interpreted in the history of man, sometimes with more success than others. For our purposes here it is sufficient to consider three of these interpretations, those of Plato, Aristotle, and the Stoics. These are not important to us here because they are prominent figures in the development of the Western mind, but rather because their attempts to find reality are characteristic of good men in general.

Since human nature can be called the roots of the spiritual life, these three concepts of it will affect the way men try to live the gospel message. The basic "spiritualities," the different ways by which we are taught to conform human nature to the gospel or to Christ, are usually the result of diverse conceptions of human nature. While this book is not to be a philosophical study of the spiritual life, an examination of these three attitudes will help us to see clearly the kind of emphasis we will place upon the relationship between nature and grace, as well as the kind of emphasis we will try to avoid.

The approach that is analogus to the philosophy of Plato puts an almost exclusive emphasis on the spirit. The fundamental position of Plato was that the soul is a prisoner in the body. In the Christian era this concept developed into a spirituality in which the body almost did not exist. When it did manifest itself, it had to be subdued, and starvation and beating were acceptable methods for doing this. Under such treatment the spirit was able to emerge— if it was strong enough.

The giants succeeded, but they will always succeed. The tragedy is that they have been put before us as an ideal, sometimes as the only ideal, whereas the disregard for the body is a way only for those who are called to go by that way, that is, for giants. A further weakness of this position can be put as a question: are giants always the closest ones to God? Is it physical endurance and strength of nerves which brings us closest to God, or is it love?

Perhaps we are taking too much liberty with the Stoics to use them as the prototype of the second kind of spirituality, the spirituality that emphasizes the rule. However, these men sought self-perfection by a severe, unrelenting self-discipline character- ized by many wise rules. Transferred to the spiritual life, this discipline produces to a great extent what it sets out to do but the result is the cold, unbending man, not what we would totally agree with after reading the passages on love in St. John's gospel. From this rigidity too, arises the difficulty of being led by the Holy Spirit who not only breathes where he will, but as he will, sometimes about things not covered by strict rule. The human mind cannot codify all the minute and delicate counsels of the spiritual life. To free the spirit from unnecessary burdens upon it is thus one of the purposes of this book.

17

It must not be thought that these two approaches are being rejected totally. There must be a definite emphasis on the spirit; to emphasize the body at the expense of the spirit would not be spirituality but naturalism or even hedonism. Likewise there must also be self-discipline, and there is no discipline at all unless there are some rules. The opposite would result in an ineffectual aimlessness, a pseudo-spirituality of moods and whims.

But there is still the third way of going to God, and it can be called the way of the whole man. This concept recognizes that man is body as well as soul. Freedom of soul is achieved by basic self-discipline but without disregarding what belongs to the body. This attitude is exemplified in the philosophy of Aristotle, particularly as given to us by St. Thomas Aquinas. It emphasizes the spirit but not at the expense of the body (which often ends up at the expense of the spirit). It also includes discipline because human nature does not always give an eager, willing response to the desires of the spirit.

This way of the whole man is more in conformity with the Gospel message because it can more easily become the way of love. It does not beat out or dry up the warmness of human love which is not only a spiritual thing, but something of the emotions and therefore pertaining to the body, to our nervous system, as well. The way of overemphasis on the spirit or on a narrow series of rules can result in a human being from whom a human kind of love has been starved out or ruled out. Usually the human goes out first, but almost of necessity the divine is diminished later.

This essential oneness of human nature seems to have found confirmation in the discoveries of modern experimental psychology and psychiatry. Although the spirituality of the soul does not fall under the competence of those studies and experiments, it is still a universal observation that what happens on the higher level of the mind (or spirit) affects the lower levels of the emotions and organs, and vice versa. Despite some false assumptions and conclusions, these sciences have uncovered a solid residue of truth available for the spiritual life. This truth is not always truth newly discovered (for St. Thomas says many of the same things), but it is put in more specific terms and is supported by clinical evidence. As Fr. Goldbrunner has pointed out, by the awareness of the forces that have caused the unhealthy mind, we can see what it takes to keep health of mind. Health of mind, we need not be told, is a not unimportant item in the spiritual life.

Each age of the world must, in a sense, find its own way to God. Each age is different, and its uniqueness must be seriously considered if the people of that age are to be successful in finding him. Wisely, it will not discard the old, in the delusion that the great minds and rich experience of the past have produced nothing. On the contrary, whatever of the past is permanent and useful it will assimilate with the new aspects of truth which are its own discovery, if it is an age of discovery.

As Christians we must not expect that all discoveries applicable to the spiritual order will have come through dedicated members of the Church. It would be a glowing experience to know that everything in the Church has had Christian inspiration, and that all pertinent discoveries have come about through the wedding of the faith with the human ingenuity of its members. But God has not left us so great a temptation to pride; the humbling truth is often quite otherwise. An excellent example is the greatest of our theologians and philosophers, St. Thomas Aquinas. St. Thomas, of course, received his great inspiration from the faith. But the framework upon which he translated that inspiration into ideas and words came from a pagan, Aristotle. It would have been unreasonable to have prevented him, as some attempted to do, from constructing his magnificient explanation of the word of God in rational terms, merely because the philosophy upon which he built his theology was not Christian in origin.

If we look at a successive age, we can see that the situation is not dissimilar. In the early days of the twentieth century some of the basic discoveries of depth psychology were being made by men who were not Christians or even believers in God. They made some great mistakes, but at the same time they made some great discoveries. At first there was opposition in the Church because of the mistakes, but we have all lived to see many of their ideas accepted, not all of them, not their materialistic, atheistic, or too-narrow background or conclusions, but the undeniable truth that came from very extensive investigations into human nature.

In this book we will not, of course, attempt to specify the page and line of these discoveries as we use them. For a practical book on the spiritual life we will rather draw from them a synthesis, a gathering together of ideas blended with the principles of the Gospel and sound theology, which will give us a deeper knowledge of ourselves as well as a deeper respect for our creator. This can be aptly expressed in the key concept of human and spiritual maturity.

Despite what may appear from the fact that we are including in the spiritual life things that are not directly of the spirit, this is essentially a book designed to make saints. Or rather it is a book to make it possible for people to pass through this intermediate state to one in which great closeness and intimacy with God is real, even when it may not be apparent. Thus it is not a description of a soul in the illuminative way but a practical guide to help it to grow. The basic groundwork is assumed already to have been laid, especially as to the manner of acquiring the virtues. Here we will attempt to show what may well have to happen spiritually, mentally, psychologically, and sometimes even physically, in the making of a saint.

This immaterial and material process is an application of a basic principle of St. Thomas' theology, that grace does not destroy nature but builds upon it. We will see how man must come to terms with his nature, and more specifically with his individual personal nature, in order to advance greatly in grace. In this way we will be formed in him who took upon himself our full nature, body and spirit, to become our way, our truth and our life.

Accepting Christ as our true model, and his grace as our higher life, we will take the necessary steps toward the fullness of union with God which is a union of love.

Part I

The Vision

Chapter 1

The Call

It is not a matter of debate, but a settled principle that God calls all men to spiritual perfection.
In the Sermon on the Mount our Lord was speaking
to a crowd of people, a cross-section of human life.
In teaching them, he is teaching all of us. And his
important words are, "In a word, you must be made
perfect as your heavenly Father is perfect" (Mt.
5:48).

There is, of course, more in this statement than
we first think. It is obvious that we are not told to
be perfect with the perfection of God. Our finite
nature can never be more than finite. But our Lord
is telling us that as God is perfect in his nature, so
we must become perfect in our own. The fact that our
nature in its fallen state cannot achieve its absolute
human perfection in this life is not an argument
against trying, and trying hard. God will give us our
absolute perfection in the next life as a reward comparable to the degree of relative perfection we
achieve in this.

The fact that our Lord addressed these words to a
cross-section of humanity brings up another point,

and for this book an important one. Not all of these men and women were alike in their personalities or their spiritual capabilities. In asking them to become perfect in their own nature as the Father is in his, our Lord was opening the way for an extensive variety of human perfection. Since each person is different, each will have a somewhat different way of being perfect, that is, according to the way each is made, although all will agree in fundamentals.

A thinker, let us say, will not have the exact kind of perfection as a man of action, and he cannot set himself to become perfect in all the details of the man of action, and vice versa. The problem of becoming perfect, of becoming a saint, is thus greatly simplified. We need look to the saints for inspiration, but not necessarily as models when they are hopelessly unattainable or unsuitable models.

God calls us to become saints only within the confines of the possibilities of the particular nature He has given us. This should be an encouragement.

This call to personal diversity in our spiritual development can be put into other terms. According to St. Thomas (*Summa Theologica* I; 63; 9 ad 3) we are destined to take the places of the fallen angels in the various choirs to which they once belonged. But each angel was in his particular place because of the way God made him. And so it is with us. We do not have to strive enormously and fruitlessly to be something we are not, something which would not make us happy even if we could attain it. The call to sanctity is basically a call to be ourselves.

There is another aspect of this call of God and one which must be brought out explicitly. Among the conglomeration of our Lord's listeners there were undoubtedly representatives of a class which, strangely, found his message appealing. These were the sin-

ners. These, no less than the others, our Lord is calling to become perfect. Some of us must be much
better than good to be good at all.

We will see strange people close to God in
heaven. We would, of course, expect to see close to
him certain ones who, we could almost say, were
specifically made for heaven. They are those so well
endowed by nature, the rich personalities, intellectual, often with noble ideals, always with great
talents, sometimes with great beauty or striking
appearance. But we won't see all of these very
close to God. In their places we will see some of the
little people, the forgotten and despised people,
if they too are not also the proud ones. For the admirable proud people our Lord had a warning, "Let
me make it clear that tax collectors and prostitutes
are entering the kingdom of God before you" (Mt.
21:31).

God's determination to have all of us close to him
can be illustrated by the parable of the great supper (Lk. 14:16-24). In the apparatus of the parable
God calls various people successively, although
in fact we are all called simultaneously. First he calls
those who were worthy but unwilling. Their excuses
identify them as the rich ("I have bought some
land"), the workers ("I have bought five yoke of
oxen and I am going out to test them"), and the
lovers ("I am newly married"). Despite their admirable natural qualities, they refused to come. But
this does not discourage God. He now calls those who
are less worthy but willing: "the poor, and the
crippled, the blind and the lame." That should, we
might suppose, include all who are going to be invited. But still there is room, and room for the worst
of us, those who can hardly expect to be invited, from
"the highways and along hedgerows," who know
themselves to be so hopelessly unworthy that they

must be compelled to come in. God means the extent of his call to be unmistakable.

The call to sanctity is not an impossible command, for God is not unfair. One reason that it is not impossible is, as we have seen, that it is a call to be ourselves and not someone else. But there is the other reason also. Sanctity is basically a call to love. Everyone can love. It is true that we are endowed with different capacities for loving, but all of us can love deeply, all can love to the fullest extent of our powers. Thus it is not impossible for each one to become perfect in our way as God, who is perfect love, is perfect in his.

Chapter 2

Invitation to Fuller Life

When our Lord said, "Be perfect," he gave us not only a command but at the same time an invitation. It is an invitation to a fuller life, to greater love. Seen this way, spiritual perfection becomes attractive. But unfortunately some of its other synonyms are occasionally less so. Such a word, and one we must eventually come up against in the spiritual life, is *the saint*.

Words have a power over us, and this one can easily have one of two effects. It can inspire one man with lofty ambition, but it will as surely fill another with fear or aversion. For those whom it inspires we have at present only one word: do not go shopping for a halo. Sanctity is the end result of much growth. We do not attain it at once, much less have we already attained it because we are inspired by it or desire it.

Those whose reaction to the word is different will be helped by an important distinction. We are not talking about canonized saints. These are in various ways proposed to us as ideals, but canonization is not necessarily an ideal. There are several unappealing things about sanctity in such a context. One is that we are immediately filled with thoughts of cruel penances, long hours of prayer on our knees, and our unlikely likeness being cast in plaster with hundreds of candles in front of it. Then too, determining to become such a saint can easily become a work of pride, a kind of external ambition which can interfere with the real sanctity within. Finally, canonization is a matter for God to decide, anyway, as he does through the many intricate ways of men by which canonization is accomplished or not accomplished. Anyhow, it is of minor consequence, for it is quite reasonable to assume that some uncanonized people will be closer to God in heaven than others whose names are prefixed with the word *Saint*. Our aspirations must always be based on the length of eternity rather than the shortness of time.

This closeness to God is what we mean when we speak of sanctity. We are concerned with union with him, principally by means of love. In one sweep, then, we do away with much that discourages us when we compare our poor selves with the great ones. If we conclude that great penances, the power of miracles, or the conversion of whole nations are impossible for us, such an estimation is not a barrier to sanctity. In our day we have the example of St. Thérèse of Lisieux to encourage us, her life so devoid of the extraordinary. But even among the older saints we also have encouragement from St. Thomas Aquinas. The witnesses at the investigation for his canonization could find nothing to testify concerning unusual mortification or ascetical practices.

The fact that these two saints were members of religious orders whose rule of life was relatively severe should not discourage us either. Although sanctity involves some restraints upon nature, mortification is not at the heart of spiritual perfection.

Neither does holiness depend on a host of spiritual exercises and practices. From one point of view, it is the submission to God's will by which we are trustingly pliant in his hands, and willingly allow him to work his likeness in us. From another point of view, holiness is love. The refusal to be a saint is the refusal to love to the full capacity of the love that is in us. If we can love, and love deeply, consistently, and practically, we can by that gift of God, and with his freely offered grace, become saints.

One of the barriers to a desire for sanctity is the note of oddity often attached to it. Saints are pictured for us as men and women of another world. They wore garments of another age, had words and attitudes which do not fit into a modern context. If we were suddenly to decide to strike out strongly in their direction, we would unconsciously fear the ridicule of ourselves as a modern apparition of an other-century image.

But of course the fact is different from the unconscious image we carry around. God wanted thirteenth century saints in the thirteenth century, but the Spirit finds fertile soil in every century and, barring a special or unusual vocation, the saints of an age are contemporaneous to that age, with the good characteristics of that age and sometimes even with its unfortunate defects.

But even if contemporary, still uncomfortable, for who has not heard that it is hard to live with a saint? Or is it? Rather, if hard to live with, do we have a saint? It is more than likely that we have a skin-deep facsimile. Allowing for an occasional exception like St. Jerome, who had enough sense to take his quick temper into seclusion and enough humility to do penance for it, we find that kindness and patience have always been predominant characteristics of the saints. In the detailed investigation before canonization, allowing always for an occasional conflict of personalities, we find the witnesses (always under oath) unanimous in attesting to the cheerfulness and congeniality of the man or woman under scrutiny. Strong testimony to the contrary would undoubtedly stop the process of canonization at once.

Oppositely, it is apt to be the person who cares very little for sanctity who is hard to live with. Selfishness is the antithesis of true holiness, and who would want to live with a selfish person? The saint surely is not envious, avaricious, unfair, or lazy. He is not afraid of hard work, he is responsible, and he can be trusted. To live with the opposite would be difficult. Furthermore, he does not brag, is not trying to keep himself the center of attention; he easily defers to others, though without being weak or ostentatious about it. The non-saint can be sad and discouraged by suffering and reverses, often sensitive to the least pain, fearful, complaining, and despairing. But the saint sees suffering as a privilege, as a sharing in the cross of Christ for his own soul and for the world. Nor will such a strong person be intolerant of the weakness of others. To be a saint he must love us.

Perhaps it is because we confuse sanctity with certain living examples of piety that we have so little stomach for it. An old priest once remarked, "I have always noticed that pious people take good care of themselves." To be merely pious means that there are still in the soul some things not compatible with full giving to God, including the illusion of being much closer to God than is actually true. Piety can be self-centered, but sanctity never. The saint must love neighbor or he could not love God.

The holier-than-thou attitude which is an accusation to the struggling part of humanity is not on the face of the saints. Often they hid their sanctity under lightness of heart and even assumed the role of the jester because they knew people expected the saint always to be somber if not morose.

The saint is happy because he is a realist. He is at home with God and with himself. He is happy principally because he is in love. And when he feels something other than happiness, he usually tries not to show it. He looks upon the difficulties of his life of dedication to God somewhat as do those who love each other and who experience suffering in fulfilling their love, as in hardship or in separation, but who would rather have the suffering than not know the love.

Chapter 3

The Promise

There is one thing about becoming a saint: unless we do, we cannot enter heaven. For it is written, "Nothing profane shall enter it" (Rev. 21:27). The difference is that some are saints at death with little or no defilement and are ready for heaven immediately or almost immediately, while others must be made ready by the perhaps long purification of purgatory. But in the end we are all meant to be saints, not necessarily by canonization, as we have said, but by being worthy to enter into the presence of God.

Perhaps one reason we do not try harder to get to heaven is that we hear so little about it. Perhaps also we have become sophistically ashamed of working for a reward. But in the Sermon on the Mount, our Lord did not think that the idea of reward was beneath him or beneath us: "Store up heavenly treasure.... Remember, where your treasure is, there your heart is also" (Mt. 6:20, 21).

Added to the silence on it, there are so many false ideas on heaven, such as sitting around playing a harp, or so many vague ideas, that we may hesitate to give all for it, as our Lord asks us in the parable of the pearl of great price (Mt. 13:45, 46). So we have a right to ask, "What is heaven like? What will a man find to recompense him for his labors, to fill his soul?"

Will he, for instance, find material treasure, real wealth or riches? If that were it, he would be disappointed because he has seen rich men on earth, unhappy and greedy for more. Will he have power and acclaim? Again he would be disappointed if this were all, for these things never completely filled him on earth. Or physical pleasure, like a real marriage feast (to use our Lord's figure) with endless varieties of food, good wine, and entertainment? These also, he knows, bring surfeit and are unsatisfying. God surely must have more than this waiting if it is to be truly heaven.

When our eyes close in death, we open the vision of our soul into life. We stare wide in ecstacy and love, trembling at what we see before us, yet yearning for it, desiring it more than we have desired anything or anyone on earth. We reach out to God to rest in love forever.

This embrace of God, this possession of him is possible through what we call the beatific vision, the vision of the blessed. St. Paul calls it seeing him "face to face," and knowing "even as I am known" (1 Cor. 13:12). In this life we see principally by faith, and always in an obscure manner, but then, as he is.

Now we must not expect that this description or any description will enable us to understand what it means to be with God. The reason for this is that we cannot, on earth especially, begin to comprehend God. We know him through his works, also by what he tells us of himself in the Scriptures, and we see him reflected, best of all, through the human nature of the God-man, Jesus Christ. But none of this is the same as the enraptured vision in heaven.

We can put this another way. We cannot expect fully to understand heaven because we cannot fully understand love. Even human love defies analysis; we break it down to its definition and we find that the definition is inadequate to describe what we feel. But we know that it is the most fulfilling thing in our nature, in our lives, and that we cannot be happy without it. It is this mysterious thing that we would have to understand before we could begin to understand heaven.

There with our unclouded vision we will see God for what he is, so many things all at once. Unfathomable love, unalloyed good, the truth itself, wordless beauty are only a beginning of the infinite variety to which our minds will be drawn in the unity of God. Just as on earth where we love what is lovable, good, true, and beautiful of his creation, so much more impellingly will we go out to him whose reality is only faintly mirrored in even the best of the things he has made. This is a basic reason why we will never get tired of heaven, because we will never get tired of God. We can never get tired of the love of a being which endlessly has the power to draw forth more and more love and admiration from us.

On earth we have glimpses of what heaven must be like. One way is the deep love that is given to two human beings who love each other. We often say that they were made for each other because their minds, hearts, and lives melt into those of the other so that there are hardly two but rather one. This experience of what is the ultimate human reality, this experience always temporary, often frustrated, sometimes betrayed, is something of what we shall have with God, endlessly and completely.

There is another glimpse we have of heaven, and we shall say more about it later when we speak of prayer. Perhaps all of us have known moments of peace in God, when we knew he was near, perhaps when we waited for services to start, perhaps when praying at night or lying awake, perhaps even when we weren't doing anything particularly religious at all. At that moment we did not need to be told that God was everywhere or that he was within us. In the moment of his presence we did not need anything else but him. Heaven is this moment prolonged forever, with the peace and love immeasurably magnified.

To be there with God is our first vocation; it is the essence of the call to the wedding feast. Blessed are those who are called and come. Blessed those whom God seeks out and who come. Blessed those who are forced to come and come prepared. As long as we come. As long as we come, leaving behind our sins, our broken and disappointed hopes, and come to him where the restless yearnings of our hearts will be filled forever, as they only can in the arms of the one who is waiting.

It would seem that in giving us himself as our reward, God had done all that even he could do to reward us. But he does not forget our nature even in heaven. The vision of himself fulfills the deepest part of our nature but not our whole nature. He is determined to give us not only an everlasting happiness but also a complete happiness. We would expect this thoughtfulness and generosity of God for it is proper to infinite goodness to be endlessly good to us. And so we expect a reward which is "good measure, pressed down, shaken together, running over" (Lk. 6:38).

These secondary or human joys of heaven do not interfere with the principal one; in heaven all things are in harmony and order. There was once a man who saw heaven, and although he was a powerful writer, he was able to speak about it only in negative terms. "Eye has not seen, ear has not heard, nor has it so much as dawned on man what God has prepared for those who love him" (1 Cor. 2:9). St. Paul is telling us that heaven is beyond description, beyond imagining.

In order for our happiness to be complete, it must affect our minds, our hearts, and our bodies. We will discuss each in order.

Our minds will be satisfied, first of all, by God himself. Truth is the joy of our intellect, and God is eminently that. But our thirst for created knowledge will be satisfied also, God never forgetting that our minds were formed to find their natural fulfillment through and in created things. Therefore, not only the questions of religion, but also those of science, of history, and even more personally, the questions arising from the mystery that is our own life — for all these God will have the answer, the truth. To the ever-questing mind of man such complete revelation is not an inconsiderably joyous prospect.

Then, although he who is all-goodness and can satisfy by himself the one basic thirst of our will, the thirst for the good, he still will leave none of the desires of our heart unfulfilled. But here we have to make a necessary distinction. The desires which we will have in heaven will not all be the same as those we may have now. A little girl, for instance, may tell us that she wants her doll in heaven. But our desires will be fulfilled, not all of them as they are now, but all of them as they will exist *then*. The most characteristic element in our desires will be their orderliness. Beyond that we cannot say much, except that we will have outgrown many of the desires we had on earth, much as grown-up little girls no longer must have dolls.

But although, as St. Paul intimates, there will be things in heaven to delight the eye and the ear, the most important human hold on our heart will be the people there. Some discussions of heaven seem almost to be contemptuous of the human side of heaven as beneath the attention of one who will have God. We will, they say, be as little aware of others as we would of a candle flame in the bright sunlight. But the incongruity of such inhumanness is shown at once by the fact that they would thus have to neglect the humanity of Christ, and that the company of the Blessed Virgin and all the angels and saints would be negligible too. But if these are not negligible (and they are not: St. Teresa never got over the memory of a vision of the humanity of Christ, and St. Bernadette did not feel a candle flame touching her when she saw the Lady at Lourdes), then the presence of our loved ones will not be negligible either.

It is a part of the orderliness of the benign justice of God that those who were our companions on earth in the struggles for salvation should also be the companions of our glorification. But there will be an important difference: all the things which separate man from man, all the defects of character and personality which make our lives difficult or tedious will be taken away. Each man and woman will be in personal perfection such as no one, for instance, could have imagined husband or wife to be even in the blinding glow of early marriage. Our loved ones will be even more perfect than we had ever dreamed, and here they are, not a dream, and forever.

But God has, besides justice, a particular mercy in the human companionship of heaven. Many of our relationships on earth are not as close as family relationships. Some of these must be fenced around with necessary restrictions, or suffer separations of distance or social barriers, or are pruned off immaturely by death. For those who go through life with half-filled hearts or empty hearts God can be said to have a special heaven waiting. This is another reason why we must understand love before we can begin to understand heaven.

Much of God's reward is paid in the very things we had to give up on earth or in which we were tempted to betray him. This is especially true of our bodies. On earth we had the words of St. Paul to encourage us: "I consider the suffering of the present to be as nothing compared with the glory to be revealed in us" (Rom. 8:18). But in heaven we will rejoice in the truth of it. "This corruptible body must be clothed with incorruptibility, this mortal body with immortality" (1 Cor. 15:53).

The precise nature of this joyful reunion of soul and body is outlined clearly in the Scriptures. And what our reason can further deduce from the Scriptures is admirably set down by St. Thomas (Suppl. qq. 75 and 79-85). The basic principle is that our bodies will be like Christ's risen body. "We know that when it comes to light [at the Second Coming], we shall be like him" (1 John 3:2). "As you well know, we have our citizenship in heaven; it is from there that we eagerly await the coming of our Savior, the Lord Jesus Christ. He will give a new form to this lowly body of ours and remake it according to the pattern of his glorified body, by his power to subject everything to himself" (Phil. 3:20, 21). Thus these bodies which we will have laid down in the deterioration of disease or old age, these bodies with their natural and accumulated defects, will arise in perfect integrity, in beauty, and in everlasting possession of the almost divine thing called youth. They will have another quality which our Lord showed at his transfiguration but chose not to assume on earth after his resurrection. This he promised us: "The saints will shine like the sun in their Father's kingdom" (Mt. 13:43).

If we are interested in reason as well as the Scripture, we can attribute the qualities of the risen body, not to direct control and movement by God, but to the predominance of the soul over the body. Thus we must understand St. Paul when he calls it a "spiritual body" (1 Cor. 15:33ff.). But it will still be a body. There will be the diversity of the sexes; we will still, consolingly, be men and women; we will see each other without shame or passion, and there will be no sexual functions (Mt. 22:30). Like our Lord's body we will be able to pass through what we call solid material as he passed through the closed doors to the upper room on the first Easter. We will be able to travel distance in a minimal time as he went back the seven miles from Emmaus to Jerusalem before the two hurrying disciples reached it the same evening. In every moment the body will feel an intense emotional joy, principally because of the overflow of joy from the soul, but also because of its own perfections and all that it sees and hears in this blessed eternity.

Heaven will be an eternity of peace, of rest from suffering, sorrow, and pain. We have God's word on that too: "He shall wipe every tear from their eyes, and there shall be no more death or mourning, crying out or pain, for the former world has passed away" (Rev. 21:4).

Chapter 4

The Response

Our point of view in heaven will be different from what it was on earth, and we can acquire some of that insight now. Many of us are content with the hope of purgatory. We take it for granted that we will have a prolonged stay there because we aren't working very hard to avoid it. We depend on the prayers which we trust will be said for us after death rather than on the strong efforts we can be making now.

There are two things against a purgatorian spirituality. One is that purgatory hurts. If we look at the difficulties of the purification whereby men do become saints in this life, we can have little doubt about the pain of purification in the next world. The second thing against waiting is that purgatory does relatively little good. It just cleans us up for heaven. While this in itself is an enormous thing, the delinquent soul is the loser all the same. We cannot merit even one little bit of additional reward or love from **God** by all this suffering. Despite the intensity, the soul is no closer to God in love and friendship; it is simply paying off its debts. Increase of merit, so as to receive greater love and closeness to God, is possible only in time and not in eternity. A practical question, therefore, is: why lose by waiting?

In the moment of judgment we will give an agonized look backward. How many things would we want to change! But then too late. We will be somewhat like an unhappily married woman who *now* would much rather that she had been parted before marriage, by force if necessary, from the man she loved so much then. Our point of view in eternity will be different, and our lives here will be different if we can lengthen our short-sightedness.

Besides the contentment with purgatory, there is another other-world obstacle to sanctity, and that is the truth that we will all be perfectly happy in heaven. All of us, from the Blessed Virgin down to the poor fellow who just got inside the door, will be filled with happiness just as a large reservoir and a small glass can both be filled with water so that they can hold no more. And so we reason: why try very hard? We can hope for perfect happiness even if we are no more than normally good, even as the man who just got inside. We feel a comfortable oneness with this man, until we realize his status. Of all the people in heaven he is the least loved by God and he loves God the least...and this forever.

We can surely imagine that the man is so happy to be there at all that he is content with this minimum; to be the least inside is an infinitely happier fate than to be the first outside. But we who still have the option of higher and lower, of nearer to God or farther, of more or less love between ourselves and God, should we be as content? On earth we constantly desire to improve our condition of life, and we ought always to improve our love and friendship with others who are worthy of it. Why not also, and even more, for eternity?

It is clear that there are various degrees in the sharing of God's love in heaven. Our Lord speaks of those who are like children, being the greater in the kingdom of heaven (Mt. 18:4). But if some are greater, then also others will be less. St. Paul says that we will be different like the stars, "Even among the stars, one differs from another in brightness" (1 Cor. 15:41). But what essentially makes us closer to God in heaven? Not intelligence, education, culture, or wealth. Basically it depends on love, on the deep love-relationship between God and ourselves as we leave this life.

Of course, many other things besides love must also be considered. The reference of our Lord to the children specifically mentions the humble trust that a child will give to a wise and loving parent. Likewise can we not also infer sinlessness and many other good qualities of children? But are not all these the fruits of love? We are also told that our good works will follow us (Rev. 14:13), and that we will be rewarded accordingly. But our good works have value not so much by the measure of what we do or how much we give, but because of the intention or the love with which we do them.

By love we do not necessarily mean an emotional love, nor do we need to think of God every time we do something in order for it to be meritorious. It is rather the habitual love that is deep in our souls, not always love that is felt. It is the same as our relations with our friends; their words or actions mean more to us than those of another, even though the friend is not here and now conscious of his love for us.

Since our closeness to God forever depends on our closeness to him in love here on earth, the only reasonable course is to love him as much as we can. This does not mean to force acts of emotional intensity, but rather to have oneness of will with him in all things, especially those that are difficult. It also means to remove the impediments to greater love. Many of these may already have been removed; mortal sin may now not be a major problem, nor perhaps even venial sin. But there are other impediments not so well recognized: too much attachment to ourselves, to our own way of doing things, to the opinions and to the things of the world. God is often crowded out of our lives or at least put in a carefully circumscribed corner. Too many voices are listened to, and so we cannot hear him. But more of this later.

The point now is to begin to love God greatly. But how do we love God greatly? A very elementary answer is another question: how do we get to do anything well? We practice it. In order to practice love, we don't need a stack of prayer books, we don't need the vocabulary of a poet, we don't even have to spend hours of time in church. All we need to do is to tell him of our love and tell him very much, to want his will very much, and to try to follow it very much. And certainly to ask for this very much. The formula for sanctity is neither secret nor complicated. It is as elementary as love.

Sanctity is often opposed by the excuse that we are too busy; we have to work. We sometimes think it is only for the professionals, that is, for priests, brothers, and sisters, or for the poor who haven't much else. But of course this isn't true. Love is not limited to any class or impeded by any condition of life. Therefore the old, the young, the poor, and even the rich can become saints because all can love.

The proof is that there have been saints from all classes, from all conditions of mankind. For instance, St. Louis was a married man, a father, a rich man. He had to rule a kingdom and go on crusades. Yet despite his involvement with this world, he is a saint.

"But my health!" Was there ever a healthy saint? The conclusion is that, since these people were mortal flesh and blood, our mortal flesh and blood can do it too.

But we should not try to face all the obstacles at once. Sanctity is as simple as growth, usually a little at a time, and sometimes we will be tempted to become discouraged because there has been so little growth in so much time. Yet as long as we put God in first place and keep him there, if we want his will first, very much first, then though it be the plodding work of a lifetime, ordinary people like you and me will wake up some day into eternity and find ourselves in the arms of God, very much loved—and saints.

We sometimes hear people vacantly ask, "Why are there no saints today?" There are, as succeeding ages will uncover. But instead of waiting for the answer of the future, there is instead a practical answer, more important to God and to me; it is that I decide to become a saint today.

Part II

Spiritual Maturity and the Self

Chapter 5

The Problem: The Many Roads

If it were not too discouraging a thing to say, we could begin the next step in our consideration of sanctity by saying that there are many ways to get off the right road in the spiritual life but only one way to stay on. In one sense there hardly seems to be a problem. We go to Mass, receive the sacraments, spend a certain time in prayer, we keep the commandments, and we do our work. By this, we are told, we can reach sanctity. And since these means apply to everybody, it therefore seems that everybody can become a saint by going the same road.

There are two difficulties with such a generalization. One is that these means are more like a compass than a road. They are not specific enough to tell us which road to take of the many we will find before us, and they leave us to travel long distances without any further directives.

This inadequacy is emphasized by the second defect of having one road for all. We are not a faceless army marching with as little individuality as if we were toy soldiers cast from the same mold. We

49

are all individuals, each of us different in the make-up of personality even more than we are in our external appearance.

Now of course we all know this. We deal with individual differences every day in both adults and children, even very small children. But still it is strangely true that in the spiritual life people expect that there is only one way to God, either by doing everything the way everybody else does, or by following narrowly the advice set down in one book, or by slavishly imitating some pre-chosen model such as a canonized saint.

What we are saying is not to deny the value of the general means of sanctification, or of wise counsel found in books, or the imitation of the saints. Especially for beginners the docile acceptance of books of good repute and the rather close imitation of the saints who can be prudently imitated has much to recommend it. But there comes a time when we are now very certain of the general direction, but find ourselves uncertain about the particular roads confronting us on our journey, or we find ourselves increasingly overburdened.

It is possible that we have forgotten that our individuality comes from God, as the result of his creation and his providence. Therefore not only our individual temperament is his work, but also the countless influences of our background have been arranged, or at least permitted, to bring about the result that we are now. We should not expect then that God through grace will do the opposite of what God through nature has taken so many pains to accomplish. Grace, we will keep repeating, builds upon nature but does not destroy it. So we should rather expect that grace will help us keep our individuality, while conforming us to the general pattern of human and spiritual life. For grace, like ordered nature, produces indeed individuality, but not the cult of self-glorifying individualism.

All this becomes clear when we look at ourselves from what we may reverently consider to be God's point of view. We know that he has made us because of love, to share his happiness. But he also made us to manifest or reflect his own perfections. This is one way of giving external glory to this one self-sufficient Being from whom all of creation must be derived as from an infinitely surpassing source and model.

Now no one thing can manifest all the perfections of God, even in the restricted sense that a creature can manifest them. This is the reason that nature is broken up into parts. The mountains tell us one thing about God, the ocean another, and the rebirth of spring still another. Yet all these things will pass away. What will not pass away is his human creation. In the eternal glory which we will give him, his perfections are meant to be reflected. And since none of us can come close to reflecting them all with equal emphasis, we must expect that he means us to be different.

There is an old saying that there is no argument against a fact. We have to accept it just because it is there. And the fact is that the most spiritually successful of us, the saints, have by no means been carbon copies of one another. We do not confuse the singing spirit of St. Francis of Assisi with another man who also wrote songs, the quiet, yet determined St. Thomas Aquinas. Even when the names of saints are similar, we know we have two greatly different persons, as in St. Teresa of Avila and St. Thérèse of Lisieux. Evidently, as we said earlier, one of the conditions for becoming saints is that we become ourselves.

We can assume, then, that God does not intend all of us to be alike, and that there is a generally

recognized necessity to draw roads on the map leading to union with God. But what happens when the
mapmakers try to draw in the roads to fit individual
spiritual lives, when they try to bring down to practice the broad principles of the spiritual life? The
result is, in a sense, unfortunate, not because of an
insufficiency of advice or even because of occasional
poor advice, but rather because of the very wealth of
advice.

The spiritual man is met by an unbelievable on-
rush and confusing diversity of spiritual attitudes,
counsels, practices, and devotions. He gets this ava-
lanche from books, sermons, retreat masters, and
friends. There is no way to stop it; in fact (within
reasonable limits) there is no reason to stop it. All
this spiritual diversity represents the spiritual diversity of its authors, and most of it fits somewhere into
the spiritual pattern of some of those who read it or
hear it. Each is promoting what seems vital or important to him, and it will probably be vital or important to some of those it reaches. We will avoid
much confusion and even discouragement if we view
the problem in this light, rather than thinking that
God is sending each one of these counselors as a
personal prophet to us, or thinking that he wants us
all to absorb and live by this often contradictory and
indigestible mass.

The failure to recognize that God wills diversity
in the spiritual life can cause both confusion and
discouragement. We often read a book or hear a talk
or meet persons who are enthusiastically pushing a
particular way to God. Their enthusiasm or their
authority makes it seem that anyone who does not
respond with the same enthusiasm, and forthwith
adopt the attitude, practice, or devotion, is less than
fit for close union with God. And this is discouraging.
But even worse, sometimes other urgings come from

equally enthusiastic or respected sources, but with a message that seems to be contradictory. At least the confused man sees that it will be difficult to go both ways.

The difficulty largely disappears when we hold fast to the basic principle of our creation, that we are made to go to God by a way suitable to our status as individuals, though always keeping to the general broad pattern. We emphasize what is our own bent, while probably also keeping something of many or even most of the other ways in a subordinate but reasonably fulfilled manner. Thus the man who is filled with a personal love for Christ will not neglect a love for Mary. Our individuality ought not to make us one-sided.

At the risk of some repetition let us look at some practical situations. We can be drawn to God *principally* by love, by service of others, by a deep sense of duty, or by our needs, and so on. Although these are not mutually exclusive, and although all these qualities make up a balanced spiritual life, one person will tend to be drawn by one more than by another. Similarly, one man will make his way to God with an emphasis on theology, another on the liturgy, whereas a third may find him in relative simplicity. As to devotions (if this word is not too poor a name for some of them), one man will find an attraction to the sufferings of Christ, another to the Blessed Sacrament, another to the Blessed Virgin, while still another is full of the presence of God. Many times we feel inferior because we cannot produce a crescendo of devotion to all of these and to others innumerable. But if we feel inferior in this basic sense, we are stopping or slowing up on our journey to God.

It is one of the glorious things about the Church that she is big enough to include all these attitudes, methods, and ways to God. She insists only on what is basic, but recommends warmly many other things, not to be considered as binding on all, but put before us for our choice as we are moved by divine instinct. It is the unwise and blindly enthusiastic man who peddles his own way to God as if it were the only way. Sometimes under the guise of freedom or renewal (his own brand of freedom and renewal) he would even tear everything else from the lives of the people of God. But this is not the way of the Church of God and, as we have seen, it is not the way of God either.

But in establishing this principle, we have said nothing about the way to find our road and to distinguish this road from the many others. To this we will now turn our attention.

Chapter 6

The Light Within Us

There are two ways in which we can find our personal way to God, or our personal vocation, to use another name. One is by looking at God, so to speak, and the other is looking at ourselves. In this chapter we will spend some time on the first, on looking to God for information about our way to him. This is not so much a call to illuminism as it may sound.

God truly guides us, even at times when we are far from him, but he seldom does it by any direct manifestation. Most often he guides us through his revealed word and through the Church which he established to teach us that word authentically. But this teaching, though indispensable, is too general for all situations. On the other hand, if the Scriptures and the Church were more specific, they would crush our personality and vitality by infinitesimal details or an infinite variety of rules to govern all possible cases. So the Church commands little and recommends much.

Such general information is like a signpost pointing toward the city. To find the exact house, we need to know the street and address. We need another light,

55

and this light has been given us by God. It is the light of reason, or common sense, if you will. When the light of reason is well developed, we give it the name of a virtue, the virtue of prudence. God ordinarily guides us by this virtue. Because our reasoning can be defective, and because we can distort its light by rationalization to get what we want, we have much need that God will thus guide our thinking.

Now, even though in some spiritual books, there seems to be prejudice against reason, we have only two other choices, neither adequate for our daily needs. One is that we be inspired directly by God in everything we do. This, besides being a colossus of pride, is open to much delusion and is justly condemned as illuminism. People who are like this presume that grace is always going to work without nature as it did for St. Paul at Damascus. But after Damascus even a St. Paul went into seclusion in the desert where the supernatural could be integrated into the natural.

The other choice is to become subject to another person; spiritual direction is a good example of this. But here we still have reason, another person's reason, operating anyway—with God's help, let us always presume—but human reason all the same. Besides, even though direction and guidance are important for every one of us, we must not become so dependent as to abdicate our responsibility of operating as a human being. Human nature involves the extensive use of reason. If we fail to develop as a human being, we will risk also failing as a spiritual being.

Guided by God through our reason or common sense, we can make many of the choices which will help us find our own way to him. Some of these choices are directly discernible by our reason. A man with a large family, for instance, cannot expect the ravens to feed them as they fed one of the prophets. A sister whose superiors wish her to teach cannot perform penances which deprive her of her ability to teach efficiently. If the spiritual life is not to find its death in the hot sands of emotional enthusiasm, it will need the quiet power of reason as the hand by which God will ordinarily guide it.

Our reason is greatly aided by our own experience and often also by the experience of others. We have known a certain course of action to succeed or to fail, to be a help or a hindrance. This experience, like reason itself, is not infallible, yet it is often a guidepost or a warning sign written in large letters which God puts along the way. And it is sometimes the only sign he places in a given situation.

The use of reason based on experience or on solid principles can help us to find many, if not most, of the roads down which God wants us to turn. Most, but not all. There are choices which are not always possible of solutions by reason. A familiar one is the choice of vocation to marriage or to religious life. Reason may make this decision for many people, and it surely will help all. But there are often excellent considerations on both sides. So in many cases the decision will depend on something else. This help is likely to be the Holy Spirit operating in the soul through the gift of counsel. This is, of course, one of the seven gifts of the Holy Spirit which are in our souls when we are in the state of grace, but which operate only rarely in the earlier stages of the spiritual life.

When with God's help we use our reason, we are operating in a human manner, and sometimes with great effort and perplexity. On the other hand, in receiving help through the gift of counsel, we operate in a somewhat divine manner. We understand simply and easily what God wants. This help is not usually given by voice or by vision, but it does not rule out human help either. We may find a solution to a difficulty in a book or we may receive advice or do a lot of thinking about the problem ourselves, all toward a satisfactory answer. But the difference between the merely human, or even the human with God's help, and the gift of counsel is the deep and abiding sense of assurance that this choice is the will of God.

Now, of course, the fact that God is willing on some occasions to help us directly opens the possibility of self-deception. In important matters, therefore, it is well to submit the decision to wise counsel. When none is available, and in minor matters not important enough for seeking counsel (such as may be the choice of a book for spiritual reading), we can first of all examine the choice to see if it is in accordance with the faith or the practice of the Church. We can also see whether it conforms to the vocation in which God has already placed us, thus involving us in the ideals and duties of that state. But once we have given due consideration, we should proceed circumspectly but without delay, unless of course delay is a part of our considered decision.

There is an area, however, in which we can prudently presume the working of the Holy Spirit, and this has to do with our more direct relationship to God. Just as with natural talents where one person will have a bent toward mechanical things, and another to more intellectual things, so in the spiritual life we find that we are attracted to one way of going to God rather than another. Thus, as we have said earlier, we will find ourselves attracted differently: to the Blessed Sacrament, to the presence of God, to the suffering Christ, to the Blessed Virgin, and so on. Under another aspect we will find our mainspring to be love of God, service to neighbor, a deep sense of duty, or something similar. The presumption is that these predominant attractions come from God, not perhaps so much by direct inspiration as by the

way we are made. And as God has made us, we must
also make ourselves. To do otherwise is to risk failure,
not to mention unhappiness and frustration.

This inner bent, it must be noted, does not always
apply to external things as to things of the inner
soul. For instance, a man will not absent himself from
the family rosary just because he is drawn more to the
Blessed Sacrament. Furthermore, it must also be
understood that this attraction is a *principal* force
within us. For example, we do not neglect the Blessed
Sacrament because we find more consolation in God's
presence in solitude. But on the other hand, always
to do the opposite, to think that we must be before
the Blessed Sacrament when the inclination is to
solitude, would damage the delicate machinery
by which we are made to operate. Of course, the
duties of our state in life will often be a barrier
to the complete fulfillment of our inclinations. But
these duties and the ideals that inspire them are
more clearly a manifestation of God's will than a
vision would be. Thus, our inclinations must sometimes find a higher fulfillment by being impeded
and then offered to God as a sacrifice for the various
needs of the Church as a whole and of ourselves
and those close to us.

A difficulty in finding our way to God can come,
strangely, from spiritual direction. Direction which
is not according to our inner drawing is likely to
become spiritual strangulation. This can happen,
not only when one is drawn in an extraordinary
manner, as St. Teresa who was almost driven out
of her mind by direction which told her that her
visions were illusions of the devil, but it can also
happen when one is drawn by quite ordinary ways.
It can come from a director who is determined to
avoid any possible difficulty by suppressing anything he hasn't experienced himself or which he

doesn't understand. Or it may be that he is filled with his own particular enthusiasm and tries to force it on subjects who are drawn by a different way.

Thus we have people who are drawn to a more interior way to God who are pushed out into a raging torrent where the liturgy is everything and the interior life is nothing. Or we have a man desperately trying to get a hold on intimacy with God who is pushed into exhausting and bewildering forms of the apostolate. Such direction is worse than none and it should be abandoned, even as St. Thérèse of Lisieux ignored the priest who told her that her simple way to union with God was an illusion.

In this middle stage of the spiritual life spiritual direction, if one is fortunate enough to find it, is usually more permissive or passive on the part of the director than it was earlier. Not all beginners are typical, but a typical beginner must leave off bad habits and make good ones. He has to be counselled about the sacraments and a bit about prayer. All this is counselled with relative ease. But as we grow in spiritual life, the differences of one soul from another become more apparent, and the Holy Spirit will take a more active part in the guidance. (In all direction he is the principal director anyway.) The attitudes and inspirations which the soul now receives are usually from him. The role of the director then becomes principally to reassure the soul that this is so, or sometimes to advise caution, or more rarely to oppose and forbid.

We should beware, at this stage, of the director who has a definite, narrow program of the spiritual life which he is trying to impose on all. Sometimes the same priest who was very successful in the earlier stages is now incapable of the delicate discernment of the wishes of the Holy Spirit. Although a director is not without his insights as to the path the soul must take, *most* of the working of the Holy Spirit in regard to the soul, he must never forget, will come directly to the soul itself.

As is easily seen, people who cannot find a director may be saved many troubles. We must not, therefore, too violently insist on being guided the way the textbooks say, by human assistance, insisting to the extent that we give up our serious efforts because no such habitual help is available. Bad direction is worse than none, and although all need direction at times, not all of us need a director. A good director is a real grace but not an indispensable one. In the providence of God occasional direction will always be made possible when needed. This book is written especially for those whose way to God may be spiritually a lonely one.

Now, having seen how God shows us the spiritual path he has chosen for us, we turn to the other way in which we can see his plan for us, and that is by looking at ourselves. We all can have a growing experience of what we are. What we are is also a road map for our way to God.

Chapter 7

The True Self

Barring some unlikely revelation from God, or an extraordinary exercise of his providence, we cannot find our road to him unless we know ourselves. A surgeon may very well be filled with a desire to bring us perfect health, but he will do poorly unless he knows, not only general anatomy, but also our particular distress, its area, and its symptoms. But even such an example is misleading for our purposes here.

Self-knowledge is a commonplace in the spiritual life, and yet it does not always carry a meaning deep or broad enough for it to have its full potential effect in helping us. Most often it is merely a search for our faults and for the reasons we commit them. This is, of course, important throughout the spiritual life, especially at the beginning. But it can give only incomplete results, and these may even thwart further advancement.

Even when such negative self-examination is not carried to an extreme, as it is by those whose spiritual life seems to consist in a perpetual examination of conscience, it can easily bring about discouragement and even despair. We see ourselves too full of defects to have much hope, and unconsciously try rather to keep God at a distance than to press on for his embrace. To avoid this, we must have not only a knowledge of our poorer side but also a knowledge of the things in which we are rich. By this is not meant only something so relatively extrinsic as opposing our bad actions by our good ones, or our failures by our successes, but a deeper knowledge which sees not only the basic defects of our particular nature but also the strong points which indicate our full potentiality. In short we must seek a knowledge of the whole self.

This full potentiality is what we will call the true self, what we can be in our strong points, though not ignoring their limitations. To find the true self, our limitations are, in a sense, as important as our strong points. We are limited, not only by the lack resulting from our own faults, but even more basically by what we lack through the design of God. The real self is what we really are, what God made us to become.

Some of us will see too rigid a determinism in this concept of being limited by the design of God in spiritual matters or in matters of personality development. We would rather think that we are endlessly perfectible on all fronts. We are told to be "creative," as if we could create our personality and our spiritual way out of unformed physical and psychical material. But a bit of humble thinking will show us that we are limited in our possibilities of development; we can develop only what we are. Or to put it in a theological concept, we can develop only what we have been given by God to develop.

For example, we are all familiar with differences in intelligence, in athletic ability, or in leadership. We all have certain gifts along these lines, but we also have certain limitations beyond which we cannot go. A gifted athlete will always be able to do more with the same amount of trying than someone else who lacks his remarkable co-ordination. And also, most of us have come upon people who are educated beyond their native ability. They have imposing degrees and they teach in schools of higher learning, but the students are soon aware that no amount of education will produce what is lacking by nature. St. Paul is fond of telling us that the Spirit bestows various gifts for the building up of the Church. This same variation, nature and grace working together, is true of each one of us in our spiritual potentiality. By the laws of self-perfection contained in our nature and in God's command of perfection, we are bound to find out our potentialities and our limitations. True creativeness then seeks to build a harmonious whole out of this specific raw material.

It is during this intermediate period in the spiritual life that a person begins to receive these deep insights into himself or herself. This period is comparable to another in the natural order of things, in which a similar kind of self-knowledge of the whole man brings about human maturity. And just as this kind of maturity does not necessarily come with the passage of years, neither does spiritual maturity necessarily come with years of sacraments, prayer, reading, and mortification. Quite certainly, spiritual maturity and human maturity will increase together. Then, perhaps slowly over the years, we get to know our way to God by finding out who we are, or as it is said, by finding ourselves. And if we do not find ourselves, whom do we find?

Sometimes we hear of people who fall away from the spiritual life, even give up the practice of religion, after a number of years in which they were considered to be more than ordinarily devout. A number of reasons may have brought this about, but surely among them was a false foundation. They did

not build a spiritual life on what they were themselves but on some imaginary picture of themselves,
even on too slavish an identification with some saint.
A great amount of intellectual and spiritual pride
may have been there, but also a false principle: trying to be what they were not.

Or we see others who may even have the reputa-
tion of being saints. We observe them, not in church
or in the security of their own mutually congratulatory
little group, but in some misfortune, adversity, or
unusual tension. How quickly the pious phrases and
attitudes desert them! How pathetically selfish and
demanding they become! What loads of self-pity do
they pour out on others! We perhaps expect this of
those who have lived an openly worldly or selfish
life, but not from those who have been following
Christ closely. Or have they? Have they not rather
been following some self-made image of what they
would like to think they are? Unfortunately, in time
of stress this will not support them.

We have an authentic example of finding one's
self and finding one's way, in the case of St. Thérèse
of Lisieux. Perhaps some of us are not drawn to her
because of her style of writing, and that cannot be
helped for she was a child of her times as we are
children of our own. But let us look at her accomplishment. Despite the chances against it, she found
herself and she found her way.

As a Carmelite she could have determined to become another Teresa of Avila, and of course would
have failed. As one who often read St. John of the
Cross, she could have taken him in the exaggerated
severity in which he is often understood, but it would
have killed her spirit. Or she could have been wafted
along in the formalized sentimentality of much of
the spirituality of her age and which, our colder age
would say, left some of its mark upon her style. But

5. *Maturing the Spirit*

she had no stomach for it. Instead she cut through the artificiality and formalism, and found instead the true core of the gospel message — to some degree, perhaps, buried for centuries. This personal way, she found, was one of love and trust, and of doing the small things which God puts into our hands instead of fruitlessly waiting for the grand occasions which never come.

The Church has recognized the creative genius of this flower that died before it could have been expected to blossom, and it has decided that this personal way of St. Thérèse was not only the way for Thérèse, but that it is a basic part of the way for all of us.

There is a further important point about her. Anyone who writes on the subject of the personal vocation or way to God ought to have a fear of distortion of his words by the thoughtless, the rebels, or the one-sided near-fanatics. How easy to distort such a simple and reasonable concept into slogans and weapons to use against legitimate authority! But such people cannot ever find themselves because they lack the insight of humility to see themselves as they are. Their self-will and their self-assured enthusiasms ever prevent this. Contrary to their failure, St. Thérèse achieved her immortal work by obedience under great difficulty and suffering. Only by these ways can the blindness be reduced so that we can come to terms with God by seeing our true selves.

The road to sanctity is never without its obstacles. On one hand those who must continually struggle with sin are disheartened by this truth of weakness they see in themselves. On the other hand those who have successfully won this battle are secretly besieged by pride and self-sufficiency in many forms. In some ways it is harder for them to be themselves than it is for the sinner. Their very success can induce them to fancy they are what they are not and never can become. But God the creator when he becomes God the judge will not ask them why they are not St. Thérèse or St. Francis Xavier, St. Vincent de Paul or St. Catherine of Siena. He is going to ask each of them why he is not the person he made him to be, with the perfection which belongs to that person.

In order not to get lost in these attractive but dead end roads, we are now going to explore some of them.

Chapter 8

The Flight from Reality

In the spiritual life we can spend great amounts of time in meditation and in examining ourselves, and yet never reach below the surface. We conclude: I am impatient, or I am sensitive, or something equally an effect rather than a cause. We do not come into contact with the real problem: what are the obstacles to God's grace, or rather, what are the barriers we have built so that grace is either kept out or reduced to a small trickle?

If we do not get below the surface at all, we are apt to end up by saying that the basic fault is pride. This, of course, is accurate both theologically and psychologically. But pride does not work in a vacuum. It sends its roots into the different parts of our human nature...or better, it uses the different parts of our human nature to keep the self supreme at no matter what cost.

This cost can be high. It is often paid for by a separation from reality. It divides us interiorly from the reality which is our real self, the only self we can ultimately be. And then the cost accelerates enormously because this unreality puts up an umbrella to God's grace.

Now, of course, people who have been in contact with the spiritual life for some time will find it hard to believe this. If there is anything they have been concerned with at all, it has been the life of grace and all its obvious appurtenances. They have read end-lessly and consulted much about states of prayer, the dark nights, the best way to make a meditation, and they sincerely seek their own betterment by being concerned about the next subject for their particular examen. And yet at the same time they are fleeing from reality because they fear to come to grips with the real problem which is the discovery of the real self. And since ordinarily we do not merely flee from something, but also flee to a secure refuge, their flight is unconsciously a flight to the supernatural.

As a priest you try to help them. You see an open-ing in the wall. Suddenly you can get behind the compulsions, the hidden fears that rule and block out grace. You can almost put your hand on the tragic lack of deep love of God brought about by not having found the true self or the personal way to him. You take advantage of the opening and you say the words. You are listened to dutifully, respectfully, but you feel the dull disbelief. Then comes the response if there is one: it is one of flight away from reality to the safe unreality they have made of the super-natural.

This is not to deny that the supernatural is real. Since God is at the heart of it, it is the most real of realities. But these people haven't gotten very far with him either. After years of religiously trying, they are moving so slowly that there is almost no motion. They are slowed down by all sorts of practices, prej-udices, compulsions, and inhibitions. We are asked why there are not more saintly people. The answer is that there are not more real people.

This matter of reaching reality is something like reaching for the truth. Well, we're all for that. We pride ourselves, or console ourselves, that humility is the truth, and all want the truth. So we say.

But the inner truth? We say we want that too. But we lack the courage to really look at ourselves. It does take great courage, and few of us can face it. So in the spiritual life we instinctively escape to where we can hold the inward vision at a distance, in the confused jungle we have made of the supernatural — if we have not made a walled city instead, quite separated from the real world.

What causes us to fear this inner reality? We often name it insecurity. It is a terrible, though often unconsciously blind state of being afraid. Those who closely study these matters say that it can often be traced back to a lack of love in early life. Since many of us have not been perfectly reared, this insecurity may be in us more universally than we think. On the other hand it may also arise from too much love. The overly-protected child is going to be insecure when his props are taken away in later life, but the result is likely to take other forms of immaturity rather than what we are discussing at present.

The lack of love in early life imprints a scar upon the inner personality. As a result we will always have the tendency to think that we are not good enough for anyone or anything. There is a lack of internal foundation. The attempt to cover it over can be compared to making the floor of a house out of paper. Since no one would want such a poor floor to be seen, we paint it over with designs, sometimes very skillfully, to make it appear that it is strong, perhaps made of hardwood or expensive tile. Psychologically speaking, we construct a false image instead of building toward the true self. Yet when stress is put upon the floor, it caves in. We collapse as a thinking human being. The result can be a deep, perhaps unconscious panic.

This gives us a key to the whole business of the flight from reality. We are not sure of ourselves because we do not love or appreciate ourselves. We do not see the true self as worthy of love or respect. So we reject this inner self. Our aversion turns to fear because we fear that the true thing which we are will be inadequate for authentic love. And so in aversion and fear we flee. This flight can take a multitude of forms because this aversion and fear are no means confined to those who attempt the spiritual life. So, many flee into sin, into the distractions of the world, into ambitious projects, into an extreme sense of duty, into many successive loves or into an unhealthy dependent love. But here we are interested in the flight into a superficial supernatural.

If we were perfectly logical, a knowledge of our insecurity would impel us toward God. And indeed even those who go only half-way with him are impelled toward him by this clear invitation in the Scriptures. From this we should know that his love does not reject us. But unfortunately the inner rejection of ourselves is accompanied by the fear of rejection by others. We fear to come close to others with our true self because, if they see us as we do, they will not love us. But unavoidably God does know us for what we are. And therefore, in order to forestall the rejection, which we unconsciously fear, we may unconsciously erect barriers against him, barriers behind which we will feel secure.

Some of the barriers are the busyness with the externals of the world, or better, with the even safer externals of the spiritual life. Along with these go the inner barriers, the building of a false image of ourselves, the painted paper floor of our house. Since this makeshift self stands in the way of the true self, it will have to be destroyed before we can have real closeness to God.

His love and the power of his grace are able to mend the essential damage done to our lives by others and by ourselves. A true foundation or an inner core is always possible because within us is ever the potentiality to be our true selves.

Chapter 9

The False Image

Our Lord has told us that his yoke is easy and his burden light (Mt. 11:30). Thus many of his close followers have been at peace and even happy despite sufferings which were considerable. But what our Lord did not tell us is that the burdens which are bitter and heavy are usually the interior burdens which we place on ourselves, or unfortunately were placed on us, or better, within us, by forces outside our control in early life. As a result we create an inner tyranny, and we do it in an attempt to hide our insecurity from ourselves and others, and we do it out of pride.

Now normally we don't do this consciously. Because of the way we are made, there is an instinctive determination to find a sense of inner security or inner worth or self-respect. Our basic motive power then is one of connatural self-love, but here it is probably working through another basic quality which is fear.

Fear, like love, is a gift of God. Ultimately we fear because we love. God has given us fear in order

to help us avoid harmful situations. Many of our reasonable precautions are based on it. But we have
other fears we don't see, and these sometimes have
a more fundamental effect on our lives than many
of the fears of which we are conscious. An example
is the deep, unknown fear of being rejected. If any
half-hidden fears have an effect on our personality,
they will surely have an effect on our spirituality.

At this state of the spiritual life, we may presume
in many cases that the difficulties of spiritual progress
are due to these unresolved fears. The surface difficulties are now largely cleared away but the deeper
ones not only remain untouched but can even become worse by secretly accomodating themselves to
the spiritual environment.

Even if our problems are there deep within us,
we are so much on the defensive that we may never
see them. But we can get glimpses of the roots underneath by the unwelcome vegetation which comes
out of the ground. One of the indications is the
presence of phobias or the tendencies to phobias.
These are quite unreasonable fears on the surface,
but must have underneath a reason for their existence
and their intensity.

Sometimes we can assign a reason, such as having been frightened by a dog, and therefore we become unreasonably fearful of dogs. But this incident
does not tell why we allowed the unreasonable effect
or phobia to take hold of us, when all that should
have come from it is a carefulness about dogs under
certain circumstances. The real cause has been the
envelopment by unconscious fear resulting from our
deep insecurity; the incident has been like a small
crack in a dam causing a flood. In spiritual matters,
scruples (although they may also arise from other
causes) can be an indication of the inner psychological vacuum of fearful insecurity.

This deep-seated fear also shows itself by inhibitions. These are a certain paralysis of our power to think, to feel, or to act. We have all seen obvious examples of this in stage fright or forgetfulness during an important examination. But in the situation we are discussing, the paralysis is so deep that the person himself is most often unaware of it. That these fears can have results in the spiritual life needs no demonstration. The psychological life of the inhibited becomes fixed as a metal which hardens in a mold; they fear to change because they dare not go beyond what they experience as accustomed safety. The spiritual life often becomes a matter of formalism, although we must not forget that the grossly uninhibited are insecure also but are trying to cover it over in a different way, often by the approval of their similarly uninhibited group.

In a sense the inhibited are harder to make into saints than those who have phobias. At least the phobia is uncomfortable and we therefore are humbled by our weakness. We also seek help from God or from others. But in the inner tyranny of deep inhibition, we can easily assume that our conduct is highly virtuous, and in our complacency we move very few steps toward God. And of course the inhibition itself paralyzes our going to God too. One of its characteristics is to impede normal, spontaneous action; it sets up barriers to the inner movements of the mind and heart. Because the spirit cannot react as it should to given situations or objects, it will not be able to reach out to God very successfully either.

Inhibition, of course, also interferes with the development of the true self, and thus with our spiritual development, as we have said. We must be psychologically free in order to be spiritually free. "The truth will set you free" (Jn. 8:32), and here is great truth: to see as unreasonable the power of the fear that binds us.

A third kind of tyrannical fear is even more hidden, so much so that it has not even the appearance of fear as do phobias and inhibitions. This is inner compulsion. Although the drive behind compulsive actions seems to be voluntary, the source is a lack of freedom within us which *demands* that we act in some manner not completely according to right reason. We see it in the spiritual life most often as perfectionism, but it is observable in other ways also, such as compulsive ambition and rebellion. Fear is at the root of it because we are desperately trying to keep our self-respect, and we are afraid that if we are less than our self-designed ideal, we will be a failure. The unreal ideal then becomes our god.

We must, of course, set up ideals for ourselves, but these should be possible ideals, not (to use perfectionism as a convenient example) a demand for personal perfection in all things *here and now*. The demand for unswerving addiction to the letter of the law even though charity and justice suffer from it, the inner demand that we must not suffer even the normal urges of unruly passion, the demand for absolute efficiency and orderliness, or something as small as the demand to say the Stations when we would be happier just making a visit—these and innumerable others wear the mask of real perfection but are really rooted in fear, too far below the surface to be noticed without special light.

Compulsions, even though at times they may be small disorders in themselves, can exercise a proportionately enormous influence over us. We can be maneuvered by them much as a large ship is maneuvered by a relatively small rudder. It is easy to see what disaster can occur when the devil finds a way to control the helm. Since his attacks are apt to be the more successful the more he can disguise himself in our weaknesses, he is likely to keep such persons under control by practicing them in their compulsions, even in their compulsions which have a good object, so that he can slowly but surely push them into compulsive action of a more tragic kind. Even small slaveries give him a hold on us. Reason and self-control are our freedom.

Our human nature more easily adapts itself to operating through symbols and images, and so we tend to synthesize our fear responses. We unconsciously form an image of ourselves as we want to see ourselves. We shall call it the false image. It exists because of a complex of reasons.

The false image is, first of all, rooted in fear, in the insecurity deep in the psyche. We feel that we are not worth very much, especially that we are not worthy of love and respect. We so easily mistake a part for the whole. We see a defect, and in our injured pride or our fear we make a whole out of the defect, instead of merely seeing it as an undesirable part of a well-endowed whole. This blind intolerance is a condition which can have come upon us to a great extent without our being at fault, and it is the work of spiritual progress and growing maturity to recognize our defects, to some extent learn to live with them, but to a greater extent overcome them, just as we would a physical deficiency resulting from an accident.

But the wounds of the psyche are not so easily recognized as those of the external body. The reason for this, strangely, must be laid at the door of God. He has put something in our nature modeled after himself who is the unachievable prototype of all creation. He has given us an irradicable love of the self. This love is basically a good thing. We even have a command to love ourselves, implied in the fact that we must love our neighbor *as ourselves*. This love instinctively, naturally seeks something in our self to love. But when our malformed inner vision sees nothing to love and respect, our tortured love-instinct closes its eyes upon what it believes to be reality and chooses an unreality to love instead.

Yet this seeking for something of ourselves to love would be a relatively simple thing, even despite our defects, if there were not another element added to the problem. This, more than the inner lack and the instinct to love ourselves, is the effective cause of the false image. This third element is the fact that our love of the self is a disordered love as an effect of the Fall. Thus our pitiful defects and our beautiful love of the self are open to the infection of pride, bringing on the fever for the unreal.

There is, of course, enough in each of us to satisfy our legitimate love of self; we are all in varied ways rich, though some more than others. But our pride either demands an image greater than reality or, more understandably, we build the false image because we *have* to believe something of ourselves in order to love ourselves. We fear that the reality is not good enough because we haven't been able to see, or haven't been shown, our true worth. We fail to see the truth because we are blinded by real or imaginary defects or by poor powers of appreciation. Thus the false image may be a desperate attempt to hold ourselves together. But in the case of tyrannical pride, even great truth is not enough for its enormous love for itself. Now the self wants to be a god. In any case we build a false image because we *want* to believe or *have* to believe something of ourselves. Often our phobias, inhibitions, and compulsions are results of the fear of not measuring up to the false image.

This image is always at least partly unreal and always unattainable. For instance, we refuse to be ordinary in any respect—or if we are convinced that we are ordinary in some respects, we demand of ourselves that *at least in this one respect* we are supreme. Our personalities turn on this as an axis. If we feel that we are not loved enough or popular enough or recognized enough, let it be. Hidden away we have a world no one knows about. Here a saint reigns supreme. Or here is the most misunderstood person in the world complete with all the glory of martyrdom. Here is ability such as no one has ever seen, and I'm going to prove it. Here is the best judgment, the most authoritative or indispensable or efficient or motherly person. Here is the bonvivant, the nonconformist, the liberator—whatever it is that we have caught onto, pride is surely at the root of it but unreality is what it is made of.

This is not to deny that such a person may sometimes have some ability along the lines of the image. In his desire for self-respect he has perhaps seized upon a part of himself, exaggerated it into a whole, and built his life around it. With so much effort we can even get some results. But the image as it stands is not the person himself. Whatever qualities he does have are not integrated into the whole of the true self. As an ideal it is always unattainable in practice. It is too pure, too goody-goody, too wishy-washy, too kind-hearted or too self-adulatory—whatever, again, constituted the falseness of the image. But we have identified ourselves with it and we try to think we are this false, idealized thing. ("This *proves* I am something.") And so we live our lives in a world dominated by a stranger we have brought in because we have not the courage to live with the reality which we are.

With the false image we live many exalted moments, but the unconscious falsehood does not make for peace. In our other moments we see that we are not living up to the demands of the false image. We are now doubly failures, failures because of our distorted view of our true self, and also failures because we have not succeeded in living up to our false image. But nature still demands that we love ourselves, and thus we are in deep conflict. We have added this ultimate tension to the already existing tensions of covering the truth with the false image and in straining to maintain the fiction.

The results of these tensions can be very great and can also be different from the causes. We are being weighed down by incredibly great psychological burdens and so our vitality often may be drained away. We may be subject to prolonged depression, chronic discouragement, discontent, restlessness, contrariness, hypochondria. We may be overly sensitive or irascible. We may become unbelievably selfish (at least *we* will not believe it) by projecting our self-hatred onto others and thus failing to see their needs and problems. Here are also the suspicious and the overly dependent.

It can be easily seen that God's grace will thus meet stubborn obstacles; the process of true growth will stop because it is a process of change. These souls resist change. They are so enmeshed in unconscious falsehood that they cannot see what God wants or they don't really want to see what God wants. We may call it spiritual or intellectual pride, and it often is; they don't want to see because they do not want to step down from the heights (as they see it) and face the lesser reality of the real self. Often they think that the pride image is God's will because they are impelled by an inner urge which they think is God's urging but is only their self-love, like a spoiled child, making impotent yet tyrannical demands.

Here we can sometimes understand how God can be so tolerant of us even in our wickedness. Our faults of pride are sometimes only a pitiful struggle to keep from psychologically drowning. And we can also understand how he can be so patient with us. He sees, as we must see, that too premature a removal of the false image would cause a worse evil, that of leaving no support at all to the psyche still insecure in its self-disbelief. Fortunately our instincts of survival protect us here and will not let us push ourselves too far or too fast in tearing out the false image unless we do violence to these instincts. Even professional help, which sometimes must be sought, must be careful in this.

We are now beginning to see that self-knowledge is not just a catalog of faults. We can see, as the saints did, that there is more of self in our best actions than we thought...and this revelation is likely to become clearer as we go on.

Chapter 10

Rejecting the False Image

By finding and accepting the real self, we will use our strength to climb the mountain and not just expend it to stand still under a burden so heavy we cannot move. This burden is, as we have said, principally the result of the false image. We wear this over our real self in order not to be in the unbearable psychological agony of having to see what we despise and yet must love. The lifting of this burden is not a matter of one vivid insight or a single day's effort. In fact it is normally the major work of a lifetime. It is our preparation for the perfection which God imposes as a command, but which is always his invitation to deeper and deeper love and union.

At the heart of all rejection of the false image must be two things. One is the knowledge of its existence, and the other is the will to reject it. Both are not so easy as we may think, not at all so easy, for instance, as deciding on some reasonable penance or extra prayer. As to the knowledge, our false image is somewhat as the Greeks said of vice, that it is unknown to itself. As to the will to reject, more things have to happen to our soul and in our soul than mere willing that the result be accomplished, just as a boy cannot add several inches to his height by willing it either. To bring about the knowledge and the rejection, we depend enormously on the providence and help of God, and we should plead for it. His power can control, not only the spiritual, but also the psychological. And since pride is often intimately connected with the false image, we should frequently ask him for humility.

There are in general two ways by which we come to this deep self-knowledge. One is by self-examination and the other is by insight. The first will be more fruitful in the beginning of our inner renewal, whereas the latter is more characteristic as we approach the end. However, both are simultaneous, for our lives are not departmentalized; and both will be accomplished or initiated by what we read and hear, and this not always in spiritual books or from spiritual persons.

Insight, however, can come at any moment of the day or night, very often at times when we are not in the least engaged in prayer. These moments have a priority over most of the things we may be doing when they occur. To the best of our ability we must give them free rein to work the good of rejecting the false and building the true that is in us. A quick mental note and an immediate strong act of the will is not the way to capture the psychological energy which will gradually work the inner miracle. One of the laws of our nature is that we must give our insights enough time to reach the roots. Since we are dealing with the psychological and not only with the spiritual, we must work according to the laws by which our psyche is made to operate.

Rejection of the false image is not accomplished, as we have said, only by strong acts of the will. Strong acts of the will are more fitting when our self-knowledge has come by way of self-examination. But even here, gentleness in handling ourselves is an indispensable condition of our growth. However, when the knowledge comes through insight, the will to reject must usually have an emotional content—not emotion forced by a determined will, but spontaneously arising from the inner situation brought about by the knowledge. Often this spontaneous response suffices for the rejection; the final act of the will and any practical details requiring extended thought are wisely left until later. Here we see an essentially different mode of operation from that produced by the knowledge which we pick up laboriously by self-examination, where the conscious act of the will and practical thinking are an immediate necessity.

In both self-examination and insight the renewing process will be aided by a certain externalization if that is possible. St. Francis de Sales suggests that our decisions will be strengthened if we take a public stand by word or action along the lines we have arrived at privately. Decisions can also be strengthened by providing the emotional support which comes by means of the senses. Such an externalization can be illustrated by a story told of St. Francis of Assisi when on one occasion he was disturbed by strong temptations against chastity. He took a long stick and laid it on the ground. "Francis, there is your wife." Then he took several smaller sticks and laid them along side the large one. "These, Francis, are your children." Then: "Now, Francis, tell me, how are you going to support all these people?"

Sometimes the rejections involved in the finding of the real self can be externalized in ways less spectacular but still filled with enough emotional content to put the whole man on the side of the insight or decision. For example, we may destroy letters, or other objects from those whose hold on us has been keeping us from God or who represent a way of life which has been submerging our true life. By emotion, of course, we do not mean extreme violence. And also, privacy is usually a wise condition for this kind of emotional rejection.

There are other externalizations, if the word fits here, which we can use in regard to our fears: the minor phobias, and also the inhibitions and compulsions which are often components of the false image. Some of these fears are now open to self-knowledge, especially since some of them are openly problems to us. It is important, of course, to be rid of these irrational fears, both obvious and hidden. Fear is a gift of God, as we have said, and many of our reasonable precautions in the spiritual life are based upon it. But there are other kinds which can prevent our progress toward God, hidden ones being the most harmful. A hidden fear of being rejected, arising from a lack of belief in ourselves, can have much more serious effects than an embarrassing fear of heights.

The discipline by which we can overcome many of our conscious fears and inhibitions is an unceasing warfare called *agere contra,* to act against. We act against the fear by *reasonable* and *prudent* disregard for the irrational fear, or by performing an act which is contrary to it. We must, of course, be careful about provoking a crisis too great for our present strength.

Perhaps some examples will help. In the case of scruples, we follow unhesitatingly and unreflectingly the advice we have been given, perhaps years previously. In another not uncommon fear situation, the unreasonable fear of sex, we may prudently force ourselves into some confrontation with the problem which will help to maintain the balanced attitude that all things which God made are good. It goes without saying that such a method of cure involves us only in things which are not only morally good in themselves, but also good from the point of view of the ideals of our state in life, or we will be involved in another and deeper inner conflict. And we also must be understood as saying that there be no close danger of consent involving mortal sin.

Because our compulsions concern actions which are often more easily reached than our phobias and inhibitions, *agere contra* can be even more successful here. We place an action contrary to the compulsion. If, for example, one is overorderly, he can leave a desk or a room with less than the desired neatness. Or if the compulsion is to save things endlessly, he can rigorously limit himself to the expectancy of need as suggested by past experience.

These are of course expedients, a *modus vivendi,* a practical way of acting rather than a cure of the deeper malady. Yet we must do what is at hand or we will paralyze the power of the healthy instincts of our psyche to bring a fuller freedom, as it will do especially by insight into our slavery and then by its rejection. It is important to maintain this unceasing warfare. Maturity is the result of winning it.

Old age does not automatically give victory or freedom from the struggle. Indeed the tendency is quite the opposite. Either our insecurity-driven slavery is overcome or we end by being progressively overcome by it. The sooner we act the better; old age does not have the energy to give to the battle, and the habits become more a second nature.

We must act gently, patiently, prudently, and yet consistently against the fears we can reach, and trust God and our basically healthy nature to help us get at the roots of the problem, the fears caused by our unbelieving rejection of our true selves, and the added fears of not being able to measure up to our false selves and false ideals.

The pain of the slavery of the false image is one of the strongest natural motives to enlist us in the battle, not to mention the even stronger supernatural motives principally based on love of God. Just as we should not want outward slavery, no matter how glorified it may appear on occasion, so we must not want inner slavery either. We have only to ask ourselves: do I want to live in pain, in interior turmoil and tension? do I not rather want peace and happiness in the truth? do I not want to be able to look at myself and love myself instead of being fearful of rejection by others? and finally, do I not want a deep love of myself so that I can go to God in the full belief that he really wants me? If we can want these things for ourselves, and want ourselves for God, we have the state of mind which will strengthen us for the temporarily painful elimination of the false image.

With the discarding of the false image, there is the growing discovery and appreciation of the true self. These two are reciprocal processes, and unless God shortens the duration, we must expect that patience will be a necessary element in our gaining our rightful freedom. Love, however, is the great motive power, love of ourselves for our full integrity and, even more importantly, love of God. Love for ourselves demands a desire to see ourselves as good and acceptable. Love for God means giving him more love and glory because it is from our whole person. And it means finding love as well as giving love. For only the free can truly love.

Chapter 11

Finding the True Self

So far we have perhaps given the impression that everyone has a false image of himself and therefore must seek some deeper reality. Despite the fact that there are some people for whom this is not true, we have waited until now to mention it. If we allowed the possibility of exceptions earlier, such candor would bring continuing blindness by providing an opening to disbelief, and disbelief especially in those to whom the false image applies in greatest measure. But now having come this far, if we have not convinced those who need the spiritual and psychological renewal, we must not hold the others in uncertainty. Perhaps all of us have some corner of our psyche which needs opening up and readjusting, but the major efforts to be described here are not comparable to the minor effect to be gained.

How do we know if we are the fortunate or the blind? The chances are that, before this point, those who need to look into the depths have been opened up already by what has been written. If not, then either there is essentially nothing further to find underneath, or this is not the time. If it is the first, we should go on carefully but confidently toward God, and without the interior struggle that the false image implies. If it is the second, the blind ones, they should prayerfully await the future in patience. God has ways of showing us the light, particularly by bringing us into a period of stress when this light of the true self is the only visible beacon pointing to safety.

The human psyche cannot exist in a vacuum. With the decaying of the false image must come the growth of the knowledge and acceptance of the true self. Anything else would result either in the substitution of a new false image for the old or, even worse, in total psychological disaster. Thus an indispensable element in our spiritual growth is the restoration of our inheritance, to the full development of our essential gifts from God. We must therefore seek out the true self.

Here certain obstacles arise. Not only is this search prevented by the same pride and disordered self-love which brought about the flight from true self in the first place, but it is also thwarted by a certain false humility which stands in the way of looking at ourselves honestly. We fear that the contemplation of our good qualities will induce pride and vanity.

We will speak at length about humility later when we see how the virtues take on deeper aspects as we approach God. We will then establish that true humility is vitally concerned with the full truth about ourselves. But now we will prompt an awareness of our good qualities from the point of view of the necessity of finding the real self.

In trying to be something else, we will fail to be what God wants us to be. In finding our true self, we will find at the same time what God wants us to become. Our good qualities spell out the spiritual capacities by which we can find our way to him. For we must always remember that God does not call us by name and tell us how to come to him. We have to find this out, as we have said, by reason, advice, experience, our reading, the duties and circumstances of our life, and by our spiritual inspirations and attractions. But all these excellent means can still end in unreality if we do not know the whole person who is expected to follow all this. The true self, if it does nothing else, will act as an objective check upon possible overstatement (or understatement) by our own thoughts and desires, always so prone to subjective exaggeration.

There is an apparent contradiction between the ideal of perfection and what we have said about the false image. The difficulty is rooted in the fact that normally we all want to become something, since self-perfection is a law of our nature. In the spiritual life, moreover, we are urged toward nothing less that perfection, to be a saint, to develop our gifts both in regard to our relationship with God and our work in the Church. What is the difference, then, between what is normal in our search for perfection and what is abnormal so as to impede the soul? The answer can be expressed in one word, reality.

To attain reality, we must be truthfully, yet humbly ready to take ourselves for what we are. This is obviously not found in the false image. In the unreality of our subjective distortions we do not, for instance, find merely a better than average intelligence, but a genius to be deferred to; not a person who is loved in varying degrees as we all are, but one who must make a conquest of all in every situation; not a man or woman influencing people by normal daily contacts, but someone pulling the strings to manipulate them like puppets; not a man satisfied to have his part in the great plan of creation, but someone who must run the show. But even with pages of examples we would not exhaust the possibilities of the unreal. They are false ideals rather than true, and their unreality is hidden from the actor who plays out his self-made part in a drama which calls for him to speak other lines.

But how are we going to find the reality, the true self, amid all the self-deception of the false image? We have already seen two general ways in the last chapter. They will serve us here also, with some additional observations.

The two ways to deep knowledge of the real self are self-examination and insight. As to the first we must feel that we are a definite person with our good qualities as well as our bad or inferior ones. This self-assessment must be honest and progressively fuller and deeper. Therefore it cannot be a matter of thinking on it once or twice while reading this book. Perhaps it will even be necessary to accept the discipline of writing down again and again what we are, with an ever deeper and fuller knowledge. This does not mean that we should be examining and writing constantly. Too frequent or prolonged introspection will have the mind tending to become more subjective than objective, and our inner vision will be blurred by the exhaustion of too much looking.

On the other hand we must jealously cherish the moments of insight, the second of the two ways, when self-revelation shines out most clearly. If these moments are neglected, the final victory cannot be won. Their demands for attention should have highest priority; the obligation to love ourselves demands this time.

While we must take the mood of the insight as we find it without trying to conform it to a "spiritual" pattern, our self-examination can profit by a situation which we can make for ourselves. This situation is our life of prayer. In the meditative kind of prayer, we find the opportunity, not only for self-examination, but also for asking God's help in using the lights received. But often we do not ask very wisely because we do not know what to ask for. This in turn is because we are not accustomed to go to God honestly; that is, we don't face him as we are. If we can face him with everything, the worst as well as the good, we will in time find ourselves quite accurately.

It may be a minor shock to be told that we do not face God honestly in prayer. After all, why try to deceive him who knows everything? Perhaps it is a question of not deceiving God but deceiving ourselves first. Perhaps we are doing to him what we do to others: we tell him what we think he might like to hear, not the honest truth, but the partial truth. So we adopt attitudes.

For instance, we make believe that a personal injustice doesn't bother us because it would be imperfect if it did bother us. But deep in our psyche the unacknowledged resentment may come out in some other form, the unreal form of a martyrlike attitude observable in hypochondria. Or at best we pray to God to overcome our feelings, and we treat them merely as temptation instead of pouring out our hearts, as the writers of the psalms did, and telling God how we really feel. We thus treat him worse than we treat our friends. We often tell them our feelings when we deeply need to relieve them, and even less wisely when we don't need the release. But our proud, sacrosanct attitude toward God will not let us approach him with the same problem except as accusing ourselves of temptation or sin, when we don't hide it completely.

Not only do we learn about ourselves through this relentless self-exposure, but we also impress upon ourselves another important truth, that God is not a picture hung on a wall in our mind, but is a living, personal being. And our open feelings give him a better chance to heal them.

We will find out more about ourselves, at least find out what we are, even if not good, if we tell God of our wants. Of course we may say that we always do this, but is it not only when it fits into a preconceived picture of what might be pleasing to God, such as praying for someone's health or conversion? Yet on the contrary we all have things we want, at least in some sense of the word *want,* some part of us which may be crying out for satisfaction that is denied by God's law or by circumstances that he could change but didn't or doesn't or won't. We will find even resentments against God, irrational it is true, but they are within us all the same. But remaining within, unseen and unresolved, they will not tell us much about ourselves, and unacknowledged, they are not going to leave us in anything but a tense peace. Having by-passed the things which really matter, our relationship with God will become duller and duller, and harder and harder.

Of course we do not concentrate too much on the things we can't have, so much that we forget the greater gifts we have received and will receive from God, or so much as to increase our desires for the impossible or for the forbidden. But still we will not see through to the real self unless we see what our full nature is, and not the pious fraud we are trying to project.

Facing God with ourselves is a harder discipline than we can imagine. The sinner must do it all the time. But those of us whom God's mercy has brought out of sin, or for whom he has prevented sin, must not take our good fortune for our real selves. Our openness to God is the primary way to self-knowledge. He can take much more from us than we imagine. We can complain to him, argue with him, weep to him...as long as we do not leave him.

Self-knowledge, as we have said, will come more slowly if it is not externalized, preferably with an emotional content. Our openness to God is surely such an externalization, but he sometimes wishes to conform his ways to our nature by providing an understanding and wise human listener. Once the soul is convinced that someone can love it even when it is at its worst, the frail, new plant of the real self can more easily emerge from the darkness underground into the sunlight of the real world.

We can also externalize the process of self-realization by writing. This has the advantage of fixing into a quasi-permanent record the results of examination and insight. Otherwise they may be forgotten and the effect nullified. We need not keep these records forever. Indeed one way to externalize our victories is to destroy the older records.

Another advantage of writing is to make more precise what may remain vague if we do not write it down. This writing requires time and work, but we must be careful lest our spiritual life become something we like to read about, think fondly about, discuss tenderly about, but for which we are unwilling to do anything painfully concrete. So we write, especially during periods of clear vision, and review this self-analysis at stated times. The things written are often revised or discarded. In the end a clear picture of the true self with its strengths and its weaknesses will gradually emerge.

While we cannot, of course, predict what will be written down as a result of special insight, there are ways to bring out the light and darkness by patient examination. We can, for instance, make various lists of pertinent facts as we see them. Not all of these lists are for everyone, and perhaps some people who are too introspective already will do well to have none of them. But they can be a help to most of us. A sample list would be the placing under one column our good qualities in the following categories: physical, talents (intellectual, artistic, etc.) and spiritual. And then list the defects in the same categories.

A word of explanation may be due those who may be surprised to see the physical included in the process of building up the spiritual man. In the first place, so far as finding our personal identity is concerned, no part of ourselves is more directly observable than our body. And then also, although the body is of a relatively low order in the hierarchy of God's creation, still it is important here in the effects which a false attitude toward it can produce in the spiritual life. Sometimes a physical defect or an imagined physical defect can cause psychological harm and therefore bring in the possibility of spiritual harm.

This possibility is all the more true because our civilization since the Renaissance has placed much emphasis on the physical. A woman, for instance, may have been told as a young girl that she was homely, or a man may have been frustratingly unathletic as a boy. But if homely, then not lovable; if unathletic, then not manly. And if not loved or respected by men, then a psychological barrier to deep love by God. It could be a great grace for her to find out in later life that she was not unbeautiful, or for him to discover that manliness has deeper connotations than the physical, even if by no other means than the common denominator that declining physical power brings to every life.

The giants can throw these things off carelessly, but for most of us our civilization is a background, and we must come to terms with its effects in us, effects sometimes with deep results in our spiritual life.

Other helpful lists may include our goals, especially where they are diverse. This is important because we are often divided interiorly so that our energies are wasted or we become restless, because of mutually conflicting goals. All the more is this true because material or public success is a demand of our earthbound civilization. Few of us are conditioned to be like the anonymous builders of the medieval cathedrals, who were satisfied that their names be known only to God.

A final list might be one which identifies the people who have influenced us for good or bad. This opens a door to seeing what we are. Our strong influences are a part of us.

The building of the real self will automatically cause us to grow in many of the virtues. For one thing, we will be freed from the tyranny which obstructs the growth of true virtues. For another, we will have special need for certain virtues and our using them to capacity will cause them to grow. We have already indicated humility and patience, but another will be fortitude or courage. The fright of seeing ourselves as we are on our less admirable side, as selfish, as moved by earthy and irrational forces more than we would like to think, this fright can be considerable. The insecurity of having to give up a false image or ideal which has been our support for years is incalculable. Added to this is the uncertainty of the future; the path is not so clear ahead as we would like to see. Hope and trust become the companions of bravery. We are brought to God by all this desolation and fear. Our weakness is compensated by his strength.

There is admittedly danger in the search for the real self, but the spiritual man must learn now that the spiritual life, as the greatest of all adventures, requires calculated, yet prudent risks. The man who buried his talent received less than praise from God. Victory alone will make it possible for us to come closer to him. His grace, and its courageous, intelligent, and diligent use, will make saints out of many who would have remained mired in their inherited and acquired deficiencies.

The process of rebuilding takes abandonment to God, a courageous thing in itself, but it is our ultimate security. In the last analysis only he can help us to make the correct choices, the proper turns in the road. Our fears must be comforted by our trust in his love for us. Our fear to see our true selves without the glitter of the false image will be lessened when we want what he wants because we love him. He wants us to be what he made us to be.

Finding the true self has many advantages. First of all, it represents a greater economy in the spiritual life. Although we will, as unprofitable servants, waste many graces, we will waste fewer. When we find what we are, what we were made to be, we are in the full flow of God's grace, and not off in the shallows.

Moreover, we will do better work. Instead of wasting energy trying to be what we cannot be, we will use our strength to develop and use what we have — and not necessarily the complete use or development of all our possibilities, as we would perhaps want, but only as God wants it.

We shall also ultimately find peace. Many who embrace the spiritual life never find it because of inner conflicts they never resolve. But peace here is not just a cessation of warfare, but a union with God, the real God, not a half-false God to fit our false image. Peace is a union with him in the depths of our being, in depths we never thought possible even in the emotional transports of first fervor.

And so the spiritual life is a lifetime of choosing, not choosing the parts of doctrine to believe or choosing which laws to obey, but a lifetime of choosing in matters which are free: what counsels are meant for me, what way of spiritual development, what way of prayer, of mortification, of reading—though not all without advice when needed. When we get to know ourselves, we learn to choose how to help ourselves, and in the bottomless depths of human experience, we get to know God.

Part III

The Life
of the Spirit

Chapter 12

By the Grace of God

Important though it is, the finding of the real self is neither the principal end of the spiritual life nor its essential constituent. The real self is a necessary substratum insofar as grace is not a substitute for healthy nature, but not in the sense that the life of grace rests on the true self as a tall building rests on foundations in the earth. This would be inaccurate because the life of grace does not take its beginning or support from nature. It exceeds nature essentially, while at the same time fully permeating it, yet always leaving it a human nature.

But even here there is only an apparent parallel: the life of nature on the one hand, and the life of grace on the other. In the concrete individual, they both make one supernatural being, as the heart of the flame completely transforms the black charcoal into a glowing transcendence of its former state.

The spiritual life is essentially a supernatural life, a life in its essence and in all its operations above the natural life which man would have without grace. This new life is the principal effect of God's love for him. He loved man so much that he adopted him. In our present state we owe this adoption to the love of God in a further sense; having lost our inheritance through Adam, we have it back again for a simple reason: that God "has loved us, and has sent his son as an offering for our sins" (1 Jn. 4:10).

This adoption is expressed by the term *grace*, a word given us by the Scriptures: "Marking us out beforehand to be his adopted children through Christ. Thus he would manifest the splendor of that grace by which he has taken us into his favor in the person of his beloved son" (Eph. 1:5, 6). We have come to call this grace "sanctifying grace." It is this grace which makes us pleasing to God, and its abundant increase in our souls is essentially what makes us saints.

Sanctifying grace is the vital element in all holiness because it makes us like to God. The more we are like him, the more are we holy, the more our wills are his in deep, habitual love. Grace therefore is not a coat of paint applied on the outside of our souls, but a new life permeating them. This life is in some way the life of God, not by our becoming a part of God, or by God's absorbing us, but still by some sort of sharing in a created way the very nature of the living God. "He has bestowed on us the great and precious things he promised, so that through these you who have fled a world corrupted by lust might become *sharers of the divine nature*" (2 Pt. 1:4). This sharing of his nature with us is the incomprehensible measure of his love for us.

In the one sense it is not difficult to see why this must be. We could not be adopted as sons unless God did raise us up to participate in his own nature. The married couple may be very fond of their dog, but they cannot adopt it as they could a baby left on their doorstep. They cannot adopt the dog because it is not human; it does not have the same nature as they. Moreover, they cannot raise it up to their own nature. But God does raise us up to a participation in his own life.

This participation in the nature of God is still mysterious even after two thousand years of thinking by our best minds. There is always an infinite chasm between a being that has always existed in all its perfection, and a being which had to be brought into existence from nothing. We do not and cannot *become* God by sanctifying grace. But we do enter into a new mode of existence. We are now something we were not before; we do not become substantially God, but through grace we take on a new relationship with him. Nor is this relationship a fixed one. We can become more and more like him; through increase of grace we increase the intensity of this relationship, as the coals glow more brightly in the fire as they absorb more heat. This is done principally by love. It is principally love which makes us saints.

Love is not the only lesson taught by a consideration of sanctifying grace. There is an even deeper one for us, our dependence, and therefore the basis for a true humility. Grace is not a created thing in the sense that the soul is an empty barrel being filled with water, but in the sense that it becomes something new in respect to God. That is, the soul is constituted in a new mode of being to which it had no predisposing merits whatsoever. Like creation itself, the antecedent boundary line of grace is nothingness in its own order, with the sole exception that we do somehow have a potentiality to being raised up. This means that it is always gratuitous; God is in no way obliged to give it by anything we had or did without him previous to its bestowal. Even the fact that it is there at all for us is the work of another, the death of Christ our redeemer.

We can understand this better by our example of the married couple and the baby on the doorstep. This baby has a right, since it is a human being, to be fed, clothed, and housed. But it has no right to be adopted as one of the family, to be treated as a son or daughter, and to be made an heir along with the other children. Yet this is precisely what God has done for us, but in a manner more fundamental than is possible in human adoption. The baby and the foster parents already have the same nature. But God has, by santifying grace, given us a share in his own nature.

Not only in respect to God does sanctifying grace provide a basis for humility, but also in respect to men. We have various strata in the Church, some necessary, others the result of conditions in society. Some of these divisions can give us an exalted picture of ourselves if we are above someone else. Yet by grace we are all basically equal, every one of us who is in the state of grace: the man who is well advanced in the ways of the spirit, and the man who has just walked out of the confessional leaving behind the reek of his sins; the delicately well-mannered nun, and the coarsest laborer; the rich man whose money brings him immediate service and attention, and the man who must depend on public charity in order to exist. As long as they are in the state of grace, they are one in being God's children or, in another sense, his friends; they are brothers and sisters of Christ, members of his mystical Body and heirs to eternal life. But without grace, any one of us is incredibly poorer than the others.

Sanctifying grace also gives us an insight into the portion of our life that will be unending. In the first place there is the indispensable need. When we are judged, it will not matter how rich we are, or how famous, how intelligent, how strong, or how beautiful, but only one thing will matter, that we have sanctifying grace, and the degree in which we have it.

"But my face you cannot see, for no man sees me and still lives" (Ex. 33:20). To see God face to face is that kind of experience, and we would be unable to do it without the relationship which begins in sanctifying grace.

The life of grace, although it is essentially different and above the life we would have by nature alone, does not imply a divorce from what we have received by nature. As God created Adam, he knew that this higher life could never make a man equal to himself, nor even to the angels in his nature, but would still keep him a man — even though now elevated to a higher kind of life and permeated with it. Nature was not meant to be destroyed by this higher life but to be developed and used in undeviating harmony. The fact that there are difficulties since the Fall does not change the essential oneness of God's design.

In the spiritual life the grandeur of grace must not blind us to the full consideration of the being to whom it is given. An abstract approach to the spiritual life, whereby man becomes a well-ordered system of sanctifying grace, infused virtues, actual grace, and the gifts of the Holy Spirit, is necessary and valuable doctrine. But in practice the guidance of man is not exclusively referable to that refined kind of common denominator. He is made of body as well as soul, and even his soul has its natural functions, limited by the conditions of the composite being which he is. Besides, he is always an individual with individual problems, traits, bents, and potentialities. A sound spirituality, therefore, must take in the whole man, and guidance must take in his individuality.

Chapter 13

Becoming More Like God

In discussing sanctity from the point of view of sanctifying grace, we are attempting to describe it in terms of the interior of the soul, as the soul is seen by God. It is grace that makes us like to him, and therefore the more we have of it, the more we are like him. We can never, of course, get so much of it that we will be even remotely equal to him because no addition of limited amounts can ever be compared with what has no limits at all.

Here we have used a facile, yet somewhat misleading, manner of speaking. We have spoken of sanctifying grace as if it were something measurable by quantity, as we would add one sum of money to another. It is natural for us to speak in quantitative terms because the symbolism of the material fits in so naturally with our human way of thinking. For this reason, even our Lord uses examples which suggest quantity, as when he tells us to lay up for ourselves treasures in heaven (see Mt. 6:20).

Sanctifying grace, however, does not consist of anything so gross as a paycheck or a promissory note redeemable in heaven. It is a *likeness*. Now a likeness can be greater or less. Quantity has little to do with it. We are closer to God by being more *like* him, a comparison which has to do with quality, not quantity. The more or less intense is this likeness, the more or less do we reflect his goodness and holiness, just as a silver mirror will reflect the light better or worse depending on its condition of smoothness, cleanness, or polish. We can thus become greater sharers in God's nature, according to the limited manner we can share in it. And thus also, we increasingly become perfect as our heavenly Father is perfect.

In a previous chapter we have discussed closeness to God in terms of love. Of course there is no contradiction here because the degree of our love also determines the degree of sanctifying grace. In that chapter also, we warned against judging our love by the emotion which may or may not be present. Now we must make a similar observation. We must not think that we lack sanctifying grace, or have very little of it, because we don't feel God or don't even have pleasant feelings about him. The truth is that, despite the occasional experience of extraordinary effects of grace, grace itself is not something we feel at all. Therefore, neither must we expect to feel an increase of it.

Grace is something which, in our present state, is unfelt and invisible even to the soul itself. Rather it is something to be believed in on the word of God. We can only trust that we have it, and we find moral certainty about this by examining our conscience and observing our actions. Of course God is free to make exceptions, and sometimes he does give us an indication of his great love. Even in the life of a saint whose experiences were quite ordinary, St. Thérèse of Lisieux, he did on one occasion show his love to the extent that she thought she would die if it lasted any longer. Yet in the final months of her life, when she was really closest to him by sanctifying grace, she had no such feeling at all, but was quite completely in darkness.

From this essential point of view of our relationship with God, we can easily see that growth in spiritual life means growing in grace, not to be separated, however, from a point of view that is closer to our ability to observe and handle, and that is our growth in love of God and neighbor and in the other virtues. Since sanctifying grace and fundamental love of God are absolute correlatives, then the more we grow in love, the more we will grow in grace, and the more we will be loved by God forever. After death we cannot grow in grace; it then receives the name and condition of glory, and the final degree of grace becomes the degree of essential glory or closeness to God forever. The increase of grace, then, is the major work of our spiritual life.

Grace is so mysterious and so unlike the material things we would have to use as examples, that the spiritual life is wisely approached from other points of view, especially that of love. But there are some deep lessons for us which can best be taught by directly speaking of grace. One is the consolation that our venial sins and our voluntary imperfections do not decrease the degree of grace already possessed. If they did, we could be in a contradictory state of soul; we could be living in enmity with God because of sin (that is, deprived of sanctifying grace) but without ever having effectively turned away from him by the choice implied in mortal sin. However, venial sins and voluntary imperfections do decrease our ability to acquire more grace, and in some sense they make it easier for us to lose all grace by mortal sin. But they still do not fundamentally destroy our relationship with God or effectively diminish our likeness to him.

If lost, grace is recovered, but possibly not in the same intensity. St. Thomas says that even with the help of the sacrament of recovery, it is recovered only in the degree of intensity of repentance with which the soul returns to God (III; 89; 2). There are other more optimistic views on this, and although the conclusions of St. Thomas are not infallible, his thinking seems to be the best we have on the subject. In any event, the fact that he may be right, or rather that he probably is right, should deter us from becoming careless about mortal sin through the hope of full restoration by future repentance. Some of the hard-earned merits of our actions can easily and foolishly be lost, to be regained only after more hard effort.

It must also be added, according to the same teacher, that a man can emerge from mortal sin (or from venial sin or voluntary imperfection, for that matter) with a greater amount of sanctifying grace than he had before, because through his sorrow the intensity of love is greater than before the lapse.

The great work of our lives, then, is to end them with as much sanctifying grace as we can, to be as much like God as we are able. This concept of the spiritual life is not so unusual as to seem a different spiritual way from what we have been discussing in this book or from what is written for beginners. There is no secret about to be disclosed as to ways of increasing sanctifying grace.

The whole of our lives, and especially the spiritual life, is directed to that purpose. Anything which brings us closer to God will have the effect of increasing it. Therefore, the Mass, the sacraments, our good works, prayers, sacrifices, sufferings, the fulfillment of our duties—anything which is a good

act and performed with good intention while in the
state of grace will not be without the reward which
is the increase of sanctifying grace. Our Lord told
us this when speaking of a cup of water given in
his name (see Mk. 9:40). The good intention, or doing
something in Christ's name, of course does not have
to be specifically made each time. A perseveringly
habitual intention of doing all things for God or
eternal life is sufficient.

Such teaching is sound but it is incomplete. If
it were to be left in this incompleteness, as is sometimes done in giving spiritual advice, it would involve a real contradiction with the observable facts.
By merely living an ordinarily good life, it would
seem that we will always increase in grace day by
day. Thus, if we all lived long enough, or if we went
to the sacraments often enough, we would all become
great saints quite automatically. But this is not what
happens, as we can see in the lives of many who go to
daily Mass and Holy Communion, these great channels of grace. A look at our own lives will underline
the same observation.

A part of the difficulty lies in the error of thinking about sanctifying grace quantitatively. If I have
$1000, and I add even small amounts to it frequently
enough and long enough, I will one day be a million-
aire. But sanctifying grace, as we have said, does
not increase this way but rather by way of intensity.
The same is true of the love of God. In the language of
St. Thomas, God makes love "to have a greater hold
on the soul, and the likeness of the Holy Spirit to
be more perfectly participated by the soul" (II, II;
24; 5 ad 3).

If an example will help in matters which are
beyond the power of natural examples to illustrate
adequately, we may take the example of penmanship.
Let us say that we can increase our ability to write

legibly by careful practice. Every time we exceed our previous ability, we have helped to form a habit of greater perfection in writing. But careless writing will not increase the quality of our penmanship. (Instead it will decrease it, and this is a reason why such examples are deficient, since sanctifying grace is not decreased even by venial sins, and therefore not by less intense acts either.) However, this example can help us understand our own lack of progress in grace, even after extensive and perhaps long use of the means of grace.

The obvious practical conclusion is to seek ways to make our actions have greater value. Since grace grows along with love of God and neighbor, the problem is to perform our actions with ever greater actual love than we have at present. To do this we must have actual graces from God, and these he gives more abundantly as we need them, desire them, and ask for them or merit them. With these our free will can perform acts which are more intense in love. But again we must warn that this has no necessary connection with feelings of love or emotional intensity. For example, a woman may nurse a sick husband for years; the love shown, though rarely now emotional, is far greater than the ecstatic days of courtship and early marriage.

Very often the spiritual life is divided into its various stages by using advancement in prayer as a measurement. This is somewhat artificial because God is free to grant any kind of prayer that he wishes when he wishes. Also there is always difficulty in fitting in some of the saints. However, things do fit the pattern often enough for it to be useful. The point here is that a higher state of prayer can mean that the prayer and subsequent actions are performed with a higher degree of love, and therefore merit an advance in grace. Indeed St. Teresa tells us that her spiritual progress was greatly increased when her prayer became that of a higher order, which (once again, not to be interminably repetitive) does not mean an emotionally more intense kind of prayer. In fact, it is quite often the opposite.

Of course we cannot demand of ourselves that we pray with a higher kind of prayer at any given time. Those who try to do so without its being given will hurt themselves, besides missing the opportunities for increasing the intensity of love in other ways which are close at hand. Love of God is best measured as our Lord has told us, by an increase in all the virtues. "You can tell a tree by its fruit" (Mt. 7:20). An increase in any virtue will bring about an increase of love of God and sanctifying grace.

Particularly useful, of course, is greater love of neighbor, since this, with love of God forms the one supernatural virtue of charity. It is well to note that our Lord practiced love of neighbor as the crowning act of his life—and also submission to his Father's will, another great road to increase.

Indeed, since love is essentially the union of God's will and ours, the intensity with which we are joined to his will determines our degree of sanctifying grace. An increase in the intensity of this union quite obviously can come in any way God chooses to offer it, for instance, in the delight of prayer or in gratitude for his gifts—not only in difficulties and suffering as we might imagine. (For we tend to have a prejudice that enjoyable things are not holy.) But of course an increase in love and grace does come greatly by the close adherence of wills implied in the endurance of suffering and in perseverance in difficult situations.

God so orders our lives that there are numerous obstacles and sufferings in them. Sometimes these are greater than previous ones, and thus they are opportunities for greater love and increase in grace. St. Thérèse must have immensely increased her degree of sanctifying grace in the disease and darkness of her last months. But even small things can increase the deep love in our soul. The closer we are to God in love, the more value all our actions have. Even the effort involved (important though it be) is secondary to the value arising from this fundamental inner love.

This necessity of having to produce always greater intensity in order here and now to increase sanctifying grace helps to explain why we do not get more spiritual good out of our Masses, Holy Communions, and confessions. The sacraments as instruments of God give grace of themselves, unless we put an obstacle in the way. Sometimes this obstacle is our selfishness, our lack of love of our neighbor, the attachment to evil or to the material, a worldly life and so on.

Mass and sacraments can also be deprived of their effectual and immediate power to increase grace by our lukewarmness, our human lack of awareness, our failure to make the best efforts to prepare and to receive (or in the Mass, to participate in the actual offering of Christ to the Father in the consecration).

The practical ways to increase the awareness and its resulting intensity of basic love will vary with each person. But we should all try to stir up our hearts by considerations of whom we are to receive and whom we are to meet each time we perform these sacred functions. Appreciation afterwards is also no little disposition for greater grace.

Occasionally one hears it said that we should lessen the frequency of our reception of the sacraments because they seem less intense than required to give us an increase of grace. The argument is that if we receive less often, we will do better, and this is especially said of frequent confession (every week or two weeks).

There are principally two things wrong with this defeatism. One is that the greater intensity, which is required for increase of grace, seems to be made co-extensive with the *feelings* of intensity and of awareness of the sacred. St. Thérèse didn't do very well with her Communions, according to such a standard. It is the will and the unfelt love deep in the soul which counts. On the contrary we have all known people who get a very intense feeling from various liturgical functions, but they fail to show an increase in the virtues, which is the best practical measurement of our progress.

Another error in the withdrawal theory is its incomplete grasp of the theology of grace. The example of handwriting which we used earlier was deficient for another reason to be noted now. When we write below our level of proficiency, we decrease our proficiency. With grace this does not happen, as we said. On the contrary *every* good action performed in the state of grace with a good intention merits a reward. This is the point missed by the minimizers. These acts of less value merit an increase of sanctifying grace, but most probably not here and now at the completion of the act. The long, glorious list of great theologians is divided on the exact time and manner in which the increase is given. But they all agree that it is given. St. Thomas says that these acts of less value are dispositions to further acts of love or other virtues until some act is intense enough to merit an actual increase for us, which is never thereafter diminished unless it be lost (see II,II; 24;6).

Thus even lukewarm Communions and confessions merit a reward, as also do the less perfectly performed duties and acts of kindness. But just as we should not give up the latter because the reward may be less, so we should not give up the frequency of Mass and the sacraments either. In going to Mass even dully, we are performing an act of worshiping God publicly and in union with others of the Mystical Body. Non-attendance would not do this. Similarly, Holy Communion is a spiritual food, and confession is a strengthening medicine. We might have a better appetite if we resort to starvation, and feel the need of medicine more acutely if we let our spiritual diseases run their course for a while, but such neglect is not likely to produce a strong spiritual life. The saints seem universally to have done the opposite.

Even if the strengthening is only minimal, it may be just enough to help us take the next step ahead; to risk having only a little less than the needed strength should be unthinkable. The value of our actions cannot be weighed accurately by ourselves anyway. It may be that our tired, plodding, and bored attempts may be advancing our souls in ways that are a delight to God and the angels.

Spiritual perfection or sanctity loses some possible fearsomeness when we see it through sanctifying grace. A man can be on the way of perfection without being entirely perfect, for sanctifying grace can exist and even increase despite present venial sins and faults. Thus we avoid expecting too much of ourselves, a fertile ground for discouragement and a reason for seeking the compensation of a false image of ourselves.

By considering sanctifying grace, we can also avoid expecting too much of others, and we can lose any distaste for spirituality brought on by distasteful spiritual people. Similarly tolerance is made easier toward old people who have led good lives but are now afflicted (and afflict us) with the faults of old people. Yet they will die, as the saying goes, "full of merits," the result of many good deeds of a lifetime. God sees all these people in their present degree of grace, and loves them very much even though they may be hard to live with. He sees through to the inner state of their souls with a clearer eye that is possible to our impatient, shorter vision. Just as he sees our own likeness to himself, so he sees and loves the same in them, the incalculable treasure which is sanctifying grace.

When the encrusted outer covering is shaken off our souls after death, all of us will shine forth, mirroring in their perfection his eternal beauty. Then how grateful will we be in the joy that we sought even that perfection which brought us only a little closer to this love. How little it will mean then that this perfection had to be sought at times in much fatigue, labor, and anguish of body and spirit.

Chapter 14

The Working of Grace

In the harmony between nature and grace there is a priority which must be emphasized. The two are not partners working together, each helping the other. This kind of partnership, though true in the sense that each must work harmoniously with the other, misses an essential causative function which is proper to grace alone. This causative and formative action, whereby the man is made into the saint, is called actual grace.

Actual grace is the working of God in our souls. We will see its function more clearly if we see the place of our souls in the supernatural order. Our souls, even though spiritual, are not supernatural as such, no more than our bodies are. Both are parts of our human nature. They begin to be supernatural because we have a destiny which is above our nature, to be with God face to face as his adopted children forever. This destiny is above our nature because our nature has no right to such a close relationship to God. Indeed, "man shall not see me and live." But since he has given us this destiny, we are in a supernatural situation.

Thus the state of being supernatural applies to us in all that we have of nature: our souls, our bodies, their different needs and capabilities. They are not now intended to be in the natural order of things, even though in speaking of them we must use the word "natural" for the sake of clear distinctions. They begin to be raised to the supernatural by our destiny of heaven as our final end, and they are raised definitely by our adoption through sanctifying grace here and now.

The help of God to accomplish every good thing we do in the state of grace is not a kind of help proportionate to or fitting in with our nature as such. Rather it is something proportionate to our final end and to our elevated state of adoption. Since our destiny and elevated state are supernatural, the help to achieve this end and to live in this state must be above our nature also. This supernatural help, as we have said, is called actual grace.

It is a movement by God which, as its principal work, enlightens our minds, inclines and strengthens our wills, but is not foreign in its influence to any part of our being and our circumstances. It is the ultimate causative element in everything we do at least implicitly for our final end. It is therefore the cause, working in and with our free wills and our whole nature, of our growth into saints.

Thus, the action of grace is not only the help of God which makes us turn from temptation and which impels us to accomplish good. It is also a formative power; like all the forces proceeding from an intelligent being, it works for an end or purpose. By it we are moved and molded by God (always freely on our part) to become more and more perfect in general, in the order of sanctifying grace and the virtues, and also more and more specifically what he wants us to become in our personal vocation.

This formation is not done in an abstract world where mathematical beings total up a higher and higher number of good deeds. The causative and formative action of grace operates deep in our nature. In the spiritual life it principally molds and reforms the rational part of us and the psychological parts of us which are not purely spiritual, and through these it even affects the physical parts of us—all that determines the way we think, will, react and feel.

To accomplish sanctity under the influence of grace and for the love of God is the theoretically simple way by which saints are formed. But in practice many of us are not capable of such a direct, frontal assault on our objective. Our individual natures have been presented to us, or we have so made them, in a condition filled with subtle obstacles to our progress. What appears to be an open field across which we can go directly to our destination is really a series of beds of quicksand which must be carefully negotiated. In other words, grace will accomplish its purpose only by enlightening us and strengthening us in self-knowledge.

This self-knowledge, the deep understanding of our capabilities and weaknesses, shows us the raw material with which grace must work, and thus helps us to co-operate with its action. Our weaknesses impede the action of grace—weaknesses which are spiritual, moral, psychological, and even physical. But it is not beyond the ordinary power of grace to take what is spiritually, morally, and psychologically imperfect and bring it to relative perfection, even causing changes in our physical nervous system by which new habits of thought and action are made easy and natural for us.

Here we are not speaking of healing disorders which would require the miraculous to cure them, although the ordinary operation of grace is often marvellous enough. Often enough grace is a true wonder, hidden in the steady growth of the natural processes and raising us up from even great imperfection on all the levels of our psyche. Not only does sanctifying grace heal the essential disorders of original sin, but actual grace must sometimes do this further psychological healing if many of us are to become saints. For, the psychological weaknesses even of normal people, not to mention spiritual and moral weaknesses, are critical obstacles to union with God. While the psychological weaknesses remain, the spiritual and moral ones tend to remain also. Even the relative perfection possible on this earth requires a relative stability in the natural substratum of our being. This relative stability, even though for some it is difficult to acquire, even though it takes much time and painful perseverance, is the eventual result of God's acting internally in the soul by grace.

Like sanctifying grace, actual grace is something essentially unfelt. Although at times we may be deeply moved in the spirit by it and even feel a corresponding pouring out into the emotions, it does not necessarily carry a placard indentifying it. It may be as ordinary a thing as reading the morning paper and noticing the sudden death of an acquaintance. This kind of actual grace is called external grace, although the real effect is by the internal action of God. In this broad sense, even our weaknesses can be used as occasions for grace. Our poor needs, our insecurity, even the sight of our sins can be used by God to open our vision and send us to him. Nothing escapes his providence.

Although dependence upon God is a property of the whole universe, it especially becomes more evident interiorly as we grow closer to him. As beginners we often half-think that our own powers are largely responsible for our successful breaking of old habits and the forming of better ones. We make this error unconsciously because we *feel* the efforts we are making, and we don't usually notice any feelings traceable to grace. But as we make our way toward knowing ourselves better and become more sensitive to the forces working for and against us, we cannot avoid the conclusion that the universal law of creation, which is dependence, applies to us in an unbelievably complete manner. Our Lord tells us flatly, "For apart from me you can do nothing" (Jn. 15:5), and we must perhaps sometimes sadly and sullenly, sometimes willingly and even joyfully, but always wisely and truthfully, come to agree with him.

The momentous thing about actual grace is that it is initial; it is the beginning from which everything else must start. God must give the first grace or we can have no grace. This is the emphatic teaching of the Scriptures: "But if the choice [the ultimate conversion of the Jews] is by grace, it is not because of their works—otherwise grace would not be grace" (Rom. 11:6). Even our prayers, by which we have so great a hold on grace, must have grace to inspire them: "For we do not know how to pray as we ought; but the Spirit himself makes intercession for us with groanings that cannot be expressed in speech" (Rom. 8:26).

Not quite so absolute is our dependence when, with the help of grace, we perform good deeds so as to *merit* more actual graces and thus to increase sanctifying grace. But even here, given the fact that we are all unprofitable servants, our sufficiency dwindles away enormously. Our dependence upon

God is so total that it would be frightening if it were not a dependence upon boundless love and power.

It is our privilege to know this love most vividly by our Lord's death on the cross. We know that our souls are safe in such love. Their perfection will come by opening them up to God's action, to the activity of grace. This is done, first of all, by submitting ourselves or abandoning ourselves and our problems to the action of grace. Even more, we ask that we may be guided, strengthened, and, if need be, healed by the working of God in our depths. We abandon to this invisible action our lives and our hopes. Our limited trust now becomes a trust for everything. We still do what is in our power, but we call upon God for help lest we fail, and we pray also for what is not in our power. "It is not that we are entitled of ourselves to take credit for anything. Our sole credit is from God" (2 Cor. 3:5).

But trust does not work alone. The completeness with which we will give ourselves into his hands, with our hopes, our weakness, and our failures, follows from the completeness of our love.

Part IV

The Gifts of Nature

Chapter 15

Things in Time

The light of faith by which we become conscious of our participation in the nature of God must not become a light to blind us. By sanctifying grace we do indeed become godlike, but never gods; we are never other than human. Yet from the very first, man has found it difficult to hold himself down to the status imposed by his nature. And the spiritual life itself, with eyes opened to heaven, can make him forget that he must walk the earth. Man tries to live in other ways than he must: if not like a god, than at least like the angels. For this reason we can call this spiritual aberration the "angelic heresy."

It was this desire to be more than man which defeated our first parents in the Garden: "You will be like gods" (Gn. 3:5). Men are helplessly limited in so many ways. We are limited to the specific, to the definite. We are condemned to plod from measure of time to measure of time. We must get up in the morning, work, eat several meals, and then must sleep again, spending an enormous proportion of our lives in unconsciousness. And through all this we see the inevitable diminution of our powers with increasing age, and their ultimate extinction in death. Instead we may want life to blaze out with the actualization of boundless vision. We long for the ecstatic moments when our powers are triumphant to the full, when we are lifted out of ourselves, when we really live.

In some sense, to want this ecstasy at times is not only commendably human; it is also an actual happening on rare occasions in each life. But to want it at all times, to demand at least unconsciously that life be made up of this in great part or exclusively, is standing unsteadily on tiptoes, reaching out for more than the human.

For us this is unreality. For the angels it is reality. Unlike us they are not tied down to the definite limits of material life nor to the chains imposed on us by time. They are not like men, who are forever being held to the consideration of details: washing our bodies, curing and preventing our diseases, satisfying our stomachs, and giving to other bodily functions their due time and care. Surely none of these is godlike, none angelic.

Not all men are affected by this angelic heresy; it is a disease usually attacking only the best of men, the best in the sense of those endowed with vision and zeal. The best of us in another sense, that is, when we are also well-balanced, are immune. Still others are immune because they are made according to a different pattern, because they have been given a love for details. Indeed their vocation can be said to be largely a matter of details.

But immunity is not always the gift of God. Others whose vocation calls for broad, aggressive action create details for themselves. These are the putterers who keep themselves trivially busy so that they won't have to do the important difficult things. And there are still others who have no argument with details because they get rid of them by sleeping through them.

In general only those whom God has fashioned to live on a higher human level can fall into the angelic heresy. And since the spiritual life will be attractive to many of these, the subtle danger must be pointed out. Such men long for the triumphant freedom of the free spirit; they grudge every second that must be put into time and details, they want to rush into some state of existence where time can be by-passed to achieve the goal *now*. A famous scientist who correctly theorized about the corpuscles of the blood made his brilliant generalization from inadequate laboratory evidence. His thesis was proven by the patient work of others. Later the same famous man rashly theorized that goat's milk produced longevity, a false generalization which grateful humanity will mercifully forget.

It requires no great insight to see that the angelic heresy is really a great intellectual or spiritual pride. In this middle period of the spiritual life, pride is our most specific enemy. And so under the disguise of spiritual intensity there is an impatience with the details of the spiritual life (or of the religious life if one is in that vocation). We want perfection without going through the steps of the virtues, the less showy virtues; we fancy the mystical life when we need the ascetical; or we think that all things will be done quickly if we will immerse ourselves in the liturgy instead of wasting time in the other parts of the spiritual life.

The angelic heresy is, in one sense, as old as the Church, afflicted by it from Pelagius to Rousseau to modern times. It is the ultimate self-perfectivity of man. It is a romantic optimism, the poetry of the free spirit, of the god who would push God aside and climb to heaven by himself on a ladder of dreams.

Instead of bringing a man close to God, as he thinks, this pride will take him farther away and without his knowing it. While he imagines that he is piercing heaven, he will be doing a poor job of living on earth. Not only will his pride cause God to resist him, as God must always resist the proud, but it will also make it quite impossible for him to love his neighbor in any way which can be called true love in either a divine or human sense. His grandiose demands will require a similar godlikeness in others. When they fail, he will cast them aside and take up others in the self-delusion that here at last he has found what he is looking for. He will not be able to tolerate the despicable details of the humanness of others. All men therefore are his to be in some sense used. This is not love, and yet without love he cannot have God.

The angelic heresy is not confined solely to the spiritual life. It is also a danger to the apostolic life. Such men want to save souls without a strong foundation for saving their own. They want to help others without the preparation normally needed. "If the grace of God isn't there beforehand, then surely it cannot be far behind. The fire of enthusiasm suffices for grace anyway." Often and sadly the grace of God, when it does come, finds a smoldering ruin brought on by this uncontrolled fire.

Now, of course, it is most necessary to want great things in the spiritual life. Our Lord left us no choice. "Be perfect," he told us. And it is not wrong to want perfection to take place in as little time as possible. But the divergence between balance and unreality comes with the understanding of the possible. God wills our perfection to be accomplished only in a world where definite times and things are an inescapable part. The spiritual life, we must keep repeating, is a growth. Time is involved in all growth, and so are details. A seedling is not at once given all the food it needs to bring it to maturity, but must take it only in the movement of time and almost atom by atom. So in the spiritual life, changes take place in a divinely ordered fashion, not all at once, but usually one at a time.

This measured necessity is essentially a part of our nature and not a punishment for original sin. Even in the Garden man was not freed from definite details and time. "The Lord God then took the man and settled him in the garden of Eden, to cultivate and care for it" (Gn. 2:15). Likewise Adam and Eve had to care for their bodies. If this divine coercion is for some people a source of impatience and even humiliation, it can be a source of grace also. To find peace, we must come face to face with God by being patient with his will. And we also come face to face with ourselves in a most fundamental stratum of our being. The acceptance of our human condition will bring knowledge of the true self. Our human nature, for all the natural glory of it, has definite circumscriptions. "You have made him little less than the angels" (Ps. 8:6), and we cannot overstep that little less.

Our lives, our spiritual lives especially, are at their best when we do not lose sight of the human. Speaking in an ultimate sense, they can be at their worst, not so much when we are most like the beasts (as we might imagine), but when we are trying to make ourselves most like the angels. For then (again speaking in an extreme sense) is when we can come closest to being like the devils. The rebellion against the order of God's creation can become a rebellion against God, the fallen angels' eternal refusal to serve. After all, this was the temptation—not that men should become like beasts, but like gods—that won the day in the Garden.

Chapter 16

Our Tools
(a) The Intellect

When St. Thomas discusses the fall of the bad angels, he encounters the problem of how a purely spiritual being could sin. Similarly he finds the problem of how the good angels could reach perfection. With remarkable insight he concludes that purely spiritual beings can reach perfection (or damnation) only all at once. In angels the intellect can see consequences so clearly that the will is able to make a final and irrevocable choice immediately. With men the situation is different.

God is mercifully patient with our sins, and our perfection is worked out by many steps. This difference follows from our kind of nature, human nature, with a spiritual intellect and will embedded in a material body. This human situation requires that our knowledge come to us piecemeal and materially through the senses before it can become a possession of our spiritual intellect. Our nature, here similar to the angels, requires that our free will can act only upon what is presented by the intellect. But unlike the angels, our voluntary processes do not begin and end with a purely spiritual act of assent or dissent, with the choice or rejection of all that this intellect can hold.

Our human intellect is wound around with influences from the material part of us. Not only is our knowledge broken up into parts, sometimes hard-earned parts, but also by the same materiality we find it more natural to look at one part at a time rather than to seek a whole or the synthesis of many parts. Our more outstanding intellects, like that of St. Thomas, are better able to do this. But a large number of men see reality in small parts, usually the parts that concern them personally, and even these parts are affected, often distorted, by further influences from the material. These influences are our instincts, feelings, and emotions.

These, of course, should not be looked upon as enemies of the intellect. They are our connatural way of operating and are intended to be under the peaceful domination of the intellect and will, thus giving a truly human form, that of the whole human being, to our contact with reality. Our instincts should lead us into rational conduct, and our feelings and emotions should incline us toward and then support correct decisions. The instincts and emotions of love and fear are easy examples of this.

But as things are in our present state, the divinely established order has been broken. What superiority of inner oneness we may still possess is either an exceptional gift or something to be struggled for during a lifetime. Our instincts, feelings, and emotions make it difficult for our intellect to see reality. They incline us to see things their way and thus they narrow our breadth of vision or they weaken our hold upon full objective reality. By their imperatives they can influence the making of our choices. They also can adversely impede the carrying out of our good choices and tragically make agreeable and delightful our bad ones. Thus for good or for evil, we work as a spiritual and material whole in everything we do as integral human beings.

Choice by choice, however, we are intended to work toward our ultimate perfection. It will help us spiritually if we understand ourselves more in our manner of knowing, choosing and feeling, not necessarily by a psychological or physical analysis, but by an understanding of the practical operation of these faculties in their relationships with each of the others. They are, after all, the tools by which we use God's grace to become perfect.

First of all then, the intellect is a spiritual faculty by which we are in contact with the truth, that is to say, with objective reality. But the intellect must reach reality, not only by the senses, but also by a complex of nerves which we know as the brain. In the brain is centered our imagination and our sensory memory, and through the push and pull of the nervous system our intellect and will are in contact with our instincts, feelings, and emotions. Our intellect can be influenced by them through their influence on the will, and thus we may not live in reality but in relative unreality.

By undue influence from the physical part of us we can live, in varying degrees, in a subjective state rather than an objective one. We become more concerned with what we feel than with what is. For instance, people who are afflicted by phobias or undue worries are thus affected because objective facts do not make as much impression on them as their interior emotional states. Our emotions, often our hidden, unconscious emotions, have the power to feed on themselves and to become stronger, so that something which ought to affect us only slightly in regard to its objective value, as the creaking of an old house at night, can become so strong as to absorb the whole consciousness, as in great fear.

The undue influence of fear is a particular characteristic of the too-subjective state of mind. The spirit does not feel secure when acting contrary to the fear-impulse or inhibitions and so, since dependence upon feeling is the essence of the subjective, the slavery to the non-real becomes a fixed way of life.

But fear is not the only road to exaggerated subjectivity. Our likes and dislikes can be enormously conducive also. An unwillingness to endure discomfort and pain can be closely connected with fear, of course, but even by itself our demand for a pleasant world can also drive us away from reality. A traitorous peace has come by the killing of truth.

Not only discomfort and fear, but all the instincts and emotions have this power to rebel against the order of creation which has designed the intellect for objective truth. We need not except, then, the most basic of all our drives, the power to love. Not to speak of the power of sexual passion, we can easily become too internally involved with the emotions which come from loving our friends. In cases where this removes us from reality, these friends are not merely people whom we like and about whom we fondly think from time to time. In a sense they actually "live" inside of us. We make them live subjectively as new creations, what we would like to think they are, rather than the real persons.

The result is a distorted image, too good—just as in the case of hatred, the image is distorted into an unreal badness. And since the spiritual life is deeply affected by those we love, to become one with a deception will hold back our progress. All our rationalizations will not help us if we are emotionally one with what objectively is a falsehood.

Since it is truth that makes us free, it likewise is a fact that untruth makes us slaves. And no such slaves can come close to God. This subjectivity is far more fundamental than the problem of daydreaming. It is a basic attitude of mind by which we retreat from confrontation with the truth in respect to God, to ourselves, to others, and to the external world.

Especially in the life of prayer, which is at the heart of our relationship with God, the subjective state can be so much with us that it is difficult to fix the attention on a real object, even on a real interior object such as God's presence in the soul. Subjective awareness of the creatures of our mind and of our moods and feelings is not only the cause of many distractions but it can also stand in the way of progress toward higher prayer.

We may erroneously think that we prepare best for contemplative prayer by becoming aware of our every inner experience, or at least by becoming self-conscious in every one of our religious experiences. But conscious attention to our feelings will result in just the opposite. Instead of looking at God quite simply (which is the state of contemplative prayer, whether acquired or infused), the soul looks at itself to see what it is doing, or reflects back on itself to enjoy the experience of enjoying. It misses the reality which is the simple objective presence of God himself.

One more situation comes to mind: the difficulty of separating true inspiration from false. The intrinsic difficulty is sometimes made enormously worse by the need to "feel" in order to accept something as true. Not only does this cause mistakes to be made in a negative way, as when the feeling of fear prevents us from distinguishing between temptation and sin, but also positive illusions are accepted as true, even as coming from God, whenever strong emotion radiates from a new idea. Such feeling (at best) often only indicates a good idea, with all the limitations of even a new, good idea, or (at worst) is associated with something irrational welling up out of the unconscious, when it is not a device of the devil. But instead, the experience is accepted as quasi-divine, only because an imperative feeling is attached to it.

The results of such self-guidance can be tragic. Obviously a man so guided cannot be consistently wise or ideally prudent. As a consequence of human weakness, even authentic inspirations must be submitted to the reasoning intellect, our own or that of a trusted guide, depending on the seriousness of the matter. They will be measured by the light God has given us, along with the even better light of the faith as it comes through the teaching and governing Church (see Gal. 2:1-10).

The dependence upon emotional states instead of the guidance of reason is in itself often the result of a deeper emotional state, that of fear or insecurity. This, we are told, often comes from a sense of rejection or worthlessness deeply experienced, probably in early life. The child is made to feel that it is all alone, but since it cannot live that way, it makes up its own world. The outside world is too hostile, and thus there follows a pitiable retreat into the subjective. A film is drawn over the intellect because reality is too distressing or too frightening.

This film varies in its ability to shut out reality, but to the extent that it does succeed, the emotions become the important thing. For something to be real, it must be felt. The motivation then is more from the feeling than from the thing. At times the mind tries to manufacture the feelings so that it will be secure and feel that it has a hold on the only "reality" it knows, which is actually unreality. In looking upon a flower, for instance, the subjective man does not let the flower bring its beauty to the senses and then to the mind where the automatic response may be the production of authentic emotion. Rather the subjective mind presents itself with an emotion ready made, an emotion which one ought to feel when looking at a flower. But of course in this substitution it is unsuccessful. We are so designed that true emotion is to be produced as a response to an object or situation, and so the forced counterfeit is uncomfortably unproductive of true satisfaction or release of tension.

The ways in which men retreat from reality are devious and some of them horrible. But any degree of it can have effects in the spiritual life. The beginning of the cure is to see the great desirability of the objective world. We must be convinced of the need to meet the real on many levels; nothing can be overlooked. If subjectivity is the ingrained habit of many years, it is not going to be broken by a mere new resolution, for instance, to be careful about daydreaming.

First, on the level of the objective physical world, we must be convinced that the greater beauty, wonder, and interest is there rather than in the lifeless counterfeit manufactured or imposed by the mind. We must see that subjectivity is self-frustrating; it is a reversal of the order put in our nature by God. Therefore it cannot lead to him.

Then we must learn to distinguish between subjective and objective states of mind. If nothing else, this will save us from many emotional depressions which have only a faint insight into reality, if any.

But more, we will be able to see truth more sharply and universally because the film is gone from our eyes. Our judgments will be based on truth and not on fancy.

Our friends, for instance, will be seen as they are. We can love the true ones more securely, and those who do not deserve the oneness of friendship can be avoided or loved distantly. In everything we see the desirability of being free, and in our true freedom we can develop in ourselves what we are. In fact, along with the successful recognition of the difference between objective and subjective must come the beginnings of a deep rejection of our false self-estimation of worthlessness and unloveliness. This underlines what we have said previously about the true self.

Finally and directly, objectivity is desirable because it is the only way to reach intimacy with God. He is real; he is not a subjectively created fantasy, but the supreme fact. And in seeking him, we will, as an invaluable aid, live in the objectively present moment to the extent that it is practical in lives that have unending needs and obligations. So much of the subjective is a reliving of the past or a projection into the future. So much of the objective is in the present. God, in fact, is only in the present.

In the spirituality of the whole man there is always a priority of function among his several parts. Even though the whole man goes to God, he must still be led, by the one power within him by which as man he must be led, and this is his intellect. Even though the will and the emotions have their important part in his life, it is first of all necessary that he be in contact with truth or he will lose his way. By truth, of course, we not only mean the truth which implies fundamental knowledge, but also that which is directed to action.

In the acquisition of truth we need help from God through the intellectual virtues, especially holy prudence, and above all the enlightenment of faith and the guidance of the teaching authority of the Church. But still, truth has only one opening into our life and this is through the intellect.

Chapter 17

Our Tools
(b) The Will

The will and the intellect were created to work together. The intellect was intended to seek after truth, the will to embrace the good. In general the intellect leads the will, for no one can desire or reject something until he knows about it. But the will in a sense can also lead the intellect. For instance, when we are attracted to someone, we desire to know more about the person.

The will is not uselessly given the power to move the intellect; much of the information which we need must come by means of this kind of cooperation. For, man is not so made that he can acquire all his knowledge by personal experience. Few of us, for instance, can travel so extensively that there would be nothing more to be learned from books, pictures, and other sources of information. Quite obviously an enormous amount of our information must come from others. We accept these facts on the word of those sources we consider to be reliable. The intellect satisfies itself about the credibility and reliability of these sources, and then the will moves it to assent to the truth which has not been directly experienced. Raised to the supernatural order, this process aided by grace is the principal guide we have for life and is called faith. It is the window we have into heaven.

The power of sometimes leading and moving the intellect is a legitimate function of the will, but it can be exaggerated into a slavery of the intellect. In the case of human faith a disregard for proper credibility in respect to those who inform us can result in credulity on our part and make us into fools. Even in the case of things related to divine faith, we can become too ready to believe reports of divine intervention, such as alleged apparitions and miracles, and thus be not far from superstition.

In another sense, especially important in finding our way to God, this leading of the intellect by the will can also debase the intellect. The intellect, in making its practical judgments, can too readily follow the lead of the will, and supply reasons of its own making to justify the action of the will. This self-deceiving distortion of the truth is called rationalization.

Rationalization is often an unconscious defense mechanism to introduce harmony when the reason and emotions are in conflict. But in the process the reason is degraded since it obeys a will which has been captured by the emotions. We want something very much and so we make up reasons for having it. Or on the contrary we may want not to be obliged to do something and so we find reasons for that. In this way our emotions and instincts lead the will and our will leads the intellect. Instead of being docile to the intellect in reverence for truth, the self-determining will forces the intellect rather to manufacture a specious imitation of the truth.

The defect here is in the will, first of all in not accepting guidance from the only faculty that can apprehend truth, and then also in allowing its own freedom to be crippled. Although God-like in the possession of freedom, the will often abuses the gift by choosing sin or other weaknesses and attachments. These not only weaken the will itself in regard to moral and spiritual good, but they also can compound the evil by putting the whole man in darkness. Unlawful and unwise choices and attachments will tend to obscure the power of the intellect to see clearly. Also, the pull toward the too subjective outlook is largely a pull brought upon the intellect by a will that has lost its independence to emotional influences.

Now of course the freedom of the will iş a relative thing; it was not given absolute freedom. Thus it has no autonomous freedom or liberty, such that it has a right to choose evil. When it does, this is an abuse of freedom. Its legitimate freedom consists in the power to choose between the various good things or choices proposed by the intellect always acting according to truth and holy prudence.

We all understand, therefore, that there are rightful curbs upon our freedom. Some of these are imposed by God, either directly, as through the Scriptures, or indirectly through our nature. Others are sometimes imposed by the God-given power residing in the Church or in legitimate government. Still others come from accepted customs of society which supply the lubrication by which man more easily lives in harmony with man.

A reasonable man understands all this. He will also understand that there are curbs which he himself must impose upon his own freedom. Examples of this are easily seen in the results of the choice of a state in life, of a marriage partner, or of a profession. Once he has made a definite choice in such a direction, he has largely restricted or eliminated his freedom to make other similar choices. He is now bound to make all subordinate choices within the framework of the more general choice. He has no other freedom but to fulfill the duties required by his state in life or profession. To recognize this and to act accordingly is, of course, responsibility and maturity.

The situation is quite similar in the spiritual life. Once we have chosen to follow Christ closely, many other choices are closed to us. Some of them, of course, are sinful or harmful, and others delay our advance. If we had a perfect human nature, we would submit with ease to such limitation upon our freedom. But our will is not under complete domination by the truth, and so we experience the attraction of what we have given up, or must give up if we would have God in the fullness possible to us. Because of the conflicting drives, some people find the spiritual life difficult, not always on account of the drives themselves, but sometimes rather on account of the indecision which results or, even more commonly with sensitive people, on account of indecision of which they only think they are guilty.

These difficulties can sometimes be solved by a consideration of the word *want*. All of us want different things in different ways. A man may, for instance, want the total dedication of himself implied in the celibacy of the religious life, but at the same time he also discovers in himself a *want* for marriage. In different senses he wants both. Similarly a man in the world may also want the spiritual life, and also experience a desire for a life of intensive sociability. But the problem is really solved by asking what we *really* want. This is ultimately determined, not by our drives, but by our will, by the free choice of our will. Then the things which we don't really want we treat as ineffectual desires. And we *make* them ineffectual by the consistent choices of our will. The various parts of our nature may reach out, but it is the will which decides what we really want.

With the will we can want in a sense that no other part of our desire system can want. The will can and sometimes must impose the higher judgment of the reason upon other parts of our nature which rebel against the higher judgment. With the freely given grace of God it is always possible for the will to exercise this control, provided that its freedom is not temporarily affected, as it can be, sometimes suddenly as in anger, sometimes unnoticeably as in a growing attachment. But of course this dominance of reason and will cannot always be maintained without great effort and even anguish, and we may feel anything but heroic while the dominance is being contested and finally asserted.

In making some of these choices, the will, because of the weakness of human reason, cannot always act with certainty. This is sometimes a cause of indecision in the spiritual life with the result of keeping the soul standing still or of pulling it apart. And yet in some things we cannot have absolute certainty. For example, how can a young man know with absolute certainty before he is ordained that he is called to the priesthood? Or how can a young woman know with absolute certainty that this man of all possible men in the world is the best choice for marriage?

The best kind of certainty which we can have in many of our choices is often what is called moral certainty. This is a certainty based on our best attempts at a solution, attempts made in good faith along with prayer and trust in God for guidance. Our consolation is that God holds us to no more than this kind of certainty, and that he judges us to have acted rightly if we act with only this. It is obvious that many of the choices by which we find our personal vocation or our personal way in the spiritual life will have to be made with just this kind of certainty, moral certainty, or sometimes even with less, an honest but tentative exploration of probability by prudent trial and possible error.

At times the role of the will has been exaggerated in ascetical literature, as if the effects of grace were only a pious afterthought. But on the other hand, it receives a de-emphasis from those who are anxious to destroy nature in order to prove their spirituality. Thus we have had advice on "breaking their wills," on "giving up our will," or on "annihilation of the will." All these have a core of basic truth in the sense that divergent tendencies in the will must be destroyed. But those who live rather by words than by basic ideas have sometimes seized upon the will as a victim for immolation by total destruction. The spiritual man thus is supposed to be without will or desires that he can call his own. Yet on the contrary, while the will must be guided and disciplined, the truth is that it must be strengthened, not weakened or broken, and this involves the capability of strong desires.

It is the man with a broken or annihilated will who always remains on the fringes of the merely pious. It takes a strong will, a very strong will, to get really close to God because the choices to be made are great and sometimes fearful. The pious person of weakened will quite fruitlessly reads spiritual books or examines his spiritual state in an attempt at self-knowledge. Spiritual books will present him with problems to be discussed, but these never become paths pointing to consistent concrete action.

The analyses of self-knowledge attract him like a magnet; he remains enamored of the pleasure that comes to all of us from thinking about ourselves. "Self-knowledge" then becomes an escape from the reality of authentic spiritual action, and becomes self-conscious introspection which is spiritually and psychologically harmful. On the other hand, the man of will uses the new self-knowledge to go to God.

The will, though potentially our strongest faculty, is a delicate instrument with laws of operation which we must observe if we are to develop its strength. A strong will, for instance, does not mean strong commands directed at oneself (or others) as if acting in the image of Napoleon directing the Grande Armée or a severe school teacher inflicting a whipping. The will operates best when we are not conscious of its operation. At times its choices can be made very gently. The book you choose for spiritual reading may be that type of choice. Occasionally our choices are made with more emotion, and this may be a good thing. But even then our actions are spontaneous and free from the approving attention of the intellect.

It is true that self-conscious self-discipline can have many good results with certain temperaments. The ever-present spirit of the Stoics and the techniques borrowed from the East, such as yoga, can be valid natural aids in producing strength of will. But anyone using such self-conscious methods must become aware of their limitations in the spiritual life. Not only do they risk turning the attention on oneself to a spiritually unproductive degree, not only do they tend to eliminate much of the sense of dependence upon God (since everything seems to depend on these self-conscious efforts), but most of all they cannot of themselves supply the element which brings us close to God, and this is love.

For those who have an inclination to use them and find them successful, they will still only build the house; they cannot of themselves put love into it to make it a home for God. Nor is the union of love

with Christ and Mary or the humble submission to
the authority of the Church a necessary consequence
of them either. Even in regard to the life of prayer,
where they may teach an admirable power to concentrate, there is danger that we will become too conscious of the operation and not enough centered in
the object.

It is like a driver who would be interested more
in the way the car is running than in where he is
going. To be psychologically authentic, we have to
will the object. In prayer, God, and not our praying
selves, must become more and more the object.

With a will operating according to its own laws
of operation, we choose without becoming conscious
of the fact that we are choosing, and our choices
can be made quietly. A good example is the handling
of an involuntary distraction in prayer. Let us suppose
that the distraction has been with us for some minutes. Then we suddenly realize that we are not praying. So far there has been no operation of the free
will except the virtual perseverance in the original
intention of praying. (This has not been withdrawn
by the involuntary distraction, and therefore the time
spent has been morally good and meritorious.)
But now the awareness of the distraction brings the
necessity of a new act of the will. Shall we now become very emotional about the situation, in disgust
call ourselves a few low-class names, and then return
to prayer? Or shall we perhaps become discouraged,
spend some time in feeling sorry for ourselves, and
then finally climb out of the pit? Or most magnificent-
ly of all, shall we deliver a sharp command and with
great determination wheel our minds back into a
closely watched regimentation?

Of course the ideal way to exert the force of will
is none of these. Rather it is a quiet and immediate
return to the object of our consideration, without

giving the slightest further attention to the distraction or the fact that we were distracted. We implicitly acknowledge our weakness without making an issue of it. We have returned to our Father without cringing, without a demand for superhuman perfection, but instead have come in the image of children who are sure of the love and understanding of such a father.

Although it by no means shuts out helpful emotion, the strong will can act quietly. Here then is a human being perfectly assured of itself, perfectly aware that no degradation is involved in reaffirming or remaking one's choice, yet making it immediately and consistently without unnecessarily disturbing the calm surface of the waters. Is not this the picture of inner strength? Who should want to break this kind of will, or to annihilate it?

How to strengthen the will? The answer, stated very simply, is to keep on making the right choices, no matter what the difficulty. If we always make the right choices, one by one, whether easy or hard, and always with as much promptness as is called for, is not this the way to develop a strong will, despite incidental failures along the way? The whole spiritual life is there to aid us. It provides many ways by which the help of God can come to us.

In practice, however, the consistent making of proper choices is not that simple. We have still to *want* to make the choices. How to want to do it? To answer, we must first see how the will operates. Suppose that one were in great temptation and at the moment when consent was imminent, a violent earthquake suddenly began to shake the building. In such a situation anyone would remove himself from the temptation very willingly — no inner anguish, no hesitation. A very strong counter-force would be operating, self-preservation, the love of the self.

The will is made so that it operates out of love; even the other motives such as fear and hatred are love with a different direction. The stronger our love for our highest good, the stronger our love for God, the stronger will be our motive for making the choices which lead us to have more of his love. The secret of wanting so many of the things we have to want, but may not want naturally, is this power to love that is in all of us.

Perfection in the spiritual life will be most easily attainable when it is directly the result of love. Although it is possible to strengthen the will by much self-discipline without much love, intimacy with God is for those who love.

Chapter 18

Our Tools
(c) The Emotions

Any mention of love as the motive force of the spiritual life brings up the third of our natural gifts, the emotions. It is not our purpose here to emphasize the fact that true love need not be emotional. Anyone at all experienced in the spiritual life already knows this, or he would not have come this far. But rather it is our purpose to show the true place of the emotions in the whole life of man and to show how to use them in the spiritual life.

There are two extreme positions in regard to the emotions. One is the stoical suppression of any manifestation of them as a weakness. The other glorifies emotion and makes our feelings the norm of judgment. We have already spoken on this latter error; any dependence on a norm so inconstant stands self-rejected before the mind of a thinking man. But the error of the other extreme is not so easily discovered, especially in the spiritual life. After all, the emotions are the cause of so many evils that their suppression seems to be the most efficient way of avoiding an undesirable influence upon spiritual progress.

Many have attempted this repression and wondered why, instead of finding God and peace, they sometimes found that things became much worse.

The emotions were created by God; they are his gift and therefore are fundamentally good. Our Lord certainly had emotions; he showed joy, sorrow, and anger. We cannot crush something good in human nature and then expect things to go on as well or better, or at worst with a slower pace in some authentic, but modified form. Human nature, and specifically our emotional human nature, is like a bar of wet soap. If we hold it properly, not too loosely or too tightly, it is a useful servant. But if we press it or squeeze it, it is likely to slip out of our hands. And so with the emotions. We crush them at our peril.

We carry self-control to extremes, to the total emptying out of all pleasure, all desire, all joy, all love of self, and we suppose this will make a saint. But in the attempted murder, nature will win out, and when the unfortunate result is not merely the drying up of our powers of love, sympathy, and enthusiasm, it can take the more sinister forms of psychological strangeness. Even where there is not a definite lack of balance, they can result in the exaggeration of harmful tendencies in those who are normal. And of course in either case you get, secretly and blindly, a really proud person. For since laughter is forbidden to them, they can never laugh at themselves.

The true solution to the problem of the emotions is neither unrestrained freedom nor complete repression, but rather intelligent control. Control can be achieved in two ways, directly and indirectly. On the one hand our emotions were intended by God to be under the control of our reason and will. On the other hand they were also created to respond to an object either exterior, as the sight of a friend, or interior, such as the recollection of the same friend. If we attempt to reassert the full control of the intellect and will, we are acting on them directly. If we bring in or remove the external or internal stimulus, we are acting indirectly.

Although we often must assert direct control over the emotions, as when we refuse to weep in public or when young married people refrain from undue public emotional display, there is some danger that too exclusive an employment of direct control will result in a suppression which is harmful. This can cause injury to the legitimate spontaneity of our nature which is a usual condition of our psychological and even physical health. It is also possible that what we think is direct control is really the irrational suppression of one emotion by another, as when the love instinct is suppressed by irrational fear. This can lead to unfortunate psychological, and therefore spiritual, inhibition. Rational and volitional control must be maintained, for man acts as man principally by the dominant power of his reason and will. But there are also the indirect means of controlling emotion, often simple and more successful.

These indirect ways of controlling emotions are concerned with the objects or stimuli which excite them. It is often easier to remove the stimulus, or remove ourselves from it, than to exercise direct control. Sometimes it is the only way, for the emotion can be so strong that control is humanly impossible, as if a man were to stand in the path of a forest fire and command his body not to be burned.

Of course, there are situations where such removal of ourselves or the stimulus is not possible or practical, and then additional help will be found in greater use of sources of grace. But even in such cases it is always possible to exercise control by directing the mind and turning the attention to something else capable of holding it. Without the attention of the mind the emotions will subside through lack of air, so to speak. For example, a doctor in examining a beautiful woman will concentrate his attention on the medical problem. Those who are tempted to anger can divert the mind to something else.

By using this method, St. Francis of Assisi overcame the emotion of disgust, by seeing the person of Christ in the leper. By this method of controlling the attention we do not risk the danger that frequent, conscious, and direct control of the emotions will result in unhealthy repression of emotional life itself.

But it would be an implied insult to the Creator if we saw the emotions only as something to be controlled, and not as a gift to be enjoyed and used. The emotions are to a great extent what makes life humanly happy — not to neglect, of course, those emotions which are basic to our welfare, such as fear and the legitimate expression of sorrow and anger. But emotions such as love, yearning, pleasure, and joy are what make our lives full in a human sense. And their lack leaves us with the problem of emptiness, no matter how interesting or successful our lives may otherwise be. Therefore, in attempting a complete suppression of emotion we are inviting unhappiness.

This risk is particularly true in the spiritual life. All of us have been warned against emotionalism, against placing our security and our prayer life on the changing lights and shadows of our feelings. But the answer is not elimination, nor only control, but wise use, and the wise directors have not failed to make use of emotion. Both St. Francis de Sales and St. Ignatius of Loyola have given us meditations in a form calculated to bring forth emotions. In this way the whole man is moved away from evil, toward the good and toward God.

In prayer we must not, in the name of higher prayer, suppress the pleasant feelings, often called consolations, which may arise. They are the gift of God to encourage us, the natural companions of love in the spirit. Indeed their removal can be a deeply felt suffering, one not to be brought on voluntarily, but only by the designs of an all-knowing God.

In connection with emotion in prayer, there must be mentioned an excess of emotion which can disturb our prayer and even cause some people to give it up. This is the experiencing of sexual passion and images in prayer. There are two unwise ways to meet this: one, by giving up all but perfunctory prayer; and two, by consciously or unconsciously repressing all emotion so that there will be no possibility of sexual feeling. The first of these is, of course, self-defeating; we cannot go to God by avoiding contact with him. The second is a mistaken course also; to strangle the emotions will render the life of prayer so difficult that the soul may not have the strength to force its way through it.

If fear or pride are not too dominant in those who experience this sexual rebellion, the following explanation will point the way to a reasonable attitude and solution. The unwanted sexual feelings are the result of the oneness of our nature. Even though the complete harmony of human nature was lost through the Fall, enough of the original oneness remains — not always, however, in the order intended by the Creator. The spiritual love that may spontaneously arise will sometimes have a strong echo in our emotional nature, and so the whole man is reaching out to God or surrendering to his love. All this is as intended by the Creator; to force ourselves to pray without emotion would be to cause a disruption of the whole affective apparatus and to prevent the spontaneous giving of ourselves to God in prayer.

But at times certain people with sensitive or ardent natures experience a further overflow, not only of the spirit into the emotional, but from the emotional into the sexual. Our sexual nature was so fashioned by God that it is ideally a love nature, this in women even more than in men. The result is that strong love can call up sexual passion. The body is participating in an intense spiritual love, but the poor body only knows love under two aspects, the emotional and the sexual. These two can be very close, even when there is no intention or desire for the sexual.

But there is nothing unworthy in this, nothing unclean; it is our beautiful nature making a mistaken response to an unintended object. In reality it may also be a sign of a more gifted nature, in the sense of being made for love.

As we have said, the response to this experience is not to give up or diminish prayer, provided, of course, that there be no close danger of certain consent. Even if the sexual feelings proceed to the ultimate, the soul still should normally keep its prayerful union with God. The secret is not to look at or notice these feelings insofar as possible, but to keep the attention fixed on him. The same is true of any erotic images which may also come to the imagination, images connected with the human nature of Christ, or with the Blessed Virgin, or merely images without reference to definite persons. Fortunately for our peace, this trial does not last forever.

Similar to the consolation we might feel in prayer is the feeling of inner renewal and freedom for our spirit that can come with sacramental confession. While we should not build our spiritual life upon emotional consolations, the psychological benefit of a fresh start made frequently can have important spiritual benefits. The feeling of renewal caused by

leaving behind even only small sins can be a psychological base enabling us to reach out to God with
more confidence and freedom.

Likewise, emotions of disgust and aversion for
sin can be useful. We do not base our conscience on
these feelings but they can influence the attraction
we may have for sin by a process similar to a conditioned reflex. Here, however, we must be careful that
it is *sin* that we are nauseated with, and not some
good part of human nature such as the sexual instinct
as such.

Because of the various reasons for self-control
we cannot permit even good emotions to have their
way completely at all times. More freedom, however,
can be allowed them when we are alone than when
we are with others. Often this is a way to get psychological release from tension, as when we weep or
externalize anger or frustration by some symbolic
action such as tearing up an unwelcome letter.

But we cannot allow our emotions to lead us. We
do not allow them to change our minds suddenly in
the face of established principles or reasoned decisions. The devil may well be pulling the strings if
we do. We can only let them flow through channels
dug out by reason. Even then we must watch that
they do not overflow their banks. This is especially
true of love emotion in spiritual friendships. To be
able to contain stronger emotions, we must dig the
channel deeper into the stability of God's love.

There is another way in which our emotions can
help us. We have already mentioned giving them a
controlled freedom so as to put the whole psychological man behind the intellect and will, by making
pleasant what is good and unpleasant what is evil.
In this we have been speaking of emotions either
arising spontaneously, as when we are confronted
with an injustice, or being induced more deliberately,

as when we present a stimulus to the imagination or memory in mental prayer. In this second way we do not manufacture emotions as such; we rather awaken them or draw them out.

But sometimes we should allow the good emotions to have their way for a while, not because we want to be ruled by emotion, but so that they may perform in our depths a work which only they are fitted to do: the healing of the wounds of harmful emotions and distorted emotions, wounds often of early origin. These depths, so named by psychiatry, are not as deep in our nature as our firmly held principles or as grace, since they are still on the emotional level. But they are rightly termed deep since they are beneath the level of our ordinarily observable thoughts and feelings. These depths cannot effectively be reached by reason, and it would be tragic to try. But good emotions, such as strong movements of love or aversion which are conformable to reason, or laughter at our own incongruities, can reach these depths and can do much to cure the ancient wounds, especially when helped by the grace of God and our attempts to find the true self.

Similar to this is the help that can come from certain inner or outward actions connected with but not arising from the emotions. For instance, we "put on" a bit when there is good news which should make us emotionally happy but for some reason, say tiredness, does not. Or we will tell God "thank you" with some enthusiasm. The reason for doing this is, just as the will affects our outer actions, so our actions (external and internal) can strengthen the operation of the will. This is not a sterile attempt to produce emotions as such, but rather to produce some of the effects which might have come from the emotions had they been in the close partnership with our rational nature, as intended by the Creator. We do this many times by smiling at people out of Christian love even though our emotions do not follow Christian love as they should.

Although it is not our emotions that are helping us, because they are not present, the employment of these externals which would follow if there were authentic emotion can do much to influence our inner life. We thus make habit patterns which make it easier for our spirit to operate; we change or maintain a body chemistry which makes for balance of spirit instead of depression. Indeed the progress toward the Christian joy characteristic of the saints may have to be made by many such forced marches. Just as the external symbols of human life, such as a wedding ring on a bride or a similar ring on a nun, can influence thought and action, so an alacrity in God's service which is willed even if not felt can make us more and more dedicated than if we dragged ourselves from one tired day to another.

Chapter 19

Companions in Glory

In considering the gifts of nature and their relationship to the spiritual life, we cannot pass over what is the most perceivably natural thing we have, and this is our body. Many words against the body have come from pulpit and pen. The words here are frankly for it.

We are justly concerned with the difficulties arising from the body, the many and great sins which proceed from it. But let us not forget that the soul is not without blame either; in fact, because there is no sin without the will, the soul is always ultimately to blame for the sins of the body. Even more, our greatest enemy is pride, and this is basically a spiritual thing. And finally, many spiritual sins are more serious than sins of the flesh, for instance, grave sins against faith, hope, or love of God and man, although fewer people commit serious spiritual sins than they do serious sins directly involving the body.

A certain attitude toward the body thus seems to imply a hatred for it. This attitude is, of course, an oversimplification, but it is not the only one. Another

161

exaggerated attitude would have us believe that the body and its instincts are good without reservation, provided that we don't hurt anyone in the achievement of our satisfactions. These two oversimplifications point out the need for a twofold attitude that is balanced, if we are to live by the truth and not by half-truth.

The first part of this twofold truth is that the body is good. It comes from God who cannot create evil. In fact he thought so much of the body that he gave it to his Son, and this through another body, that of the Son's mother. On the other hand, the body has suffered the more manifest effects of the Fall. It has various impulses which are not now under the complete domination of the reason and will. We often tend to think only of sexual passion when we hear this, but there are surely other difficult passions, such as anger and fear.

We cannot forget this twofold truth of goodness and weakness. If we forget the essential goodness of the body with its various parts and instincts, we risk becoming unbalanced. Our bodies and their instincts are too close to us, too much one with us, to be written off as if they didn't exist. Of course, not every lack of balance denotes an abnormal person. We all carry around with us certain attitudes which are not quite the objective truth. But nevertheless, there is here a risk of abnormality which may have consequences in the spiritual life.

But of course we forget the second truth at our peril also, even at greater peril because of the two evils, abnormality and sin, sin is the worse and is ultimately the worst of all evils. Yet we are incorrect to put abnormality as an opposite of sin; sanctity is not built on abnormality, but often sinfulness is. At any rate, although the effects of the Fall vary with different temperaments and become less as we grow in the spiritual life, the sober truth is that none of us can trust himself as if he already had a glorified body.

We can see the basis for this twofold attitude in the Scriptures. St. Paul, for instance, is very eloquent on the dangers: "But I see in my body's members another law at war with the law of my mind; this makes me a prisoner of the law of sin in my members" (Rom. 7:23). But St. Paul also speaks eloquently on the love we must have for the body. When he is counseling on marriage, he uses the love of the body as an example: "Husbands should love their wives as they do their own bodies.... Observe that no one ever hates his own flesh; no, he nourishes it and takes care of it as Christ cares for the church—for we are members of his body" (Eph. 5:28-30). In Christ we see a willingness to sacrifice his own body, but not without reluctance and surely not with hatred of it. And indeed if his body were hateful, would he have given it to us in the Holy Eucharist?

The importance of our bodies in the spiritual life is enormous. So very many graces come to us through them, even the first and most essential grace, our adoption through baptism. All the other sacraments also involve our bodies, especially the intimacy of the Holy Eucharist by which Christ's body is taken into ours. By our bodies also we have received our instruction in the faith: how to know God, how to love him, and how to reach heaven. Indeed our whole faith rests upon a body, the one that Christ joyfully took up again on the first Easter.

Likewise in living our faith, the body is an indispensable companion. Through the senses we can come to know God better by our appreciation of the beauty of nature, not excluding physical human nature, the marvellous and beautiful thing that the body is. Furthermore our bodies show forth the soul's love of God. We praise him by voice and by music. We show our love for him by the many things we do for the love of our neighbor. We fulfill most of the duties of our state in life through our bodies. And even when our bodies are not at their best, we accept their discomfort and disease in reparation for sin, not to speak of voluntary penances which we also do with our bodies.

And of course, there is a superior kind of dedication which some are called upon to give to God by the total offering of legitimate sexual love and pleasure, an offering especially pleasing to God because it is a gift, not of something impure but rather of great excellence.

There is also another way in which the body is of importance in the spiritual life. This is the way of honest appreciation. It is not a slave to be driven nor a prison to be endured. St. Francis of Assisi is often quoted as calling his body "Brother Donkey" but in later life he called it "Brother Body." We have already mentioned that our self-identity can be greatly advanced through an appreciation of the good qualities of our bodies, if not of what they have here and now, then of what full perfection they will have in heaven.

The acceptance of our physical endowments is a crucial point, not only of our personal identity, but also of necessary self-love. In the spiritual life it is easy for self-hatred to disguise itself by a hatred of the body. Sometimes even well-intentioned mortifications are mistakenly thought to be performed for love of God, but are really done out of self-hatred symbolized by punishing the body.

On the contrary, a sound spirituality ordinarily requires a sound psychological foundation. If we think of ourselves as something hateful, we will with difficulty make ourselves ready for love by God. A true union of love demands that each know that he is lovable to the other. But if not lovable to self, then logically but mistakenly, not to others or to God.

Since psychological inadequacy sometimes involves the body, or at least is sometimes reached through the body, it is sound spirituality to go to God through a prudent love for the body, not only by maintaining reasonable health, but also by appreciating its perfections — or as we said, the full perfection it will have in heaven.

St. Thomas goes so far as to say, "With the same love with which we love God we ought to love our bodies also." But of course we ought not to love the evil effects of original sin and our disordered tendencies. "Rather by the desire of love we ought to long for the removal of such things" (II, II; 25;5). It goes without saying that this love should be guided by supernatural reason, and not by a pampered indulgence or a superficial sensuality or even worse, an idolatry of the self expressed through the body. Like all other things, the love of the body must lead to love of God.

St. Thomas finds his chief reason for a supernatural love of the body in the fact that it is destined for eternal life. In heaven, of course, we will be able to love it without the unfortunate dangers of this life. In this final destiny we have another indication that God himself is the source of the spirituality of the whole man. Heaven is not the liberation of an imprisoned spirit, nor after the resurrection is it a renewed toleration of a reluctant union. In divine fittingness the whole man now receives the reward for which on earth both soul and body worked together.

How wise, then, to understand that we are by God's adoption one supernatural being with our bodies! Instead of contempt, hatred, or shame for what God has made, we accept them as companions, not always willing, not always reliable, but still our companions in a companionship of love which is to last, except for an interval which will seem short, for all eternity.

Chapter 20

Male and Female

There is a danger of not understanding ourselves, and therefore of not understanding our spiritual problems, if we do not appreciate the place our bodies have in the spiritual life. The danger is only increased when we also fail to appreciate our bodies in their specific nature as sexual bodies. Although certain psychiatrists are in error when they attribute so many of our troubles to an exaggerated, often unconscious fear of sex, they are basically right in that if we are greatly unbalanced in this, it can have harmful psychological and physical effects which we may not recognize. And these effects can also be felt in the spiritual order.

As an example which is obvious but not typical of those who have made deep progress in the spiritual life, we have all come across people who are afraid of their own shadows, so to speak, because they will remind them of something impure. Surely these should never be held up as ideals, nor should we think that such fear of our bodies is saintly. Chastity and continence are saintly, but exaggerated fear is not.

An overly fearful chastity, like a false modesty, does not come from God. If it does not come from unconscious psychological disability, it may come from the devil. Or it may come from both. The devil may want to draw us into some psychological extreme so as eventually to destroy or hinder our spiritual life. The end hoped for may be something as simple as discouragement with even ordinary temptations or, more cleverly, a spiritual pride which sees itself as advanced so far in the spiritual life that the flesh and everything to do with it is despicable.

This pride is, of course, a characteristic of the angelic heresy. But pride never achieves its own satisfaction. Either the result is contradictory, for pride is a breeding ground for temptation as well as a blindness to occasions of sin, or the result is a certain sexual insensibility which is mistaken for true progress but really is psychological repression.

Perhaps in some of these souls the devil may be playing for the highest stakes. Because of their superior spiritual potentialities, they are worthy of his greatest attention, and he would be a very poor devil if he did not give them his greatest attention. These are the souls who can love more than most. With them often, more than with most people, the sexual instinct and the emotion of love are closely knit. This is not to say that the emotions aroused by love of God will always call up a sexual response in the manner described earlier. But the very act of giving ourselves to God in prayer, since it cannot but be done spontaneously in a human manner, has a psychological similarity and an unconscious connection with the sexual instinct.

This similarity and connection is obviously different in man and in woman. For a man, his manner of giving himself to God is basically a going out to him, for this going out is the fundamental characteristic of a man's way of loving. For a woman there is more generally an acceptance of and a surrender to love. Now of course, neither as sexual beings nor as spiritual beings are these attitudes exclusive; psychologically we are fortunately a happy inclusion of both. But the point here is that a great fear or aversion in regard to sex can extend itself in the unconscious to anything which has a similarity to sex. As a result the prayer response in a man or woman can become rigidly cold by unconscious inhibition.

The same effect can be noticed in dealing with our neighbor. Instead of a wholehearted, yet prudent observance of the second great commandment, we can become cold people or shackled spirits, tortured by this unknown fear. Saying this is not to commit the exaggeration of excluding other causes for coldness and inhibition, but it still is true that if we crush the sexual instinct, whether consciously or unconciously, we can at the same time crush out the fire and warmth which we are meant to give to God and man.

The sexual instinct is unavoidably a part of all of us, but in some it is a more pervading part. And by this we do not mean to disparage such people. Sex so much a normal part of us that it affects the whole man as nothing else does except situations like extreme hunger, thirst, or danger to life. Even normal sexual attraction involves deeper and more pervading responses in our nature than a normal desire for food. The capacity for self-expression in a fundamental manner involving the whole man, involving the most powerful instincts of possession and surrender, all enwrapped in the impelling urge for complete love and union—this does not allow us to treat it in the same category as we would an ordinary response to food and drink.

All this describes its permeating power as an instinct but does not emphasize its nature. It is fundamentally a love nature. The only union in which it finds its lawfulness and its perfection is the marriage union, in which a man and a woman pledge each other love and devotion for life. In marriage the sexual act is meant to be a spiritual love act expressed in physical terms. This is the immediate end of the ideal marriage relationship, each giving to the other of themselves in pure and unashamed abandonment. That God by this act further intends to bring into the world children for the kingdom of heaven is an ultimate objective end of the act, but love is the usual immediate concern of the souls and bodies in this embrace.

This fact of love, while it shows forth the goodness of the Creator in giving this fulfillment to mankind, also shows us the danger to ourselves if we are not mentally adjusted to see its presence, its full purpose, and its beauty. We are too much one thing with a need for the fullness implied in this instinct. Thus if we have a fear or dislike for it, we will not be at home in our own bodies; mere existence with our bodies will be like being married to someone we fear or hate. We will be pulled apart psychologically, and when it does not develop into more serious effects, the inner conflict will use up energy uselessly and like other unresolved conflicts can leave us perpetually tired without our knowing the reason.

In the spiritual life a lack of appreciation of our sexual nature may seem to be a minor thing, but it is not. In finding our true selves, we cannot help but find ourselves as male or female. We must accept our bodies (and those of the opposite sex) precisely for what they are. If we do not, our respect for our manhood or our womanhood is at stake.

We are never exclusively spiritual creatures but always this precise man or woman. Our bodies with their maleness or femaleness are ourselves along with our souls. If we do not love and respect these bodies as male or female, our respect for our particular selves will be destroyed. But if we destroy nature in obliterating our masculinity or femininity, we are giving grace an enormously harder job to do.

All this has been said with the fullest awareness of the dangers inherent in this instinct, or of the shame so inextricably attached to it when it exhibits a torturing or embarrassing rebellion. We are not urging forgetfulness of danger or license of action, but only an appreciation and honor for the gift as God designed it and intends its use. In this sense, then, we hate sin and sinful tendencies, but we love what God has made.

Now, of course, it is one thing to see all this ideally and theoretically, and another thing to see it in practice. Although the beauty of sex is a gift of God, we do not react to this beauty as we would to a sunset on the ocean. Leaving out the question of sin, which may be basically settled at this stage of the spiritual life, we can become more involved in the deep attraction which flows from the sexual instinct than its value merits. We, both married and unmarried, can open ourselves to a partial obliteration of the beauty and eminence of the spiritual.

To use an example only a few steps removed from the sexual, we can form judgments on others and on the conduct of others which are based upon physical charm rather than on the higher truth, the spiritual qualities of the solid virtues. On the other hand, we can fail in being alive to the presence of Christ in those to whom we are not attracted physically or emotionally. Our love for physical charm and beauty can become such that we feel only horror for physical defects instead of finding reason to love as we love the suffering Christ.

This does not mean that we must shut out all appreciation of physical beauty, but rather that we must so limit our observing and enjoying it that it does not encroach upon higher things or upon the freedom of the soul. This freedom can sometimes be impaired even though we try to justify ourselves that we seek only beauty or the glory of God.

It seems best to divide the remainder of this chapter into considerations of sexuality in the spiritual life of the married and the unmarried, although not with such a rigid division that what is said to the one will not be of value to the other.

First, for the married. The appreciation of the sexual instinct has sometimes been too limited by an obvious truth, that marriage is a remedy for the rebellious nature of man since the Fall. Yet even for spiritual people this truth is important, and a mistaken asceticism should not prevent them from taking this remedy when it is at hand. But beyond this practical truth lies the full and wondrous plan of God in giving this instinct to man.

Through its manifestations, ideally seen and exercised, it carries man and woman out of themselves and into an intense relationship with each other. The loneliness of human life is broken down and the two are temporarily one in body, and because of the union of bodies, more permanently one in the spirit. There is a fulfillment of man and woman, not only in the sublime procreation of new life which carries the imprint of themselves, but also in the giving and receiving of love for the person through the symbol of the sexual union and its concomitant expressions of affection.

Even in the spiritual life married people should not neglect the practical results of this love and pleasure. For them the sexual life is a source of grace. Even the pleasure involved can be a great support in the difficulties both of life and of personality. To hold off the pleasure in a mistaken form of self-denial, while merely externally co-operating in the act, will not only put oneself outside of the providence of God but will probably be an injustice to the partner and a slow cooling off of spontaneous love. On the other hand, discouragement, aimlessness, and personal insecurity can be dispelled by the love which raises the spirit through the enjoyment of the physical.

Yet, although so many erroneously stress sexual fulfillment as if it were life's supreme aim, the truth is that the spirit must prevail. The sexual life must lead to greater spiritual life. "In contrast, the fruit of the spirit is love, joy, peace, patient endurance, kindness, generosity, faith, mildness and chastity" (Gal. 5:22, 23). These and many more are all higher than sex, even in its acceptable sense.

Admittedly we are here presenting the sexual life as an ideal picture, the way God has designed married love. In practice, however, and for many reasons, the ideal is not always attained. On the contrary, the sexual life can become an added burden even when there is no fault in at least one of the partners. This is what St. Paul may be realistically referring to when he spoke against the extremists who would forbid marriage: "Should you marry, however, you will not be committing sin.... But such people will have trials in this life, and these I should like to spare you" (1 Cor. 7:28). In such circumstances the way of the cross is obvious.

Moreover, the full panorama of married love is not limited to the marriage act but takes in the fulfillment of the duties of love toward spouse and children. Married love must always rest upon higher motives than the physical, on something more stable than the intricate human passions of two people and the inevitable changes in physical attraction and powers.

We should not expect that the sexual relationship in marriage, whereby body and spirit are united in one act of love, should be a barrier to grace. Rather it is a means of increasing it. We grow in grace, not only by doing difficult things, but also by pleasurable things taken with the right intention and moderation.

However, the sexual instinct has inherent dangers, and these are not only the obvious ones of sinful abuse. The soul can be blinded to the need of a deeper life by too great a preoccupation with sex. If one tries to make it an end in itself, the result is always a deepening emptiness. But even when it is brought into the general framework of God's plan, its attraction can be so delightful that there is no great desire to go to God or to go deeper into oneself. The dispositions of God's providence are sometimes so arranged as to take care of this, and obviously grace is able to overcome it. But married people will do better with this tendency of sex to over-attract if they are on guard against it.

This pull toward the purely physical or toward the sexual experience as aesthetically isolated in itself is a disharmony resulting from the Fall. Neither the sexual instinct nor its essential attractiveness is the result of original sin. St. Thomas teaches this clearly and convincingly (I; 98; 2). Nor is the great pleasure an evil effect, even though in the sexual ecstacy a man and woman are beyond the self-possession of reason. "For reason itself demands that the use of reason be interrupted at times," as indeed it is in sleep (I, II; 34; 1 ad 1). But the danger to the spiritual life is in the tendency of the physical to make itself the dominant part of the experience or, a more refined and more elusive danger, in the tendency of the love experience to make itself the sole end. Yet neither physical experience nor another human being is comprehensive enough so to hold us without eventually harming us.

As to the excessive pull toward the physical, this must be compensated by seeing the situation in the light of love and beauty. Tenderness and consideration of the partner are important in bringing this about. Love of neighbor as oneself will prevent sexual expression from becoming egotistical self-expression instead of human fulfillment. This is the great value of externalizations of love and tenderness, that they have no other reason (as such) than to express and symbolize love for the other.

But there must be a further compensation for the pull of the aesthetic appeal of sexual love as such, if the married partners are to grow greatly in grace. This compensation against the over-attractiveness of nature does not mean that the husband or wife must inhibit the pleasure, or through a false idea of virtue or modesty become reserved in the supreme joy of giving and receiving the things of sexual love. What it means is that God be brought into the situation, at least in intention before and in thanksgiving afterwards, that the things done be done in his sight, that the ecstacy of sexual love be further deepened by offering him the love for this beloved creature in this intimate manner, and that the surrender of the self to the other be done in him. In this way the spirit soars to him; as a result of this experience his goodness is discovered in depths most profound, and love for so good a God increases proportionately.

In speaking now to the unmarried, we include all who must live without sexual satisfaction, even those who are in this state, not by their own choice, that is, not called directly by God, but who are called to it by God through circumstances. However we are more particularly addressing the dedicated unmarried, whether in religious life or not. These have made an offering of the lawful sexual life they might have had in marriage. The offering is not a small one; it is often reckoned as heroic. But it is not always thusly reckoned. Instead it is sometimes said that by the celibate life we become frustrated men and women.

Such an opinion does not show an understanding of psychological frustration. Frustration never occurs when a higher part of our nature is able to impose itself *reasonably* upon another part. For instance, even though we may be hungry, we wait for the food to be served. We are not emotionally frustrated just because we don't go out and gobble up the food in the kitchen. The heroic, when it is wholeheartedly embraced, does not frustrate but ennobles us.

We are impressed, for instance, with the heroism of Nathan Hale who regretted that he had only one life to give for his country. We do not think of him as a man under great frustration as he walks to execution to give that young life. We can imagine how a frustrated man would act. He would plead, he would cringe, he would flatter, he would be willing to betray. But Nathan Hale valued life, not for its existence, but for its worth, for what he could do with it.

Likewise we who choose to follow Christ perfectly, who "follow the Lamb wherever he goes" (Rev. 14:4), who want a unique union with God and service of our fellow man at the expense of other things we might want, we too act nobly and rationally when we follow our light with an open heart.

The beauty of sexual love and its inherent desirability, while always the exclusive, actual realization of the married, nevertheless is for the dedicated unmarried not a sterile consideration. On one hand they will not think themselves so superior to sex that they will despise it. For this they too were made by nature according to the design of God. They will see their sexuality as a blessed part of their nature, and their offering of it as a gift from God because of his choice of them. On the other hand their appreciation of it will not be reflected in an envious thirst for what they may not have, nor in fruitless and hopeless longing, but in gratitude that God has given so great a gift to humanity, while not forgetting that he has given a greater gift to them.

Their appreciation of what they have freely given to God will result in a greater dedication, provided that this appreciation be kept within reasonable bounds. But given a deep spirituality and the good will that goes with it, they will be closer to God through this knowledge and appreciation than if they were to view the sexual relationship as grossly repugnant in an effort to dull its attraction. Despite the occasional inner conflict and emptiness, there will be a sustaining gratitude for being chosen by God to come to him directly, without the support and privileges of married love and companionship.

For both the married and the unmarried, there is the central fact that we cannot live without love. Love is needed for our full development. We need to be carried out of ourselves and into the spiritual being of another. For many this need is greatly filled by the love of marriage; others find an answer in true friendship. But no human being is able to fill us completely. There is a deeper love needed to do this, the love for him who is love, who made love, and who made us to love him.

This is a love which never grows faint because of the inability of the other to fulfill us to the depths of oneness and understanding. Nor does the ability to enjoy this love depend on powers which must inevitably diminish, but upon our soul which is ever young. It is a love which grows always stronger and more intense, even if in hidden ways, as we become even more like the Beloved himself.

Chapter 21

Men and Women

To appreciate male and female on the level of their sexual relationships is an important insight, but it is far from being the whole picture either in ordinary life or in the spiritual life. The two sexes have other aspects which reach into every corner of their lives, including the spiritual. None of us are neuter. Thus if grace and nature are to work in harmony, the psychological difference of the sexes cannot be ignored.

It takes only a little thinking to see that the male approach to almost everything is different from the female. But clear as this idea is in general, in the spiritual life the distinction often becomes blurred. As a result, there can be deep and unconscious conflict or frustration.

On one hand, the woman is guided in the spiritual life principally by men, as is fitting because of the man's generally broader vision and greater freedom from emotion in judgment. But the man has his own way of going to God, and the male approach can unconsciously become the ideal

179

toward which the woman is asked to work. For her this can be as difficult as climbing a smooth, glass mountain.

On the other hand, the man, because of his more independent nature will seek to find his way to God more by his own study, reading, and thinking than by frequent contact with a director. But in this process he will find many admirable books, even indispensable books, written by women or by men whose chief avocation has been to direct women. For him these feminine attitudes come somehow to be understood as the spiritual life. But being a man, he senses the incongruity of a female man even in spiritual disguise, and he loses stomach for spiritual reading even when he doesn't lose heart.

Now of course, we can draw the lines between male and female too sharply. The truth seems to be, and this is a major premise of at least one school of psychiatry, that we all are a mixture of both male and female. This is true to a limited extent physically, to a greater extent psychologically, and therefore we should also expect it to be true spiritually. This should put us on our guard against a conscious adoption of masculine traits in a man or feminine traits in a woman.

The incongruity of this (for instance, a deliberately cultivated deep voice in a man or fluttery mannerisms in a woman) is observable to all. In trying to project masculinity or femininity, not only do we run the risk of a particularly deceptive false image, but we also can be covering up an anxiety over our masculinity (especially) or femininity which is probably better met out in the open than covered up with self-assuring disguises which do not solve the crucial uncertainty.

For this reason we are not making any attempt to set down here what are the characteristics of man

and woman, or what should be their dominant
attitudes in the spiritual life. It is probably true that a
purely male or female person would be a psychological monstrosity. A mere consideration of the
male's characteristic desire to be *somebody* or the
female's possessiveness is enough to show the point.
It goes without saying, however, that the portion
of the opposite sex within us must never be in habitual dominance so as to submerge our real sex. This
would be a psychological inversion which would
make impossible a true personality and an authentic
spiritual life. But outside of this, far from being un-
sexed, we are enriched rather than impoverished by
what God has normally given us of the opposite sex.
If nothing else, it helps to maintain lines of communication and understanding between us. And this is
no small benefit.

So instead of anxiety or rebellion, there should
be peace and acceptance of ourselves as we are
made. For in a well-orientated man or woman, the
qualities of the opposite sex will not make either
appear to be members of that sex. In a man the feminine part of him will be projected in a masculine
manner, for an effeminate man is hardly a man.
A true man, on the other hand, can be gentle, sensitive, and understanding without giving up one
bit of his masculinity. Our Lord was surely such a
man, he who in his masculinity was powerfully
combative against the Scribes and Pharisees (See
Mt. 23:15-39).

Similarly a woman will project in a feminine
manner such more masculine qualities as independence and a broad, non-emotional approach. Examples of this would be St. Catherine of Siena,
St. Teresa of Avila, and Queen Isabella, all powerful
personalities but still, delightfully, women.

We have already mentioned that the difference of sex will affect our relationship with God in prayer. Besides a way common to both sexes, there is built upon this a man's way and a woman's way. But beyond a word of caution, that one not try to adopt attitudes here, we do not intend to pursue a subject which depends so much on the make-up of the individual and on his search for personal identity. In any case, even in the love of the sexes, a man delights in receiving love from a woman as well as giving it. Thus in the spiritual life a man, for all his independence, must receive from God not only grace, but if the man will humbly allow it, also love.

Sometimes our fearfully adopted attitudes of masculinity or femininity can become major obstacles. Thus out of fear of being womanly, (or sentimental, as he may call it) a man will content himself with a relationship with God which is kept at an impersonal distance by an admirable adherence to set rules and functions. Yet the truth is that love is a major masculine province. Compared to woman, he has only a little less of the ability to be completely absorbed in love, but lacks none of her depth in it. Thus he need not fear that love in the spiritual life will make him feminine, because loving is one of the best things that a man does.

Likewise, a woman may fear that she must challenge man in the spiritual life in order to avoid being submerged in a world frustratingly masculine. She will hesitate in this if she recalls that the most spiritually successful of all purely human beings was a woman, and that this woman succeeded, not by trying to be a man, but by being a woman.

Yet love is for women especially. What we look for most in a woman is the power to love. She may have all the other qualities: beauty, personality, intelligence, diligence. But if she lacks the power of giving in love, we have less than a woman. On the contrary, if she lacks many of the other qualities which we would desire in an ideal woman, but has a deep, sustained power to love, and power likewise to transfer that love into devoted service, much of her lack can be overlooked.

Herein women excel men. A man must divide himself between those he loves and his work. The heart of a true woman knows no division. And because she is all that she is more exclusively than a man, she can be the best thing in the world as well as the worst. Thus, fittingly, God made the very best of his creatures to be a woman—his Blessed Mother.

The difference between man and woman more clearly shows itself in their personal and social relationships with each other than in their relationship with God. The two sexes were designed to work in perfect harmony, the one in great measure supplying for some lack in the other. But often the actuality is the opposite of harmony. So, since we are obliged to love our neighbor, the fulfillment of this commandment can be aided by an examination of the fundamental forces involved. These are present, not only in marriage, but also in spiritual direction and friendship.

Consigning woman to a subservient role, as was or even is done in some civilizations, is an oversimplified solution of a complex problem. When man uses woman principally as his servant, as the mother of his children, and as an object of sexual pleasure with few if any civil or social rights, he is in a sense safe from her. He dominates and to a great extent controls her. If he were to give her more freedom—so it may have been reasoned—it is she who would dominate him. And he instinctively sees the incongruity of that. So being the stronger, he endeavors to prevent it, not always successfully even in the most male-dominated social organization.

Woman, it must be admitted, has been given deadly weapons which she can use to dominate her surroundings. Man is instinctively attracted to this creature which God has fashioned to fill him as no other can, as mother, as mate, as confidant. This attraction is increased to over-powering proportions when he is filled with love for this woman. Then it can amount almost to worship. Thus there is enormous potential power in the hands of woman.

One of her weapons obviously is her body. She can dazzle man with it, even when she does not bargain with it. In marriage, to give her the choice of surrendering to him or not, or where the commandment to submit is observed, for her to do so in sullenness or passivity, is to put her at an enormous advantage. The list of selfish women who have dominated men by the flesh alone is probably long and sad.

The second weapon given to a woman is the man's own sense of justice. Even though he is often thoughtless when dealing with a woman, he can be brought to the light by his sense of justice if this is not inoperative. On the other hand, the woman does not usually see things in broad perspective, being made by nature for a more limited world, the home. Thus she tends to seize the immediate goal rather than to weigh one thing carefully against another. In a self-willed woman this difference can work out so that she forces her immediate concerns upon a man by storming her way through, and on other occasions she will win her way by appealing to his sense of justice. The area in which he operates as a man can thus become smaller and smaller.

Her third and most powerful weapon is given her by man directly, and this is his love for her. He loves her more than anything else on earth. He wants to please her; he wants peace with what he loves so much; he wants and needs love from her. The unscrupulous woman offers this at a price. To have her love, he must surrender what is most precious to him, his manhood. Obviously this is too great a price.

If all women were unaffected by selfishness and shortsightedness, they would use this power wisely for the good of man and the family. As it is, it is sometimes cynically said that a woman must manage the man without letting him know that he is being managed. But how many women can conduct such subversion without the man's becoming aware of it, even unconsciously?

This is not being written to exonerate all men and condemn all women. Men's faults, however, are notoriously obvious. What is sometimes not obvious are the insidious forces working at his manhood. These, though hidden, can drive him into open opposition or callous disregard for a woman who, innocent and abused though she may appear to others, is trying to rob him. Man, being the stronger, cannot permit this, and this is a reason, among others not at all understandable, that he has sometimes forced woman into a secondary place by making her a creature apart from his higher pursuits, a lower form of humanity who is to share only one side of his life, the sexual, and do his work for him.

But as we have said, this is an unsatisfactory solution to the problem. Principally because of the Christian revelation, woman's place has become higher than at other times in our history. Through her restored dignity, ideally at least, we can see the marvel of this creature somewhat as Adam must have first seen Eve. Woman has been given this dignity again in the New Law because she has also been offered the light and grace to use it wisely, and this means that she use it to be a woman.

Like many problems this one can best be solved by Christian education. The basic teaching is given by St. Paul in the epistle to the Ephesians, and although this applies specifically to marriage, it is equally true for many other man-woman relationships. The man is to rule but not to dominate. His rule is to be characterized mostly by love, and St. Paul writes down powerful metaphors to express that love: "Husbands should love their wives just as Christ loved the Church.... In the same way must husbands love their wives as their own bodies" (see Eph. 5:21-33).

The woman is to be a companion and yet subordinate to the reasonable rule of the man. But her subjection is not because of force or custom, but rather out of love. In this, in general, she can find happiness because her God-given womanness instinctively looks for strength and guidance from the man. Since she is a woman, she will be happy only by accepting her womanhood.

However, when her dignity and the power that goes with it are not wisely used, and if he cannot reasonably change the situation, a man must withdraw from the situation to the extent that is in his lawful power. If it is a case of spiritual direction, direction has already ceased in fact and must do so in appearance. In marriage (and even to some degree in friendship) a man's obligations generally do not allow such complete withdrawal. Instead he salvages his manhood, his inner manhood to the extent possible. What compromises he makes must still keep this treasure intact; such is the will of God who gave him the gift of manhood. But he must make some compromises with life anyway; no one gets all he had hoped for or planned. Yet he never makes them so as to find himself against God or the Church for the love of woman. He accepts his situation as Job accepted the complaints of his wife. He prudently avoids topics of friction, and sadly he must withhold the secrets of his heart when he would want so much to share them. Sometimes this situation arises because of mere incompatibility, but if it has come because of the dominance of the woman, she has bought her dominance at a great price both to him and to herself.

The man, however, is not without his more subtle faults in regard to the woman. In a sense it all began with Adam, who was moved toward the first sin principally because of the pride by which he wanted to eliminate God. But his pride also involved Eve. His great love for this perfect woman made him want to be the beginning and end of her life and interest. He wanted to be her god. We are often made familiar with the possessiveness of woman, but a man can demand a sort of idolatry while being openly most devoted and considerate. He demands that her whole life be centered on him. This is probably pride and insecurity both at once, but it gives a woman little chance to be herself as a human being or a spiritual being.

It is essential that man realize that he is important; in some sense his manhood depends on this realization. But he must also see that he is not so important that other human beings should become his satellites. Indeed, man must reach out and almost bestow the sense of dignity and worth upon her whose love, understanding, and help he in turn needs almost irresistibly.

Man is apt to forget that woman has needs which he must not fail. Part of this forgetfulness is male blindness, male ego, if you will. But another part can be traced to an illusion brought on by early impressions. One such impression is the apparently limitless capacities of the woman he knew as mother. Another is the fact that later on he found it necessary to pursue woman, to woo her, and to offer himself and his future as the price of possessing this creature for his whole life. Then after marriage, if she is a competent woman, her competence will not disabuse him of his illusion of her apparently inexhaustible strength and consequent independence. All this may easily make him think that woman is a more exalted and self-sufficient being than she really is. Sometimes this apparent self-sufficiency makes him doubt his masculinity in which protectiveness is an instinctive part.

In such situations, where his primitive role of protector and provider is not easily evident, a man must reason his way toward adjustment to the situation rather than pull the woman down from her position. He will discover that the most competent woman is a dependent being simply because she is a woman. She is apt to feel loneliness more deeply than he, and therefore to have greater need of his interested company. Unconsciously she is always questioning herself.

For instance, women take things more personally than men; they apply to themselves even general statements not intended to have an application. In this way they are weaker than men, but often more clever at hiding it and more aggressive in defending it.

In this realization of woman's deep psychological or emotional dependence, a man can find an outlet for his masculinity. He is still and always protector and provider, although here on a higher level than physical or material dependence. Therefore he must

give woman love, admiration, praise, and attention—all sincerely. This is the psychological food
which she must eat in order to be what all women
are meant to be, in some reasonable sense: queens
and princesses. She must be made to feel what she is,
because she, even more than the man, finds it difficult to come to the realization of her worth by
herself.

There is always the romantic tendency in marriage and in friendship to think that love by itself
is enough; all difficulties will be solved by this
alone. But the sober truth is that every successful
marriage and friendship requires the constant carefulness which the philosophers have called the
virtue of prudence. This use of our practical reason
(or in woman, the short cut to reason known as her
intuition) will do more to keep love alive than oceans
of sexual passion in marriage or great compatibility in many areas in marriage and friendship
alike. We must constantly be thoughtful and vigilant
in what we say and do, and the manner in which
we say and do it. This care is one of the offerings
that our intellect places on the altar of love.

One final word must be said on the relationship of the sexes and here it concerns the dedicated unmarried perhaps more than the married.
For them the attraction and love of the opposite
sex is based on emotional and psychological grounds
which nevertheless have honorable roots in the
physical. Thus are we created. But the attractive
body, especially the attractive feminine body in
respect to the male, is not of the highest value in
the plan of God. The whole spiritual order of grace
and the virtues comes ahead of it, not to mention
many other things in the social, political, and econom-
ic order. Even when the body has been abundantly
endowed with beauty or handsomeness, this like

youth itself must pass away. But the spiritual order does not pass away. In a world where the emphasis is placed on youth, beauty, and glamor, a man or woman will find it necessary to weigh such things to keep a spiritual balance.

This is not to say that the only evil effect of the attractive body is the temptation to lust. If it were this alone, the pull to evil could well be thwarted by an appeal to the aesthetic, at least with good men, for in these there is an instinctive appreciation and even a reverence for the beautiful body. But the effect of unguarded and excessive appreciation may end, even in good men, by their being blinded to the faults and deficiencies of the person. This may well be a partial blessing in married life but otherwise it can result in tragic errors of judgment. Like our father Adam, whose full use of reason was probably blocked by his excessive love for Eve, we may be held by an unconscious fascination of the physical, even the good physical.

There is, then, a reasonable fear of the body of the woman by the man, and a similarly reasonable fear of the body of the man by the woman, especially when the attractive body is that of a person who is encountered frequently. This fear is not because the body is evil; rather by underlining its goodness and beauty, we are indicating its greater attractiveness and more subtle danger to those in the spiritual life, that is, to those who would be repelled by any attraction to evil as such. As a consequence, since our souls, and the difficulty of keeping them pointed toward God, are so important, we must carefully arrange our lives, must control our eyes, our thoughts, and our affections, and must dress modestly, even when there is no danger of sin. But there must not be so much fear

as to make us cold or without appreciation. By living close to God, we will find, not always without
difficulty, the balance between carefulness and
warmth in living among those to whom we are attracted by the design of our nature.

Chapter 22

Symbols

Our humanness never leaves us in our pursuit of the life of the spirit. We are ever flesh as well as spirit, and the way to the fullness for man as a principally spiritual being must always take into account this material side of him. God, it seems, has given us little choice. The great channels of the grace which makes us more like him are seven things of a material nature, the seven sacraments. These are signs, perceivable by the senses, which give grace when used as instruments by God. He did not make these sacraments purely spiritual things. He made them to fit our nature so that we might arrive at salvation and sanctification according to the way he compounded us of matter and spirit both.

There is another way, dissimilar but important, in which we are meant to find him, and this is in purely natural things. The experience of most of us even is that at times we can find him better in nature than in purely spiritual attempts to reach him. Thus we can see him in the quiet of the evening, and it is not without reason that he was pictured as "moving

about in the garden at the breezy time of the day"
(Gn. 3:8). We can see him in the vastness of the ocean,
in the awesomeness of a mountain, in the delicate
beauty of a flower. At these times our hearts will
not really need the urging of Scripture:

> "Bless the Lord, all you works of the Lord:
> Praise and exalt him above all forever"
> (Dn. 3:57 ff.).

There is still another way in which the natural
is important to the spiritual life, and this is by way of
symbolism. This has always been a part of human life,
as we can see from the stone age paintings on the
walls of the caves and on down to our own times in
which the flags of the nations stand for their ideals
and history. In all religions it has its part, this too
dating at least from the walls of the caves. Even those
Christian religions which have tried to eliminate
symbolism must by the law of Christ make use of the
symbols of cleansing from sin by the washing in baptism, and of food for the soul by some form of the
Lord's Supper.

Thus, because we have advanced beyond the
beginnings of the spiritual life, we should not think
that we have no need for other symbols of our religion
such as pictures and images. There is in some of us
a tendency to associate these with some almost
superstitious people in the Church. The truth is,
however, that in some form or other religious symbols
are companions of our human nature throughout the
whole spiritual journey. Not that we remain solely
or even principally with the symbol. Some superficial people (and these not always the uneducated
or the unenthusiastic) emphasize the outer sign
while neglecting the total reality underneath. Symbols are meant to lead to this reality, never to become
a substitute for it.

Similarly some overly intellectual people are repelled from images of Christ because they are not actual in the sense that the infancy and crucifixion, for instance, are not the way Christ is now in his risen body. But a little thought will show us that, although the outward condition of his humanity has changed, the person, the Divine Person, is still and always was the same. Thus we can, in the best of theological accuracy, put ourselves at the scene depicted. When we pray at the manger, when we offer ourselves as a gift along with those of the Wise Men, or when we sorrow for our sins at the cross, we are there in a true spiritual sense. Our Lord, in the sweep of the knowledge which he had of all things, saw us there.

In the Church we are constantly brought face to face with the crucifix, not so much a representation of an historical event, but as the most awesome symbol of God's love for man. Similarly the Sacred Heart is not so much a representation of the physical organ which pumped blood through the veins of the God-man, as it is a symbol of God's love personified in the universal symbol of human love. Our Lady is not only the mother of God and the most powerful advocate with her Son; she is also a symbol of the dignity of womanhood, and it is principally through this symbol of what should be, that the status of womanhood was raised in Christian ages above the level of even the enlightened pagans. Finally, there are the saints. Even though we cannot follow their steps in every detail, they do show us what direction, at least, our own should be taking.

An excellent example of God's providence fashioning a saint to be a symbol is St. Francis Xavier. His world-wide vision was worthy of St. Paul himself. In this he would always remain a symbol even though, like St. Paul, his work never accomplished a fraction of his hopes. But even more. He died on his way to

China. By taking him in action instead of in repose, by calling him home on a lonely island instead of in Europe where letters he never received would have ordered him, God has left us a symbol, a light to help us to see better into the darkness of a still unconverted world.

But lest the symbols of the saints should be too distant for us, there is in the Church a living symbol we may see every day. This is the symbol of the garb of those in religious life. The varied attire of these people, surely not all saints, certainly all struggling for salvation and sanctification like everyone else in the Church, symbolizes a dedication to the service of God and man. This was well understood by St. Francis of Assisi. He once invited a brother to accompany him to preach a sermon. They walked from one end of the town to the other, and then walked back again. When the brother asked when he was going to preach the sermon, Francis replied that they had already preached it. By their clothing and their demeanor they had preached the allness of God. In an age which tends to submerge religion by the sight and sound of so much else, and to treat it as a totally private matter, we have great need of such symbols.

Perhaps we can use this example as a stepping off place into the next development of our subject. As an example then, to see a nun publicly in her habit may well inspire us, at least unconsciously, toward a higher world. But if we were to see the same nun publicly walking around in a bathing suit, for instance, it might well symbolize the opposite of what the religious habit is designed to inspire. Not even great amounts of unrealistic optimism about the goodness and purity of the human body, or great outpourings of misguided zeal to be "one with the people," could prevent the destruction of a needed symbolical relationship — and perhaps the destruc-

tion of much more besides. This uncomfortable
fact, however, is not a plea for a return to exaggerated
ways of symbolizing modesty, this help to man's
spirit in controlling the flesh. It is rather an example
to point out to everyone a fact not always obvious,
that if we do not have one kind of symbolism, we
are likely to have another, and often an undesirable
kind.

Yet any such warning against the loss which
might come by careless imprudence or by the excess of mere convenience should not push anyone
toward a shame of the body. Such a danger is perhaps
more present to those who are unmarried than to
those who are married. In marriage there is a normal
process which tends to dispel false shame. There,
where ideally the body is enjoyed in the context
of love and procreation, the wedded partners can
easily come to a deep love and respect for their
own body and that of their partner. But those who
are unmarried, and especially those whose dedication
to God implies a permanent renouncing of marriage,
cannot reach this appreciation by this kind of experience. They can only look upon it at a distance,
as they would admire a magnificent painting, with
intellectual and perhaps chaste emotional response
to its beauty and innate desirability. They can also
give God a reverent gratitude for the knowledge
that, although they have agreed upon a more exclusive love of himself, they are by no means eunuchs
in a physical sense, but have the same nature as those
who know by experience wedded love and parent-
hood.

They may at times feel shame, considering their
dedication, in feeling instincts which rebel against
this dedication. But these are instincts which, though
God-given, are now acting blindly according to their
nature, instincts which would be most honorable

if these unmarried persons were husbands or wives.
Our beloved but fallen nature does not change
because of a higher vocation. Thus it may be necessary for them to resolve this shame or they can
become involved in deep emotional conflict. There
is an honorable, though limited, symbolism in the
flesh, and all must see it, especially those whose
use of the flesh is generously returned as a gift
to God.

Although we ought to have a legitimate love
for the body, our own and that of the opposite sex,
and although the appreciation of our own body can
be a source for finding personal identity, the body
can only in a limited sense become a symbol for us.
It is true that our manhood or womanhood is shown
in our bodies, and from this we might think that they
can provide a focal point for the symbolism needed
by our nature to operate efficiently and smoothly.
In an ideal world this would be true. But as things
are, the body tends toward a symbolizing of its own
powers (particularly of its sexual powers) which
on one hand are not expressive of full manhood
or womanhood, and on the other hand even lead
away from this fullness.

The body cannot be fully expressive of manhood
or womanhood because it does not as such reveal
the most important part of us which is the soul;
the intellect remains unseen, and it is a commonplace that a beautiful body may house a will so
selfish that one would almost curse the body that
hid it. But on a higher level there is a further deception if we exaggerate the symbolism of the body.
There is an inborn and normal fascination about sex,
and it is difficult to avoid its exaggeration even
when we think we are balanced on the subject.
The lie that it tells is that we can have through
sexual love or through mere sexual experience the

perfect fulfillment or transcendence which our nature seeks in being made for universal good. But this expectation is always false, and thus any undue admittance of sexual symbolism will lead to a subtraction from the higher transcendence which the soul of man can find only in union with God.

Nevertheless, it may be useful to point out the legitimate, even if limited, symbolism of the body. Our own body, in its sexual structure, has a necessary and primary relationship outside the person, to another of the opposite sex. But it can also have a deep meaning to the person himself. In the first place the sexual part of us somehow is a symbol of the fatherhood of God. In the male body especially is this true, for the Father in all power brought forth the Son. And in the spiritual union of the Father and Son came forth the Holy Spirit, equal to them in nature. Thus do we have an inexpressible and essentially surpassing prototype of sexual procreative love and union. Such is the nobility of the bodies of married and unmarried alike.

There are other legitimate symbolic meanings also. For the man there is in his sexual nature the symbol of strength, not the strength of the wild animal, but a human symbol of spiritual strength that makes the man a man, and likewise of a strength that knows tenderness in love. Thus are all men to look upon themselves as having the nature of fatherhood, and of this the masculine body is a noble symbol. For the woman her body symbolizes the more gentle beauty and the desirability of this complex creature who is simple at least in this, that she must somehow be wanted and loved if she is to be happy. Even the deterioration of time is not a permanent darkening of our appreciation because we will have all the beauty and integrity of our bodies back again, young again, for all eternity.

By such an appreciation both men and women not only avoid the conflict with their own nature, but can even help open the way to God. A feeling of repulsiveness for what we are can hardly but produce an unconscious barrier to others, and this includes God who must always see us as we are. Bringing our bodies to him, so to speak, we can more easily find him in our personal oneness which includes a love and appreciation of all the areas of our being, spiritual, emotional, and physical.

Yet this symbolism of the body cannot become a cult of sexuality. Our dominant symbolism must always be supernatural; the least amount of the supernatural is essentially greater than all our natural perfections, necessary and helpful though the natural may be in its own right. Besides, the flesh has for us other symbolism than the honorable. Careless and frequent disregard for modesty (according to one's state in life) will make a man or woman come into contact with the potential rebellion which tends to assert a domination by the flesh over the spirit. Too frequent a concentration cannot but bring forth an urge for the fulfillment or sexual use of the body. This urge is not always confined to a lawful use, even when this is possible, but pushes toward imaginative (at least) circumstances of fulfillment divorced from all other considerations. This tendency is obviously more harmful in those who have chosen to live without sexual fulfillment or upon whom abstinence is imposed by circumstance.

Thus the sexual cannot ever be a principal symbol for us but only one included in a whole where it is possible of assimilation. For we are drawn to what we accept as symbols; they become guideposts to our lives. Even though our bodies do symbolize our manhood and womanhood, the deeper truth is that the body is a lower thing than the soul. Therefore an emphasis on what is physical (even though good) will tend to draw the soul down to this level, whereas it is important that the lower (especially the sexual) be drawn up to participate in the higher. This is even true in marriage where even lawful sexual freedom must be continually raised up to the aesthetic and to the spiritual through tenderness and spiritual love. For, given liberty without the guidance of the higher, the pull of sexual nature will be away from the higher things, natural as well as supernatural, so completely is it mixed into our nature by God's creative wisdom and love.

These dangers in a cult of sexuality are obvious, but more delicate ones are not. By any great preoccupation with ourselves (easily possible because of the instinctive or unconscious attractiveness of sex), we may become too introspective, a dangerous thing in spiritual as well as psychological life. Or, observing false shame or fear of sex we may try to reform our nature all at once by an unwise confrontation with all sorts of sexual situations designed to tear out that shame or fear, hopefully without danger to ourselves or another. Or we may command that we become balanced by force of will alone, or analyze ourselves to the degree that we intellectualize our sexual nature, depriving it of its essential physical and emotional elements.

All this results in destroying the legitimate, though necessarily limited, autonomy of this part of our nature; we squeeze out of our conscious life an emotional content by which we would be enriched if we had proceeded more slowly, gently, and quietly. Even when we do not foolishly risk going beyond our moral or spiritual strength, we can end up by turning a difficult and delicate sexual intricacy into a psychological chaos. The intellect cannot pull all the strings, using our body as a puppet. And so these words on sexual symbolism are meant only to be like a seed put into the soil to grow in darkness and come to light in the form of many strong insights on the way to full emotional and spiritual maturity.

We have said that, being human, we cannot live without symbols, and that if we do not live by one set of symbols, we will live by another. Those in the spiritual life will find themselves under constant fire from symbols which are impossible of assimilation, or at least of full assimilation. The artillery most often used will be that of advertising, through all the media of communication, together with small arms fire from individuals who have acceptance into groups we are told we ought to admire. Thus a certain material article becomes something more than its intrinsic worth or use; it represents something further, often something as intangible as an unconscious desire for freedom from responsibility, at any rate always something portrayed as desirable.

We are all familiar with the status symbol represented by a home in a certain locality, by an expensive car, or by the ability to say that we have been here, read this, or eaten that. But a certain kind of advertising goes even further. We are not merely asked to try a certain product for its real or imaginary benefits. We are also shown situations where those who do as the advertiser suggests are seen to be gloriously happy, the insinuation being that if we will only use the product, we too will be similarly gloriously happy. Of course, no thinking man would admit that such a projection would be true. Does anyone, for instance, think that the people who are portraying the happiness in the advertisement are actually that happy in real life? Yet such fantasy works its purpose, so great is the power of symbols.

The danger is, the truth is, that if we too abandon ourselves to these voices, we will be working against our own peace. Using false and unreal symbols, we will soon project ourselves into the attitude of mind represented by the symbol. It is not so much that we are using some of the things of the world but rather that we unconsciously make ourselves into something represented by the symbols, and this something, besides being alien to reality, is also alien to the spiritual life. The two sets of principles will destroy inner peace.

A spiritual man in the world must to some extent conform himself to the world, and the same is true in a lesser degree for those in religious life. (These last are by no means immune from deception by the world; they too have pride of life and pride of the flesh, and could want to see themselves in situations which promise glamor, fun, or freedom compared to the relative drabness of the externals of their state.) But those in the world must conform more because of their peace of mind. Very few are called, for instance, to be as indifferent to clothing as a religious can be. Such radical non-conformity, even if it were always a virtue, would mean going beyond their spiritual strength. Also, if they dared to be very different, their children would suffer from the taunts of other children, and perhaps come to hate the very things that the parents too zealously practiced.

The use of the good things of the world is important to the layman also because he, more than the religious, is called by his vocation to be "all things to all men in order to save at least some of them" (1 Cor. 9:22). But ordinarily, at least, we will not save our neighbor if we represent a way to God which will be unnecessarily hard for our neighbor to follow. On the other hand "being all things to all men" does not mean the adoption of all the symbols of a knowledgeable worldliness. Instead it would have the opposite effect of confirming others in their worldliness. And it might deprive them of a needed symbol of other-worldliness which they cherish even though they do not as yet follow.

Often too, our attempts would become ridiculous or even mildly shocking as if a responsible married man were to decide to become an expert at the race track, or a demure woman suddenly to take up drinking and smoking in her gayest manner. A part of our self-knowledge is to learn that certain things don't fit us or our vocation for we too may be created to be symbols for others.

Our way of acting can be a symbol even for ourselves. The authentic externalization of our essential personality or of the ideals of our state in life is a symbol for our own support and even guidance. We can only be at peace when we are externally living up to the ideals of our state, whether it be that of a religious, a parent, or whatever other state to which we may be called, including in this also the ideals of the professions.

In the end the salvation of the worldling must come, to some extent, by seeing the essential emptiness of the supports upon which he has built his life. He must see for himself that his is an attitude of immaturity despite its sophistication. His blindness is a human tragedy which can be appreciated fully only by those who are free of it — unless it be also by those who in moments of clear insight see themselves as make-believe instead of the real persons they were created to be. By the grace of God they can come to see themselves as yearning for God with great, empty hearts and tortured souls, empty and tortured by what they thought would fill them but could not.

The tragedy does not revolve around this or that material thing, perhaps good enough in itself or

204 MATURING THE SPIRIT

at worst somewhat unseemly for a spiritual person. It is the symbols of the world which have been accepted, the song of its false freedom that has been listened to. It is these borrowed, usually unconscious, attitudes that erode the soul and bring discontent and frustration where the Lord promised peace. What is to be done to prevent or heal the disease which can be very deep?

Those in religious life have a great advantage here as in many other things; their lives are surrounded by useful symbols, and they often have a long tradition to strengthen these symbols. The spiritual man in the world also has his symbols every time he walks into a church, but he will do wisely also to have others in his home or on his person. This, of course, does not mean that we should overload ourselves or our surroundings with any excess, nor does it mean holding on to all things from the past no matter how anachronistic to our times or unsuitable to our circumstances. Some of these things, or even an excess of suitable things, can become emotionally and reasonably intolerable to us and a stumbling block to others. We must never forget that in such matters we have a God-given freedom that can resist the propaganda of the narrowly overzealous or of our own insecurity.

But on the other hand we must not give up too easily too much of our heritage as if the world just began yesterday. Certain psychiatrists see deeper links with the past than we are generally aware of. The past of mankind is in some sense ourselves, and if we cut ourselves off from these roots, we become sick in the spirit. However, in any case, if we eradicate all but the least common denominator between ourselves and good symbolism, we make our spiritual task harder, and open the way to a less desirable symbolism. We rob ourselves of an aid which mankind has always found necessary, even before history was recorded, the material which is symbolic of the spiritual. No one goes to God by spirit alone. This is part of his way with men.

Chapter 23

The Care and Use of
the Gifts of Nature

A gift properly implies appreciation for the gift. This is shown, not only in gratitude, but also in the care and use of the gift. The application of this principle to the gifts of nature is obvious, but the spiritual life makes us aware of an additional facet of our obligation: the gifts must not separate us from the giver. On the contrary, we must so care for and use them that they not only do not keep us from him, but rather lead us to him. If we will think of this idea in terms of one married partner giving a gift to the other, we will see, beyond need to explain, that this is true.

There is a balance, sometimes a very delicate balance, between the love, care, and use of God's gifts of this world, and the restraining of ourselves in respect to them. The elation we may feel in being made as we are, or in being given so many things for our use and enjoyment, must always be sobered down by the rights of the giver. His rights imply a certain control and restraint, such that we never lose sight of him who is our first love and that we always use his gifts to grow in his love.

By seeing as choices of love any conflicts which our nature experiences concerning this world, we have at once avoided the unhealthy darkness of totally negative prohibitions and also given ourselves a working principle by which we can use creation with a relative freedom and joy. This principle tells us that in the spiritual life we can use and love whatever in some way brings us to God. What does not do so, even indirectly, we discard and avoid. As examples, there are created things which help us directly, such as a spiritual friend, and there are other things which help us indirectly, perhaps something as earthly as a cup of coffee in the morning or a warm bath at night.

Despite the earnestness of a one-sided optimism, the spiritual life cannot help being partly negative. We must sometimes say no, even to good things, or we will be undisciplined for the battles to be encountered in making our love a fitting thing for the holiness of God. Detachment, as this restraint or control is sometimes called, has this negative aspect. It is a willingness, put into practice whenever necessary, to abandon whatever would keep the soul from advancing here and now to God. Besides helping to prevent separation from God in the use and enjoyment of his gifts, it also prevents us from overusing or abusing them.

This same virtue is also called mortification, a word which implies a death. "The man who loves his life loses it, while the man who hates his life in this world preserves it to life eternal" (Jn. 12:25). If we use physical death as an example, we can see why metaphorical deaths are necessary in the spiritual life. In regard to physical death our faith tells us that our true happiness is in the next world. Even when this truth is firmly accepted, how unwillingly would one take this step if it were a stepping out of an interesting, healthy life filled with all the acquisitions required for graceful living. God in his merciful providence often prepares such people for their heavenly inheritance by reverses and disappointments, by loneliness after the death of loved ones, or by disease and old age.

In the spiritual life he also does much of the work of metaphorical death for us. However, in the early and middle periods, he expects us to do some of it ourselves according as our vision becomes clearer. He does more of it by himself later when matters become more delicate or are concerned with hidden depths unknown to the soul itself.

From this we can see another aspect of the process of mortification or detachment, this a more positive one which has the name of purification. Purification is primarily a positive concept because the word implies a purpose. In the spiritual life we are being purified for love. Thus we not only avoid the use of things which are harmful to love, but we also become careful about our desires. We become more and more desirous only of those things which increase our love, even indirectly, and we reject those which do not. In this way our love is made free. We can love God more and more, and more and more purely, that is, more and more for himself.

In this sense the whole idea of detachment can be treated positively. We can see it as our positive conformity to God's purifying will, or as our abandonment to God's will for our spiritual good. These are more perfect concepts than isolatedly negative detachment and mortification, since they are more immediately involved with love. But the negative concepts are exceedingly helpful also because they face us with the details of the task to be done. We will usually go to God faster if we work from both ends, negatively as well as positively.

We so often think of detachment in the context of material pleasures that we are not aware of deeper and broader tendencies that also must be put to death. Our principal work in the spiritual life is to remove the obstacles to grace, and these are many more than things like food, drink, and entertainment. Our intellect, for instance, must be disciplined, both by curbing its tendency to dissipate itself on interesting non-essentials, and to teach it to be humble in the face of truth regardless of its source. Also, the will reaches out with a multitude of desires, plans, and ambitions. Many of these need to be weighed, or even prudently tried, to test them against the universal, humbling norm, the inescapable mind and will of God. In other words, the renunciation so important to the spiritual life always implies a scale of values rather than a concentration upon the elimination of the pleasurable. It is the exaggerated concentration upon the more easily seen outer world, and the neglect of enormous faults inside, that sometimes has brought upon the spiritual life the accusation of hypocrisy.

Furthermore, by seeing detachment in the light of love, we will avoid the effect of becoming hardened both to God and to the needs of our neighbor. Instead of making us cold, distant, and severe, our purification should really mean a softening of our hearts by elimination of the selfishness and the undue influence of our appetites and passions.

Detachment or mortification has other refinements, also more important than giving up this or that useless comfort. Another of these is detachment from our moods. The moods of discouragement or self-hatred, for instance, are unhealthy states, spirit-

ually as well as mentally. Therefore it is an excellent
kind of detachment to fight these things with both
spiritual and material means—not only the spiritual
means because sometimes more solitude and attempts
at prayer will result only in a deepening of the unhealthy mood. We should not shun certain lawful
natural means, including added pleasures. Detachment at times from our set patterns has advantages
in the spiritual life.

But the fact that there are deeper things to be
mortified than those which appeal to the senses
should nevertheless not prevent us from giving
attention to these also. Man has so been changed
by the Fall that the pleasures of the senses are especially able to draw him from God. Our desires and
affections go out to them, and if we are not careful, we are easily drawn from wanting God with the
intensity of which we are capable. We have only one
heart; all things must fit into the love of God and
help to unite us to him, or there will be less room
for him in this heart.

Therefore detachment is something not only for
beginners, but also and always for those who have
gone on the rest of the way. It must, like every
habit, become a second nature. Thus it becomes
easier and more agreeable. Our purpose here is not
to list mortifications in detail. Each life is an individual adventure with individual circumstances and
problems.

The process of detachment or purification is
usually a gradual one, as growth (to which it is ordered) is usually gradual. God does not want all
mortifications all at once, here and now. Nor will he
ever want all possible mortifications of anyone, even
though they may indicate great and difficult self-
conquest. For instance, he did not want St. John Vianney, the Curé of Ars, to undertake the mortification

THE CARE AND USE OF THE GIFTS OF NATURE

required of a Trappist monk. He wanted the mortification required of a dedicated parish priest. Similarly, for a husband or wife, or for a religious who must teach or nurse, he will not want the asceticism of the early Fathers in the desert. The spiritual life is not an endurance contest; it is a union of love.

Those in religious life usually have certain mortifications spelled out for them by their rule and by the ideals of their state in life. They also have superiors whose duty it is to watch them for any dangerous excess. Those in the world are not so fortunate, but with the help of a prudent confessor or director they may be able to reach their personal balance of use and detachment. But even when they can find such a man, there are many things too trivial to bother him about. Reason itself can often make judgments as to whether this or that is a help or hindrance to God. This course, guided by prudent trial and error, is obviously the only course for those who do not have someone to help.

Married people sometimes develop an overly tender conscience on the pleasures of sexual love. Or they may have a false modesty about certain aspects of physical lovemaking. Their urge then is toward detachment to the extent that the relationship fails to do what God intended, to be a vehicle for love and a release from daily tensions, not to speak of failure in love of neighbor, in this case the marriage partner. Although the marriage relationship must be brought totally under love of God, as we have said, this does not mean that God is against normal pleasure of the most intimate and ecstatic kind. After all, it was he who made this pleasure and bestowed it as a gift. More than most pleasures it has the power, if it is brought into an open relationship with him, to draw the partners closer to him both directly and indirectly.

This is not to say that there should be no restraint here at times too, for no one is expected to take all possible pleasure in any category. But an intense enjoyment and desire are not incompatible with the heights of spirituality, since spirituality depends principally on love.

Similarly, and this for women especially, some people in the spiritual life feel guilty about giving care to their physical appearance, their figure, and their attire. For married women such care is a duty to husband and children. For those in professional life it is a part of their means of livelihood. For all it is an important symbol of self-respect. One of the dangers of the spiritual life is that it can easily disguise an unhealthy self-hatred under such things as mortification or penance. However, we must never take so much care as to make our appearance the major concern of our available time, a cult of the body. Youth is a thing almost divine, but no one possesses it forever. Outside of a special vocation to special care (or an opposite vocation to special neglect) we should patiently work to preserve what was given by God so freely in youth and early maturity.

Sometimes we read expressions in spiritual books or prayers that seem to demand a totality of actual detachment, "to give all," as it is said. But we must understand that total detachment will never be actual; it will rather be potential, in the sense of our willingness to give God whatever he might ask. And of course, the extent of actual giving is always based on our growth in the spiritual life. Potential giving, however, means that our desires are fitted into the supreme desire of our lives, the desire for God's greater love.

It is also said that we should take no pleasure in any created thing. But, of course, this is not true. As it stands, we could take no pleasure in our spiritual love for the Blessed Virgin, who indeed is created. Rather we should take no pleasure outside of the will of God, often expressed in our own broad needs and the needs of others. We are not forbidden to enjoy creatures, or else the spiritual friendships of the saints would have been harmful. But we may not set our hearts on anything in creation that stands in the way of God.

Thus, when we read or hear statements on the emptiness of all things and the total desirability of God, we must not take them outside the context of the whole of our lives according to God's will, or outside the context of our present spiritual development. Many of the sayings of the saints had validity only in the latter part of their own lives, and perhaps even then, were valid only as expressing a particular insight or mood of the moment and not intended as a pattern or attitude for all the variations of living. The psalms, for instance, often tell us of magnificent trust in God, but the inspired authors also let us look into their souls to see the human fear and discouragement that was a part of their lives.

Some use of creation for enjoyment, call it recreation if you will, is a necessary part of the spiritual life, and all life for that matter, and St. Thomas therefore gives it the dignity of a virtue (II,II; 168;2). Human nature is not capable of an arduous ascent of the mountain without periods of relief from this and other tensions. We will climb better if we learn wisely to change the pace of our lives according to our needs and temperament, always understanding this to be done in ways which do not result in a serious or permanent dissipation of our spiritual oneness.

In order not to stagnate or become stultified spiritually (or mentally and emotionally also), we must on some occasions do something not included in our set pattern of life. While a definitely scheduled day has obvious advantages, we can become victims of a numbness which not only makes it harder to pray, but also prevents us from seeing the needs of our neighbor or, seeing them, to do anything about them. This is a limited field where change for the sake of change becomes a virtue. Sometimes God himself will provide the needed change, for he is in many ways unpredictable. We must therefore not look upon all intrusions upon our routine as if they were crosses. They can keep us flexible to God's will and can help us to avoid the rut of stagnation.

Sometimes, however, it is necessary for us to act to bring about change. We then change our pattern on some occasions, even though a habit-formed rigidity cries out against it. This change may take the form of more recreation, on holidays, for instance, or a change in scheduling or doing our work. Our souls are thus kept pliable for the changes God will want to make in them by his grace — and in the process we may discover a better or wiser way of life.

It is not out of place to append here a word on reparation. By this we mean not only the reparation owed to God for our own sins and misuse of grace, but also reparation for others, for the world, if you wish. From this period in the spiritual life until the climax of perfection reparation for others may become more and more a reason for the evils that God permits to happen to us. And we need not wait for what God permits or sends; we ourselves can also choose. The best reparation, of course, is love. Love best makes up for lack of love.

Similar to this is the acceptance of suffering and the practice of self-denial for the good of the Church. As with reparation (indeed, as with everything we do), we make our offering in union with the Christ who first made it for all, but who wills also to allow us to be associated with him in this work (see Col. 1:24). As with our redemption, God sometimes wills that prayer alone be insufficient; only the love expressed through suffering is acceptable for the purpose. This is a high form of apostolic activity available even to those who can have no activity.

In reparation and sacrifice, as well as in detachment, we risk the danger, not only of going beyond our physical strength, but also beyond our emotional and spiritual strength. A wise counsel, then, is to avoid permanent commitments unless the resolution or practice has successfully endured the test of duration of time. We proceed by trial and by correction of errors. Our basic rule of testing all our resolutions, whether over the long haul we are brought closer to God in the practice of the virtues, can be enlarged to include an observation of our peace of soul. Peace can be a sign of God's grace in the matter at hand.

Peace is, of course, often misunderstood for ease and pleasure. But on the contrary, even though a thing may be difficult, we can still be at peace about it, generally speaking. If we are not at peace, it may be well to re-examine our steps. This obviously applies only to matters which are voluntary. In matters in which we have no choice, we must bring about inner peace by prayer, thought, and will. This rule of peace is not a perfect rule, but it is a good one in the difficult, never-completely-settled problems concerning the care and use of God's gifts through nature.

Although the gifts of nature are not supernatural as such, in us they are in the supernatural order both because they share in our destiny and because they are used in the giving and receiving of grace. Our detailed consideration of them will help us to use them with greater certitude and less floundering, in order to become saints through the acquisition of God's higher gifts which are grace and the fruits of grace. It is to these higher gifts which proceed from grace that we now direct our consideration.

Part V

Gifts of Grace

Chapter 24

Foundation for Sustained Action

To have to put things in some logical order is a human necessity; our minds cannot grasp the whole of any extended subject and so must see the whole through an orderly arrangement of its parts. In regard to the spiritual life many attempts have been made to put order into the whole by dividing it according to the obvious fact of growth or progress in it. Thus we have the useful division of purgative, illuminative, and unitive periods. But when we come to determine what essentially constitutes each of these divisions, we can easily leave the obvious reality for something less certain.

The result sometimes is confusion, not only for those who are more concerned about where they are in the spiritual life than they are about growing in it, but even for those who reasonably understand that a prudent knowledge of where they are can help them to know what to expect and how to proceed more efficiently.

The chief source of confusion seems to come from the tendency to identify the three periods of the spiritual life with different kinds of prayer. Thus if one is experiencing a certain kind of prayer, he is automatically in a definite stage of the spiritual life and vice versa. Much argument by learned writers has been the result, and a review of such debate would be out of place in a book which is meant to be a practical guide. It is true that there are some reasons for generalizing about prayer and other interior phenomena and that there are many cases which will adequately fit the generalization. But the irreconcilable fact remains that there are also many which do not.

The truth found by experience is that God sometimes chooses to give graces of prayer to souls who are not in the particular category assigned by the textbooks. Conversely there are souls who do not have an habitual hold on higher prayer, and yet they are saints or close to it. St. Thérèse of Lisieux seems to be a good example; her life, which we know better than those of most other saints, does not at all seem to be a steady, discernable progression from simple meditation to the highest, habitual contemplation. If we are to make these three divisions of the spiritual life have a meaning that can be put to practical use, then we must search for a different essential constituent than that of the three degrees of prayer.

In our search we can use no better norm than that given us by our Lord himself: "You can tell a tree by its fruit" (Mt. 7:20). This norm not only tells us the difference between the sheep and the wolves; it also can identify the better ones of the flock from the poorer.

Our actions, then, would seem to be this norm. But actions themselves are too scattered in time and in variety, and any computation of them would involve too much attention for them to be a norm by which to judge our spiritual state. Also, even exceptional acts can be performed occasionally for a short period by meagerly spiritual persons, and this may quite completely confuse the issue. Thus it seems necessary to go one level beneath the actions to a kind of goodness which is habitually there. This foundation for sustained action, whereby we can judge our spiritual state, is the virtues.

Such a stable norm has at least three practical advantages. One is seen in those souls for whom God is apparently making a greater bid. On these he lavishes much love and other gifts, such at times as we would expect him to give as rewards to those he loves because of great present likeness to him, the Beloved, in grace. And yet these are souls whose imperfection is at times appalling. If they were erroneously and proudly to consider that, because of these graces of prayer, they were in the last stages of the unitive way, they would eventually end up in spiritual disintegration.

A second reason for choosing the virtues as a norm for judging our spiritual state has to do with the deceits of the devil. He has too clever an intelligence for us always to be able to discern his activity in the matter of prayer and spiritual sentiments. Yet he cannot and will not completely counterfeit virtue because he cannot bear to lose his chance for victory by too successful a deceit. He can never divide his house against itself; we have our Lord's word on that.

The virtues, then, especially humility, patience, and charity to neighbor, are far better criteria than all the phenomena of prayer, and all the extraordinary mystical phenomena as well.

The third practical reason for choosing the virtues as a norm of spiritual progress is the fact, as we have just said, that even extraordinary *acts* of virtue can be performed on occasion or for short periods of time. These may be the result of special

graces of God given for some needed occasion, or
they may be the result of an abundance of fervor at
the beginning of a conversion to God. Less ideally,
they may sometimes be poured out almost as an unconscious love-offering to a spiritual human being
by someone who feels that such actions must be produced (or imagined to be produced) in order to win
and keep the attentions of human love. In all these
cases, and probably others, deep supernatural virtue
may not exist. At best, and dangerously for those who
must judge, there are sometimes only the bare beginnings.

In practice this norm of the virtues will center
around the principal one of love of God. The beginner, or one who is in the purgative state, will be
principally concerned with the obstacles to love
which he finds in his life. This is, of course, a simplification. He cannot and ought not try only to work
negatively, that is, only to oppose his weaknesses.
He must at the same time work very hard to acquire
the good habits or virtues leading to greater love of
God. But his dominant awareness and effort must be
toward elimination of his weaknesses, for if it is not,
he will find that his defects stand consistently in the
way of his progress.

A man progresses into the next state of soul, the
illuminative, quite imperceptibly because there are
no sharp boundaries which can be easily recognized.
But he will find that his principal concern has become a more positive strengthening of all the virtues
so that he also grows in stability in his love for God.

In the third stage, or the unitive way, love becomes more and more the dominant characteristic of
his life. This is not apt to be a different motive
from what it was at the very first, but now there is a
deep oneness which he knows to be different from
his previous states. Love dominates and permeates

his life as expressed through the virtues and especially love of neighbor. All centers around a compelling passion, or at least an all-absorbing determination, for union with God. Thus in all of the three states it will be easily seen that we will have better and more consistent victories over our weaknesses, and greater progress toward union with God, when we live and grow in love and consistently ask for increase in it.

Since, therefore, the depth or strength of the virtues is the best practical norm by which we may judge our progress toward God, it is well to make clear what they are. It would be simple and quite true merely to say that they are good habits in our spiritual and moral life. As an example, we have already dealt with one of them in the last chapter, when we spoke of detachment. We can easily identify this with the supernatural virtue of temperance. But once we mention virtue as supernatural, a certain simplicity of concept ends. Here even those who are well-read in learned books are sometimes unable to see the picture clearly. And so, more to avoid confusion than to direct towards specific action, we must speak briefly about supernatural virtue.

The problem may be put in terms of a practical situation, as it is by St. Thomas (see I,II; 63;4). For a man in the natural order of things, let us say a good pagan, the norm for his moral conduct must be right reason. This enables him to live free from the extremes of too much or too little in the innumerable ways in which life encounters a need for such decisions. For a Christian this norm taken by itself, is insufficient, not so much because it is so hard for man to reason rightly in moral matters, but rather because it does not carry him high enough. Reason as such cannot operate accurately in dealing with judgments and decisions on matters which are above reason.

For instance, merely natural reason will regulate the matter of food insofar as a man takes care not to harm the body by excess or by deficiency, and thus prevent it from interfering with the operations of reason and with the duties of his state in life. But the Christian must look to a broader and higher meaning of temperance. His aim is not the good life of reason. "What I do is discipline my own body and master it" (1 Cor. 9:27). The body must be made subject so that the love of God and the accomplishment of the works of God find a minimum of resistance. The necessity of fitness for work is perhaps obvious. But even more important and not always so obvious are the demands of a life by which a man must purify himself for close friendship with an all-holy God.

In this we are in open confrontation with the spiritual inertia of many Catholics who have been educated in philosophy, even those who have received this education in Catholic institutions of higher learning. Their reading in ethics does not sufficiently take them beyond a merely reasonable norm which might have been the guide of the good pagan. Thus their religion and their intellectual life are not completely in harmony, and the message of the Gospel is hindered instead of helped by their education even when this philosophy contains no direct error. Their love of God can thus to some extent be blunted by collision with good, but insufficient, criteria for their practical judgments. St. Thomas, it may again be pointed out, although he uses reason extensively, does not make this error.

Rather than the merely reasonable, which is a wide road leading to spiritual mediocrity and apostolic indolence, we must be guided by the attitude of mind expressed in the beatitudes. Here the blessed, the happy, are not those who have all that a comfortable life can give. Rather the blessed, and therefore happy, are those who do the humanly difficult things, such as being poor in spirit and being meek or gentle. Blessed again are those who are in sorrow, at least unconsciously, over what they have lost of life, and those who hunger and thirst for what is just and right. Blessed also the merciful, the pure of heart, and those who work for peace with their difficult neighbor. And even happy and blessed are those who are persecuted in the cause of right.

And in all this we are called happy because we will have a reward which is principally friendship with God, but always includes more, both in heaven and on earth. Our basic happiness even here is meant to be supernatural, an ideal not to be achieved in a day or a year, however.

Yet even though our lives must be a reflection of the teachings of the Gospel, and thus would be only poorly served by reason unaided by faith, this does not argue for the abandonment of reason as a guide. This would be a vacuum of intelligence and, of course, be intrinsically impossible if we are to operate as human beings. Thus to say that the merely reasonable is insufficient does not mean that we recommend the unreasonable. There is a divine quality about reason in that it reflects the mind of God. If $2+2=4$ is a complete and valid conclusion of reason on earth, it is also the mind of God in heaven. And so St. Thomas does not hesitate to adopt very frequently the reasoned conclusions of Aristotle, the greatest of the pagans. Nor should we hesitate to use our intelligence in the spiritual life, providing that our reasoning is enlightened by our faith, that it is always the higher reasoning leading us on to greater fitness for the love of God.

The need to assimilate the natural into the higher life of union with God brings us to a further truth about ourselves if we look at the virtues as the basis of our operations. First, there is the obvious observation that we can have some, even many, of the virtues without being in sanctifying grace. A man in mortal sin may still have the virtue of honesty, chastity and so on, many of the habits of a good life. We would call these virtues imperfect because the man has lost his oneness of spirit by losing what binds him to God who is his final end. For that reason his virtues are apt to be less than stable also.

A second truth is that the good habits we acquire by our repeated efforts and experience are not able *by themselves* to be the basis of our operation in the supernatural life. These are a valuable and necessary substratum for our actions, but they do not give us the intrinsic ability to operate above our nature as we must in our life as God's sons and daughters. And so, besides the virtues acquired by experience and repeated acts, another kind of virtue is required, the infused virtues which are impressed into the soul by God along with sanctifying grace. They are thus distinguished from the acquired virtues by their origin.

The infused virtues are also distinguished from the acquired ones by their essence. They are essentially supernatural and thus could not exist in the soul of a man in mortal sin as can the acquired ones. We must have these supernatural virtues because otherwise we would be faced with an impossibility: we cannot operate above the limits of our ability; no one can lift a mountain. In the life of grace we are no longer merely men but we are adopted sons and daughters of God. Our moral and spiritual life is now essentially different from what it was before we received grace. We must therefore be able to act in this higher life beyond the capacity of our natural powers. This is the first point, but there is another.

Even in the spiritual life we are still human. As human beings we are designed to operate in a human way, that is, our actions must normally proceed from habits, even in the life of grace. Therefore since the acquired habits are not sufficient to do this, God, who is not deficient either in nature or in grace, infuses the supernatural habits into the soul along with sanctifying grace. Thus we have a supernatural basis of operation at once proportional to our supernatural destiny and at the same time conformed to our human manner of acting.

The existence of three of these infused virtues is guaranteed by the Church (Council of Trent: sess. 6, ch. 7), the three virtues which have God directly as their object. We are used to saying that faith is a gift, but the same is also true of divine hope and love. By these three theological virtues our intellect and will are made capable of a supernatural destiny. But the same need to be made capable also applies to other of our natural powers. They too require that they be raised up and strengthened by habits given for this same destiny since the gap between the natural and supernatural is such that no natural power can bridge it alone.

The infusion of these virtues is something like their being created in the soul, but there is one difference. Creation, strictly speaking, always starts from nothingness, whereas our souls and all their powers do have a potentiality to be raised to a higher manner of existence or operation.

Although the infused virtues differ in essence from the acquired virtues, we must not think that they are different in every respect. In fact each infused virtue corresponds to an acquired virtue so that both work together, and usually unobservably together. It is not impossible, of course, for the infused virtue to act without any previously acquired virtue, for as St. Thomas says, "God can produce the effects of secondary causes without these secondary causes" (I,II; 51;4). God sometimes does this, perhaps in the case of those who receive an extraordinary amount of grace in the beginning of their spiritual life. But it is not his ordinary way of working with us.

We would perhaps desire that our spiritual life be more simple than this duplicating of virtues seems to be. In actual practice, however, it still is simple because we do not become conscious of the two kinds of virtues when we are acting; we merely look to God for help in prayer and we do our best to follow our lights, thus acquiring strong habits. But the time spent in this discussion will help us to see our spiritual life better than if we thought it to be all grace or all nature. As for simplicity, we may well ask whether anything living is really simple. The living thing most familiar to us, our own body, is a mystery even to ourselves.

Using the virtues as a norm to judge our progress can sometimes be misleading, however, because our idea of a virtue is sometimes inaccurate. Even when we do not make the word synonymous with purity (or vice with impurity), we sometimes consider that these virtues are habits which control only our emotions or appetites, such as fortitude does fear and sobriety does drink. But this leaves out other very important virtues, such as justice which forms a good will in giving everyone his due, and holy prudence which guides the reason in its practical judgments. This last is in one sense the greatest of the moral virtues; all other virtues must in some way be influenced by it except the love of God. But even there it has indirect influence, as when we determine the time we can give to God in prayer.

In this virtue of prudence we can see the harmony which exists between the infused virtue and the acquired one. The first is infused into our soul, and on the other hand the work of a good part of our lifetime is spent in growing in the acquired virtue which we often know as common sense. Under the influence of grace the higher prudence will have the leadership. The law of love received from supernatural revelation requires more than the merely reasonable even when this is supernaturalized by a good intention. When it says, "You shall love the Lord your God with all your heart, with all your soul, with all your strength and with all your mind" (Lk. 10:27), the careful moderation of the merely reasonable is left behind. Holy prudence, on the other hand, is just as much against rashness, for instance, as is acquired prudence. Indeed the infused virtue will often have to consult the experience of the acquired virtue in order to see what is unreasonable. Holy prudence will also form its judgments in the light of the teaching and governing authority of the Church. The way of love does not eliminate what God has put on earth to guide us. In the quest for God in almost unbelievable friendship, we make our reasonable choices with all this in mind. And some of these choices will not be entirely comfortable.

There are perhaps a few people who will object to this emphasis on the virtues because they like to think of themselves as being nothing and of their dependence upon God as being total. They misunderstand the meaning of total abjection and despoilment and think they should have nothing, not even strength, within themselves. For them all things, strength and counsel for instance, should come directly from God into an inert void, so to speak. And by so thinking, they believe they are giving more glory to God.

The truth is, however, that God intends some of his gifts to be permanent, even though others are meant to be transient. For example, actual grace, which is given to accomplish a definite good, is always transient. But sanctifying grace, to use the best spiritual example, is always meant to be permanent. The virtues, both acquired and infused, are also meant to be permanent. The infused ones are given to us along with sanctifying grace, but they cannot normally operate unless there is a substratum in our acquired habit patterns. Surely God would not bestow such gifts and then desire us to be in a state in which they could not operate. He does not want to move us like robots. He surely does not want us to be permanently in moral weakness or emotional instability in which every temptation or every fear is a major crisis. We sometimes see this kind of mistaken spiritual people, and they do not endear outsiders to the spiritual life. They are tossed to and fro, in danger of drowning from the small waves upon the sea of life. God does look down and inevitably support their weakness, but the weakness is still apparent in their anxieties, fretfulness, in their lack of peace and depth, and in their same foolish errors of judgment.

On the contrary, the virtues really do not make us less dependent upon God. We still always need actual graces to produce the acts of each virtue, just as the best gasoline engine needs some outside force to start it and also fuel to keep it going. A poor engine, on the other hand, will not run well even with good fuel, and thus God's graces are partially spoiled or wasted, and little progress is made toward him. Our humility is safeguarded by the fact that the strength of these virtues comes only through his gift. And even with the strongest virtues, we are in absolute need of his constant help, through grace and through his providence, not only for every act of the virtues, but more especially for final perseverance itself.

It is therefore a mistake to think that dependence upon God is in opposition to a strength of our own, since our strength, both actual and habitual, is always something which has been given. Certainly God wants us to build deep, stable foundations in our souls so that we can have an inner peace even in great trials and dangers. But this peace and stability can come only from the abiding presence of all the virtues, these infused and acquired habits by which we act correctly and even heroically under all circumstances.

Chapter 25

Growing in the Virtues

It is an insight into the relationship between the natural and supernatural to see that their most evident co-operation is in the growth of the virtues. As to the supernatural, actual grace and the providence of God are the effective causes. Sanctifying grace is the soil in which the virtues must live in order for them to have the power to bring us to God forever. Nature has its due share also, but in a harmony largely brought about by the virtues. In the otherwise disorderly conglomeration of the pushes and pulls of instincts, senses, and desires in our difficult composite of flesh and spirit, we can see the orderly design of a competent God. It is principally the virtues which put this discernible order into our nature.

From one point of view it is sanctifying grace which makes us like to God; from another it is the virtues. These are the habits, supernatural and natural, which can make us perfect in our operations so that we do not have a bare supernatural existence by grace alone, but are endowed with all the powers needed by such an existence as well. By the virtues we become perfect as men, as our heavenly Father is perfect as God.

In our desire to become closer to God, we may long for a "once and for all" conversion to him whereby we would put ourselves firmly and forever on the level of our highest aspirations. This was the way of the angels, but it is not the way of men. With us our perfection is a growth, usually a gradual growth, often as imperceptible as the day-to-day growth of a plant. Thus we must again and again repeat and deepen our choices and our dedication. Sometimes this happens through repeated falls from our previous level of attainment. Sometimes it comes about by an ever deepening insight and embrace of theoretical and practical truth, of the rightness of the good, and of the total desirability of God. Not too infrequently it will come by both ways, through the lowliness of our mistakes and the clearness and attraction of the light. God is not held to any single way of acting. Since he is the effective cause of the spiritual life both as it proceeds from grace and as it proceeds from nature, he can use or provide special circumstances to increase this life within us, not only by increasing sanctifying grace but also by increasing the virtues, both infused and acquired.

With the infused virtues the increase, though illusively mysterious as are all things of grace, is apparently simple. The infused virtues increase along with sanctifying grace, or in other words, along with our essential love of God. Just as we need these virtues to operate at all on the supernatural level, so a greater participation in the nature of God by sanctifying grace will require an increase of these supernatural habits in the depth of our souls.

Although the acquired virtues work smoothly with the infused virtues, their way of growth is different. Since these are things of nature, we must expect that their growth will come by natural means and dispositions, always however, in the spiritual life at least, through the actual grace of God and his providence. Their manner of increase, then, like any habit must come about by repetitive acts, especially by acts which can raise their strength or power so that future acts of these virtues will be performed with greater ease, with a fuller grasp upon their present situations, or with an extension into broader or higher areas and circumstances, such as avoiding all voluntary imperfections.

Thus the difficulties of our lives are an excellent means to increase the acquired virtues as well as to grow in sanctifying grace and love of God by which the infused virtues are also increased. On the other hand, if we do not exercise a habit by frequent acts or do so only by acts of an inferior grade, the acquired virtue may come near to dying, and thus the supernatural habit will find great difficulty in operating. It needs not to be repeated that spiritual perfection is not the sole work of either the acquired virtues or the infused virtues, but of both together.

In the increase of the acquired virtues by repetitive acts, the body has an important part. Although all responsibility must ultimately come from the free will acting under grace, the will would have a difficult task if it had so to move nature to physical responses that all our actions were always unexplored territory, if it had so to produce them as if every time they were something entirely new. Thus, the acquired virtues, to be virtues in nature, must have a necessary response in the nervous system of the body. We then can act according to our reason and our will with relative ease even in difficult things, just as we now accomplish with ease the once difficult act of being able to walk. To the body we owe the "memory" of how to proceed in the operation of the virtue so that even arduous action can become a pleasure, at least to the spirit which thus extends its legitimate control over the unwilling instincts and passions of the body and thus reaches out more securely to God.

The body can also be a help in the increase of the virtues by way of a disposition which is called temperament. In this we are not created equal. Rather as St. Paul says, "Still, each one has his own gift from God, one this, and another that" (1 Cor. 7:7). Consequently it will be easier for some people to acquire a particular virtue, let us say the virtue of fortitude or of gentleness, than it will for others. St. Thomas calls these qualities of temperament the "natural beginnings" of the virtues (I,II; 51;1). They are not the virtues themselves, and so we sometimes find people who are excellently disposed by nature in some manner, but do not really have the virtue in any depth. There are certain kindly people, for instance, who are not kindly when it will cost them something which they are not now inclined to give, as their time or active help.

Yet these dispositions are an enormous help and the result ought to be deep virtue because we do not measure the strength of a virtue by the difficulty of its acquisition but by its ability to perform. However, when a virtue is difficult because of an opposite temperament, the merit is greater because the effort, and presumably also the love, is greater. Thus even our poorer dispositions can help bring us closer to God.

It must be related here that the deepening of the virtues by repetition and the actualization of our natural dispositions is ordinarily accomplished through the judgment of our reason. Grace ordinarily works in this human way, that we are not enlightened and guided by God directly, but by him through this light he has given, this light in turn perfected by the very important virtue of holy prudence. Growth in the virtues, therefore, also has the growing awareness of the voice of reason as enlightened by faith. And as with every virtue, we strengthen this influence of holy prudence by following its insights with due promptness, rather than blindly following the call of unguided instincts, prejudices, passions, and desires, even when we choose to call them by the name of love.

So far we have been speaking of the ordinary processes by which the acquired virtues are increased in us. However, "God does not work by necessity of nature, but according to the order of his wisdom" (I,II; 66; 1 ad 3). Thus he is not limited, and may choose to increase these acquired virtues by situations or events which are graces coming to us through his universal providence. Such graces can be observed, for instance, when in some extraordinary way we see his protection or even his punishments. Such a grace may even come out of our sins or our laxity. It can come at hearing of the death of someone close to us; it can come when hearing from a doctor of our own death in a few years or months. It can be the seasons of grace such as Christmas or Holy Week and Easter, especially if they were prepared for.

In all these situations and the limitless others that God has available in his resourcefulness, he can cause, not only an increase of grace, but also a change in our psyche by which we are naturally turned away from evil or toward a higher level of good. Of course, all these are only a disposition toward the virtue and not the virtue itself, and we are not to waste our days waiting for them to happen. But such events do point up our need to abandon ourselves to God continually in our spiritual life, and to pray much that *he* will bring us closer, even by graces we do not deserve.

God similarly is not limited when it is a matter of the infused virtues. These, as we said, grow along with sanctifying grace and supernatural love. They thus will grow by means of the great channels of grace, which are the sacraments and the fruitful participation in the sacrifice of Christ in the Mass. They will also increase by means of all the meritorious actions which increase the acquired virtues, especially as they proceed from love. (But perhaps they will not increase immediately, since we may not merit an increase of sanctifying grace immediately, as we have said earlier. God may save up the merits of actions which are not sufficient to bring us closer to himself here and now.) And of course, besides all this we should ask and hope that an increase of grace and the infused virtues will come to us for no other reason than that goodness of God which we call his mercy, by which he gives what we totally do not deserve and have not earned. It is the nature of love to wish to give this way, and in our love for him we must not be too proud to want and to accept undeserved generosity.

Since God is free in his working in our soul, perhaps it is through this increase of the infused virtues that we sometimes almost suddenly find ourselves in possession of a degree of virtue for which we had hardly worked or had worked fruitlessly for years. It may be that the infused virtue is now leading the acquired one. Perhaps also this is a reason that increase in the virtues generally becomes easier as we grow closer to God in grace and love. The case of St. Alphonsus Liguori, who as an old man suffered the temptations we might expect of a young man, is an exception, and his condition was probably brought on by physiological causes.

Normally however, the infused virtue does not work except in conjunction with the acquired virtue, and only to the extent of the facility provided by the acquired virtue. From this we will see the necessity of the sometimes painful steps needed to increase these latter virtues. Usually "a subject does not acquire all at once a firm and difficultly changeable disposition," which we call a virtue (I,II; 54;4 ad 1). And even though the infused virtues do not decrease (just as sanctifying grace does not decrease), they can lose their power to produce acts leading to greater merit by the deterioration of the acquired virtues. Thus in the virtue of temperance in food and drink, for example, a man who has just spent Lent in acquiring greater control over his appetite has a greater degree of the acquired virtue. But if he were to become lax during the rest of the year, this virtue would diminish without having lost any of the infused virtue. But this would make it more difficult for the infused virtue to operate, and therefore the man would be less capable of increase in grace.

The practical conclusion to all this is the determination never to give up in our efforts toward increasing the virtues. To stop trying is to allow victory to the contrary forces of spiritual and psychological erosion so that the virtues may in their practical sense even disappear. Then all of God's normal giving of grace will be like trying to force water through a pipe that is plugged at one end.

Even a considerable growth in the virtues does not mean an uncritical casting off of the helps used to arrive at this point of growth. In many cases this would mean pulling up roots in the belief that we were casting off burdens now unnecessary. It may well be that some of the helps and practices of our earlier spiritual life are now unnecessary and even harmful to a new insight as to the way to God. But we should make ourselves relatively certain before we cast anything off. Certainty is found by clarity of vision, some tentative experimentation (for about six months to a year, at least), and fervent prayer for light.

As an example, some people in the spiritual life no longer think it necessary to examine their consciences as to the number of their sins or their specific classification or circumstances. God, they say, is not an accountant; he is a lover. Quite true. But God is not the only one in the picture. We are also involved, and *our* love should prompt us to search out and confront in some detail whatever is displeasing to him. Far from being alien to love, it is an admirable human characteristic to take this care, just as a husband or wife should not only love each other but also should attempt to find the causes of friction, the obstacles to greater love, and to remove them. At the same time, however, we will be on our guard not to let the examining process become more predominant than the love and the vision of God as lover.

If all our acts of the virtues were filled with the fullness of the love of which we are capable at the time, we would come closer to God with an ever-increasing acceleration. Our progress is not meant to be exactly like climbing a mountain. In such an ascent we would go more slowly as we approach the top both because of the more difficult conditions and our increasing fatigue. The ideal is rather that our acts of the virtues should merit an increase of grace, and then with this increased degree of grace, or increased friendship with God, our next act of the virtues would merit more than the previous one. Thus our pace toward him should be ever faster and faster.

Nature provides an excellent example of this in the various inverse square laws; gravitation and radiation, such as light and heat, are governed by such a law. If God were to be considered to be our sun, so to speak, then our attraction toward him, our speed, and our absorption of light and heat (shall we call these grace and love?) would increase enormously as our distance decreases. At half the original distance, for example, we would experience not twice as much, but four times as much gravitational force, speed, and intensity of light and heat; at one fourth the distance we would receive sixteen times as much. Now, of course, we have no way of knowing the mathematics of the increase of grace and love, if indeed God operates according to any such pattern. But still the principle of increase in grace, in basic love, and in the infused virtues is nevertheless well illustrated by this law.

A final lesson can be drawn from this same natural phenomenon. The example of the sun is really a poor one because we would not want that much closeness, that much light and heat. So the example breaks down. God is all goodness; love and closeness to him are our greatest joy on earth — except for some of us, and to some degree all of us. Because of our poor understanding of him and of happiness, we unconsciously fear closeness to him as we would the burning sun. And so we do what our earth and the other planets do, we do not move directly toward him; we move in a transverse direction which puts us into an orbit that is sometimes closer, sometimes farther, but is kept within very safe limits. We allow ourselves to be turned from our path by other considerations than the love and happiness that he is. And yet if we would have love and the happiness that only lovers know, we must go ahead blindly, trustingly, either in eagerness or in determination, trying to fill up every one of our actions with the kind of love which will make the distance between us ever shorter with increasing acceleration.

Chapter 26

A Deeper Perspective

       The spiritual man, intent upon immediate success in the spiritual life, may sometimes be impatient with the complexity of the apparatus by which he is expected to achieve success. In his praiseworthy desire to reach as close to God as he can, he wants a direct way, and the fracturing of the spiritual life into the various virtues seems to be unnecessary and even destructive of the spirit of the gospels. This spirit he is apt to interpret as something extremely simple. Even when he does not turn this desire of oneness into one-sidedness, he will wonder why we cannot be satisfied with something like love of God and neighbor, which our Lord affirmed to be the whole of the obligations of the law and the exhortations of the prophets.

       The answers to this are both theological and practical. First and theologically, the virtue of love or charity is one by which we have a direct relationship with God himself. We love him personally and directly. No other virtue does this. But love, although it is the greatest of the virtues, does not have a direct relationship with other things which are also of essential importance. For instance, it does not directly

241

tell us how to solve our problems, but the virtue of holy prudence does. It does not directly tell us that we must speak the truth, but the virtue of justice does that. Love of God likewise does not pertain directly to the problems arising from our sexual nature, but there is a virtue for that too.

Love indeed has an important relationship to these virtues and to all the others. But it cannot be the same thing, the same habit, as these virtues both because it primarily and directly concerns God himself, and also because it is possible to have many of the acquired virtues and not have love of God. An atheist, for instance, can be scrupulously honest.

Secondly, the practical answer to the desire for an extreme simplicity. To take our spiritual life apart and look at it in the light of the virtues can have the effect of making our efforts fit reality. We will not be likely to live a dream by which we think we are saints merely because we claim to love God very much. Through the virtues we will see what God wants of us and where our real problems lie. We then will seek means to bring ourselves up to the measure of Christ which is still lacking in us. Indeed the way of the virtues is only an orderly way of looking at the perfection we must find and imitate in Christ. If we read the Scriptures, we will find not only the love of God spoken of, but every other virtue as well. And our Lord by his words and actions is a summation of all of them.

The relationship of love of God to all the other virtues is close and vital. Love of God is rooted in sanctifying grace, and this gives it a common life with all the other infused virtues. The acquired virtues, since they can exist in some degree without love of God, do not necessarily share this oneness of common life. But for a man in the spiritual life they are integrated into one whole, as we have said, and they too share with the infused virtues a specific relationship with love of God. We can now ask what this relationship is.

One of the effects of growing in love is that it imprints its image on so much in our lives. This transformation is noticeably prominent in our acquired habits of right thinking and good conduct and becomes more characteristic of them as we grow in spiritual life. These, while not differing in kind from what they were when we began, have become stronger, principally by being more permeated with love. They all have a firm dependence upon love of God, and we can observe this clearly if we look at what love does in a familiar human situation. The love of a woman for her husband and children is the dominant driving force in her life. Her work for them, her carefulness for their moral and physical welfare, her prudence with money, her efforts to make the home pleasing and happy—all these in an ideal woman flow from her love.

In much the same way does the love of God affect all the other parts of our spiritual life. It supplies the motive power by which we perform the acts of all the other virtues. The more intense the love, the more will we be honest, truthful, brave, pure, and so on. This for the infused virtues surely. But the acquired virtues, which depend partly on our natural dispositions and early training, will tend also to follow the same leadership of love. In fact, generally speaking, the acquired virtues will grow under no other leadership in areas in which we are naturally weak.

The acquired virtues are connected together in love of God because love gives them their direction toward God. By our desire for God, by our earnest wish to please him, they become purified of their imperfections and of the limitations which a purely

human virtue would have by depending on reason
alone. Nor do we rest in a partial victory wherein we
now successfully avoid sin. We affirmatively seek
deep spiritual union with God. We offer for love our
whole mind and heart and our whole life.

We will be able to see love of God at work in the
virtues if we select a few examples from the spiritual
life. In the first place, we will understand how important is the other part of this virtue, which is love
of neighbor. Because we love God, we will love his
children, Christ's brothers, in a love which does not
depend on compatibility, usefulness, or anything else
by which we would love naturally.

Then also in our life of prayer, we will not seek
to aggrandize the self by concentrating on the many
pleasant details which can so occupy us: the exact
state of prayer we are in, or getting in our many small
devotions and practices. We will see that at the heart
of the spiritual life is a sincere and practical love of
God and neighbor. Sometimes the spiritual life can
become a confusion of irrelevancies, and even con-
tradictions, because we fail to understand the relative
importance of the various counsels, practices, and
even the virtues.

Then in the matter of detachment, by love of
God we lessen the power of other loves over us in
those things which are opposed to it. Love of God also
helps to give us a balance in this difficult matter. Not
only does love supply us with a warm and reasonable
motive as against the cold severity of self-perfection
or self-hatred, but it also is the measure for our
detachment.

Detachment is not an absolute perfection but
only a relative one. It becomes perfect, not in increasing the number of things we have given up, but only
in relation to the love of God. As we have said earlier,
those persons and things whose attachment keeps us

from God here and now are to be eliminated as far as possible, but not those which bring us closer to him even indirectly. Like all the virtues, detachment takes on a refined aspect under the influence of love. No longer is sin the only practical norm of judging our attachments, but rather the ever more delicate understanding of what is demanded if we would have greater closeness in love. For instance, we do not avoid idle curiosity only as voluntary imperfection or as a discipline to train ourselves to avoid and reject sinful occasions, but now also to free the mind for God.

Love of God is also at work in the very important virtue of humility, a virtue which comes so hard to human nature. Better than any other consideration, it is this love which makes us throw away our false ideals of thinking and acting, for otherwise we cannot possess him who is worth more than all the unreality on which we may have been depending. The void unconsciously feared in stripping ourselves of our illusions is no longer feared, for this love is a friendship and therefore there is a mutuality about it. God cannot love us unless there is something in us to love. Yet he does love us; we have his word on that, and we get to know it by instinct also. Despite what we secretly know about ourselves, he sees something in us that attracts his pure and limitless love. Growing in love then means growing in our ability to live our own truth, and thus we are at the heart of the virtue of humility.

Love also puts a rationality into otherwise meaningless lives — lives filled with contradiction, loneliness, failure, suffering. Love is at work here, even though its voice is sometimes almost inaudible. The love of God makes hard things easy, and unbearable things bearable, just as Jacob worked for seven years to win Rachel, only to have to work seven more years because he was tricked. It makes us respond with a patience that is not negative, as if the spiritual life were all suffering or all dark night. We suffer because the Beloved asks, and only what he asks. And in many lives, as well as many times in each life, love supplies the answers where reasoning fails.

Indeed the whole idea of human perfection is transformed by love. We must go beyond mere self-perfection as an adequate motive in the spiritual life, and yet we cannot refuse this powerful human instinct as an ally in our progress toward God. One of the things which keeps us psychologically alive is this urge to want to be better. Now of course, we can't continually become better in certain things, for instance, in physical strength or in ease of learning. And furthermore there are also a number of things we don't care to be better in; they are not worth the effort. But to be alive, we still have to want to be better in some way, and with advancing years, along with deeper perspective, it has to be something worthwhile.

Are we not thus enlisting enormous natural forces to help our spiritual progress when we determine that the highest and best of all perfections is centered in the love of God? And it will be this same love of God which will keep spiritual perfection from becoming only a sterile self-love.

The virtues take on a greater luster as we approach God. They become more permeated with the love that is their life. They also fit together in a harmonious whole. As beginners, when the virtues were being acquired more laboriously, the process might have seemed like constructing a house brick by brick. But now in relatively secure possession of all the virtues, the result seems more like the parts of a living person. But in a sense it is even more than this. Christ is living in us, not in our artificial adoption of the mannerisms of speech of biblical language, but in his making us more our-selves, what we are meant by God to be, and by our conforming our life to his, by our showing in our life the virtues that were in his. Through the suc-cessful acquiring of the virtues, the gentle domina-tion of love will lead our difficult nature to the relatively easy harmony and inner peace which we want so much. Love is both the end and the way. Surely then, to increase in love, and in all that leads to greater love, must become our deepest and most constant petition before God.

It is one thing to speak of love and peace, and another to be able to give it. In these pages we can speak of it, but only God can give it. We can speak of the value of love, and to some extent of how to go about finding it. We can say with St. Paul, "God's own peace, which is beyond all understanding" (Phil. 4:7), but these are only words unless we can experience it. For this we ourselves have to go to God, in the manner in which Philip invited Nathanael to go to Christ: "Come, see for yourself" (Jn. 1:46).

Many of us have brought our troubles to a quiet church and left them there. We were unburdened, not always by thinking them out before the Friend we find there, but sometimes by seeing them dis-appear merely in being there with him alone. But in the spiritual life we come to understand deeply that we do not meet our God only in church. We find him everywhere by only turning our hearts to him, not always in a spirit of fervor but sometimes only in a spirit of faith. Unlike the good loves of this earth, which are filled with the many varieties of separation, we can be with this Friend merely by wanting to be. And if we are never far from him, neither will we ever be far from love and peace.

One final word. Even though in the spiritual life we need to emphasize love, we must not do so at the expense of something even more necessary. We must be careful that in saying that love will make us perfect, we are not really trying to go to God by our own power. Our love, we may be unconsciously saying, will overwhelm the obstinacy of our nature, and this will be sufficient to force our way toward God. But love itself is not enough; it is not the basic effective cause either of our perseverance toward salvation or of our sanctification. Only actual grace can do this; grace is always the essential effective cause.

Grace comes in so many ways, as we have already said, but insofar as it depends on our asking, we must constantly pray for it, no matter how great our love. In fact we must pray for it especially if we would increase in love. But along with grace, greater love will make us use grace better and enable us to receive more of it.

Chapter 27

Love of God

The love of God is intimately involved with belief in God. In the first place, unless we somehow know that he exists, we cannot love him. But faith also tells us what kind of God he is, and thus gives birth to the assurance that our love is not a hopeless love. The pages of the inspired word tell us over and over that God is truly all that God must be, such as powerful, wise, and just. But the dominant message, especially when he reveals himself more fully in the New Testament, is that he is a God of mercy and love. And also, for reasons he knows better than we, he is intensely interested in us.

From almost any point of view we are insignificant. Our earth by its raw powers can overwhelm us in our weakness. Our precious life itself depends on things as cheap as water and as free as sunlight. We are the tiniest of atoms compared to the size of the universe. And yet to God we are something beyond value. All the galaxies of burning stars which he has splashed across the cosmos are nothing compared to one man. The stars may explode in his heavens and it concerns him not at all. But let mankind sin, and he sends his Son.

If one of us sins, he is there with his grace immediately. If we persist, he loves us enough to correct us by punishment. Our daily misfortunes find him ready to respond to our prayers. Our lives are under his care, in ways we do not always understand, but still under his care from beginning to end. This kind of God gives us hope that we are not forgotten in a difficult world nor abandoned as our planet is dragged along by its galaxy into ever dark emptiness. Indeed he tells us explicitly that he even wants our love.

Man's association with him is pictured by God as an essentially simple thing, that is to say, a personal relationship between God and the race, but even more fundamentally between him and each human soul. At its lowest it is a service of fear; at its highest it is a oneness of love. Man must ever come to God drawn by these two forces, fear and love, but the only one which will bring him close is the attractive power of love.

Although God is our father both by nature and by our adoption through grace, there is a higher relationship between us, and this is the love known as friendship. True friendship always seeks to give something to the friend. St. Thomas (II,II; 23;1) tells us that God's friendship for us is shown by the fact that he wishes to share his happiness with us, especially when this friendship reaches its consummation in the next life.

Our love therefore is not a love which is one-sided, we loving him as a remote, disinterested, all-perfect being. It is rather a love which is mutually shared, his love giving us first and gratuitously the ability to love him, and then that love accepted by him as the most important thing in creation to this being who really needs nothing, not even our love.

In giving us his friendship God has given us his greatest gift, for even God cannot give a greater thing, except when he gave the Son and later the Holy Spirit. But once given, we act most laudably only when we give ourselves fully to it in return. I must accept the fact that God wants me, that he made me because he wants me, that he wants me because he sees something in me, either actual or potential, which draws his love. This is the law of all friendship.

We will accept this fact of God's desire for us more easily, more wholeheartedly, if we depend not only on his word in the Scriptures, but also on a realistic appraisal of what we are or what we have been given. Thus a knowledge and love of the true self will induce us to believe more deeply in God's desire for personal friendship, for "the love with which a man loves himself is the exemplar and root of friendship" (ibid. 25;4).

It may seem contradictory to say that love of another, especially of God, must have a beginning in love of the self. It is so easy to construe love of the self as a completely selfish love, a self-centered love which loves another principally for what it gets from the other. On the other hand, a truly mature love consists principally in giving. But with love of God, as with human love, this giving will be done better if we know ourselves to be lovable and wanted, not in an egotistical admiration of self but in the truth founded on the gratuitousness of God's giving in the first place.

Even though our human status before God is such that we can give only what we have been given, it is still ours to give through the gift of God which is our free will. Even though we may in many ways be overwhelmed by the misery and emptiness within us, each of us has the wealth of the person which

God has made, and made for himself so that he could love and be loved in turn. Thus, to give ourselves wholly, we must know that we have something to offer that the other will really want. There is a fear of loving, a fear of giving, because of the fear of not being wanted.

The more we know we are wanted, the more will we give of what is alive in ourselves, our joys, our fears, our interests, our sadness, even the things we think are funny. We will know that they are of interest to God because they are part of ourselves. The way to union is this all-inclusive kind of giving.

This giving is not a perpetual "giving up" of things so that we have nothing in this world or the next. Nor is it a giving for the purpose of receiving some favor in return; that is barter, a business transaction, and not friendship. Rather it is a giving of the most precious of all gifts, the gift of oneself. This is as true of friendship with God as it is of human friendship.

It would be quite simple to say that the more we love God, the more complete will be the giving of what is ours. Yet there is a certain lack of wisdom in such a concept. The subtle implication is that our love must be entirely other-centered, wholly altruistic. But with love of God even as in the best of human friendships, there will always be the instinct of our nature which seeks our own happiness. Thus we are made by God. Even our best loves are somewhat self-centered; they become less admirable only when they are predominantly concerned with self.

We all have a love that is based on need. In its lowest and least desirable forms it loves only for what it receives, as for instance, solely for the pleasure that comes from loving. Something like this often happens in the spiritual life, and it is called first fervor. But even in the noblest of us there are needs which love fulfills, which we would be fools to deny and foolish to resist. In its highest form this need-love, or need to be loved, fulfills us by conferring upon us a sense of our worth, a sense of appreciation of ourself, because we are something in the eyes of another whom we respect, whose love we want because we value the person of the other.

This need-love is necessary for us if we are to overcome our loneliness. For this we need the love of others, and in our deepest nature we need the love of God. This need-love of him can become a most compelling love even as we grow in spiritual life, and we would be unwise to neglect it in favor of an exclusive attempt to have the highest love, love of God for himself. This need-love for God includes needs as individual as the need for him sometimes forced on certain people by the circumstances through which he calls them, the fact that there is no one else to fill their loneliness. Or it can be as universal as the need implied in his providence over all of us in a universe whose forces are overpowering. But it is both personal and universal in a love-need for him implied by our humanly unfillable emptiness.

Our will is able to love only the good in things; even in our sins we love the apparent good that is in them. But our will, reaching out to so many good things, finds that no one of them nor any succession of them fills it to permanent satisfaction because they do not fill up the ever-remaining potentiality for the all of good things. There is always an eventual emptiness for more or for other good things. Only he upon whom created goodness is imaged, he who is all-goodness in himself, can quiet this humanly incurable hunger.

There is what we may call the irresistibility of God, irresistibility if we do not turn our eyes from it by our own contrary desires and fulfillments. It is true that he does not immediately appear to be supremely lovable in the same way that a beautiful woman is immediately seen to be beautiful. But reason and faith, and the grace which works through both, are able to impress this truth on us. As irresistible we shall see him in heaven, and irresistible we can sometimes find him in prayer on earth. For so he is.

To be a love worthy of God, he must be loved for his own sake. Or to be more theologically specific, he is to be loved principally for his goodness, as he is good in himself, and not principally because he is good to us. All other reasons for loving him are secondary and follow from this, as St. Thomas tells us as he analyzes love for God with his intellect (II,II; 23;5 ad 2). But in our direct loving of God we do not greatly need the intellect, other than to know only a few things about him. It is love itself which supplies our vision. The will, as we have said, must sometimes lead the intellect, but never to the exclusion of the ultimate guidance of the intellect, for this is the disease of the fanatic. But love, which is principally in the will, can reach out to God, can find oneness with him in ways in which the intellect can never know and indeed would disrupt if it tried to understand them.

Despite the importance of an enlightened need-love, the perfection of love is to become principally other-centered. We can easily see that a predominantly self-centered love must end in frustration. No human being can possess the right to have his whims, desires, and even all his needs made the principal basis for friendship with God or even with other human beings. Even children, whose love is often like this, cannot receive it as much as they want. Such a love means the disintegration of the person who tries to give it, and of course God cannot do this. Our growing closer to God implies growing in a love that is principally for the other, for him, in that we desire his will, his glory, in that we continually choose his love as our highest good. Our legitimate self-interests must come under that.

The giving of mature love is therefore essentially a choice. It is not merely a feeling; it is a decision. It is an act of the mind and will to give our lives, ourselves, completely into the hands of this other. Our love consists in this choice or preference for God rather than in any pleasant feelings or emotions.

Our emotions, valuable though they are, cannot determine our love either for God or for anyone. A love founded and nourished on emotions will at best end up in a sentimentality which often is a glaring contradiction to what true love is. For this kind of people religion is made up only of sweetness and light, and where no sweetness is felt, there is no light. God is looked upon only in the meek and humble dimension of an emasculated Christ. Since, then, a false god has been manufactured according to their liking, these people are free to live their lives according to their own feelings. When a commandment or a counsel becomes too hard, when loneliness or unfulfilled desires pull at them, when there is the embarrassment of not being able to agree with the crowd, how easy to say that love is all that matters anyway, as if God were only a mirror of our wishes instead of having a mind of his own. A mind with sometimes incomprehensible ways, he even tells us.

Thus, to love at all adequately requires courage. This holds for loving other human beings, and it holds especially for loving God. Only if we have this virtue, will we be able to face the truth that God has a hard core, that his love must reach into our lives and cover every bit of it. "Anyone who loves me will be true to my word" (Jn. 14:23). If you love me, live the way I want you to live, or it isn't love.

On the other hand it is love which will give us the courage as it gives us so much else. While the full ability to love depends on the full development of our spiritual maturity, love itself, only a little at first, can make us take the steps toward this maturity because we *want to* enough. A child learning to walk falls and falls. In the beginning of our life of love we may crawl; we then try walking, yet keep on falling and falling. But if we keep on trying, in the end we will run.

What we have said earlier about increasing in grace applies also to love, since they both increase together in the depths of the soul. Therefore, not everything we do merits an increase of love here and now, but only when God in his wisdom sees fit to increase it. Yet, as with sanctifying grace, we should in general increase in love as our life moves on. Since actions performed with greater love will always merit even greater love, we should, by recollection and purity of intention, try to do everything with this kind of love so that our meriting of increase may be constant and rapid.

Such intensity of love most likely will not usually be emotional intensity, and may not even be easily discernible. It may be as unlike what we think of as love as the anguished choosing of him in a difficult situation or even in failure, or taking deeper breaths of love in an atmosphere of monotony. It is always a loving of himself and his will, increasingly more for himself than for any other good reason.

For increase in love we need the grace of God. "No one can come to me unless the Father who sent me draws him" (Jn. 6:44). We obtain this grace by wanting it very much and trusting very much that we will get it through all the means of grace, especially the Mass, the sacraments, and our prayers. By making increase in love the first purpose of our lives, we indeed "seek first the kingdom of God and his holiness," and we will find that "all things will be given us besides" (cf. Mt. 6:33). We put this full giving of our heart ahead of all our other loves, our other plans, our other desires, our ambitions for the fulfillment of other gifts less important, and we will find, in not being concerned with these to the detriment of love, the best way to their fulfillment...or non-fulfillment when their fulfillment would be a mistake.

Loving God does not mean inaction. Even the saint who wrote, "Now I guard no flock nor have I other office, for now my exercise is in loving alone," did not find it so, nor did he mean it so (*Spiritual Canticle*, XXVIII, St. John of the Cross). God has plans for us which we must first of all find (or recover), then pray about, and finally bring to success, if he so wills, with much determination and stress. But we never lose sight of our greatest personal good and duty, growing in love.

In the end we should hope to love God in the degree that he deserves to be loved, and this measure of love, as St. Bernard tells us, is to love him without measure. We should want to love him as much as he can be loved by this human heart. Love of God has no limits; this virtue can always increase. The limits imposed by our reason are not limits on love itself, but only on certain circumstances of our love, such as the time we may spend in prayer. It would be a false fear and a lie of the devil to consider that we had ever reached the limits of the union we can have with God, for love has no limits of its own.

Chapter 28

Love for Others

We must preface the remainder of this section of the book by stating that it is not our purpose to consider all the virtues or even all the important virtues. This has already been done in our book for those beginning the spiritual life.[1] What was said there about the virtues is still valid and will always be so, no matter how far we progress. Therefore none of this will be repeated, or even summarized, insofar as is compatible with the purpose of this present book, which must itself be a consistent whole. A man in this period of the spiritual life no longer needs to have the virtues spelled out for him; in fact by the grace of God, more than by instruction, he will acquire an ever deeper insight of his own into their need and into ways of increasing them. However, he still has need of guidance and encouragement in respect to certain virtues more important to his present situation in the spiritual life.

Therefore love of neighbor is not now to be treated so much to tell how or why, but, principally

1. *Beginnings in Spiritual Life* (New York: Doubleday, 1967).

to give two warnings. The first is a common hazard in the spiritual life. Our spiritual endeavor can so absorb our outlook and energies that we may unconsciously become self-centered. Our soul and God exist almost alone in the universe. How contrary this is to the will of God is seen by the fact that, although he has obligingly given us two great commandments, they are both summed up in one virtue. The supernatural virtue of charity includes both love of God and love of neighbor; by this supernatural virtue we love our neighbor principally because we love God. Therefore, since this one virtue must move on two fronts before there is increase, quite obviously we are working in vain if we try to grow in love of God without growing in love of our brothers.

Supernatural love is one virtue principally because, as we have said, love of God and neighbor both have the same motive. God is loved for himself, for God; our neighbor is loved for the same reason, for God, in the many ways that there are to love someone for God. This love of neighbor, like love of God, is a gift of God. He has given us reasons for loving which are universal, which cover all cases, a much greater gift than his gift of loving for particular reasons, such as relationship or compatibility. For God has given us the power to love all men, despite our natural or acquired dispositions against many of them. We love them all as God's children (at least potentially), as brothers of Christ (by his own word), and (hopefully) as companions in our enjoyment of God's love in heaven.

Sometimes, however, we do not value this gift of grace as we ought because we are impressed with the need for other virtues, such as those which so obviously affect our relationship with God, like humility, or those which have to do with our peace, like courage and trust. Or we seek higher prayer as a gateway to closer union. And yet, no other virtue can bring us so close to love of God because no other is one virtue with love of God. And conversely, no other ordinary failing we are now likely to encounter can keep us from God so effectively as failure in this. All the other sins we are now usually concerned with, even taken together, do not have the guilt before God as do our sins against love of neighbor. Of all the sins we usually confess, he wants this eliminated the most. Of all of them this is the principal reason why so many relatively good people never come closer to him.

It is this love of our brothers that is at the heart of the gospel message. A man might find it easy to love the God who sent his Son to death for him, but he might forget that this Son was not sent only for one man. Therefore, "I give you a new commandment: love one another. Such as my love has been for you, so must your love be for each other" (Jn. 13:34). The love of Christ for each of us is the measure we must try to equal in our love for all others.

We must use our knowledge of the relationship of God and Christ to all men to remove what is opposed to love. Our unloving thoughts are best kept out by thoughts of love based on God's gift of love to all. Our words will no longer oppress our brother, present or absent, as if he did not pertain in some way to God and to Christ. We will know that, unless he has committed some rather serious sin, our fault in criticizing him is greater in God's sight than his. And even if his sin is greater and we have no proportionately great reason for discussing it, our sin stands before God regardless.

As for our actions, a love of God that understands God will no longer allow us to live in a world walled with mirrors that reflect only ourselves, as if others of our acquaintance were not sometimes overburdened and could use our help, if only that of a kind word or prayer when we can do nothing more. And our concern for spiritual progress will not be an occasion to forget the many unknown people who are sharing the cross of Christ in intense and almost hopeless suffering.

In return, this love of our brothers will bring us much, for our love is not without self-interest. When we are urged by our Lord, "Be compassionate, as your Father is compassionate" (Lk. 6:36), the plain truth follows that "the measure you measure with will be measured back to you" (v. 38).

Our self-interest, however, must be limited. We ought not seek from our actions the reward that comes from human praise or other human return. If we are doing for God through the needs of our neighbor what we cannot do for God who has no needs, then we must be content with the return that God will give. We should therefore not be discouraged when we receive no human return. Christ did not stop just because the nine lepers did not come back, or just because the apostles could not watch one hour, or even because of Judas' kiss. Nor does he stop giving to us, mercifully, because of our own sins and infidelities to grace.

Love of neighbor is therefore a gift by which we can love those we find it hard to love but must, and those we greatly want to love unto eternal life but, without the gift, could not. We must grow in this love if we would grow in love of God, but not so much as to come to minimize love of God. There are some who do, and to them we address the second warning. For them love of neighbor is everything, and God seems to get very little either of their time or their attention. And yet, love of neighbor by itself does not make a Christian; others, even those who have no faith, have done great things for humanity. The Christian is bound by two great commandments, and the first, our Lord tells us, is also the greater.

Thus, even though there are great divergencies in the personal vocations of different men, they must all be ways to God. If they fail to be this, then either the way itself, or our judgment that it is our way, or our conduct in this way must be re-examined. Through all the various ways by which we can imitate Christ, we can be led only one ultimate way and that is to the Father.

There is one other aspect of love of neighbor which is important to those who have come this far in the spiritual life, and this is love for true friends. We usually have no difficulty in seeing this kind of love as a gift of grace, for besides the general reasons for which we must love all men, or even the particular reasons by which we see God's goodness reflected to us in our friends, we love them principally and sacredly because they are his special and personal gift to us.

We have already written much on friendship, and again it is a primary purpose here not to repeat. But those in any stage of the spiritual life always have the same problem. Although they know they must love their enemies, they may have doubts that they may love their friends. The doubts can be both doctrinal and practical.

St. Thomas offers a common formulation of the doctrinal problem. "Some say we ought to love all men equally as regards affection, but not as regards outward effect" (II,II; 26;6). That is to say, we should feel the same amount of love, preferably a cool, level type, toward everyone, but as to outward effects we will help this one more than that because this one needs it more, say, because he has a broken leg. St. Thomas answers this with a bit less than his usual gentleness. "But this," he says, "is unreasonable. For the affection (of the virtue of) charity, which is the inclination of grace, is not less orderly than the natural desire which is the inclination of nature, for both inclinations flow from the Divine Wisdom" (ibid.). In the broad sweep of deep insight he sees the loves of our nature: parents for children, children for parents, all the loves within the family, all the other good loves of man for woman, and woman for man, the loves of friendship of man for man and woman for woman; he sees these not as a confused interplay of the forces of survival or biology, but as the orderly creation of an orderly God. Things are meant to be the way they are (not, of course, the serious defects that got into the system by way of original sin) and so, just as we do not love all people equally in the order of nature, we must not expect it in the spiritual life either.

Another doctrinal objection comes from a defect, that of the too-spiritual, the misunderstanding of the true ideal of "giving ourselves wholly to God." Briefly we may respond that there have been some of us who have done this very difficult thing, giving ourselves wholly to God, and these have been the saints. But their lives tell us again and again that they were also able to give themselves to others in friendship. And who succeeded best of all in giving himself wholly to God? It was of course our Lord, considered in his human nature. Yet he who loved all loved some with a special love. And we are asked to learn of him who is the way.

We are called to follow Christ in different ways and different degrees, for no one man can follow him completely or perfectly. And so the exercise of friendship will vary in different men. But in any case, "giving all to God" means only that we be willing to give

him whatever he may ask, without constantly thinking that he may be asking something as valuable to
our spiritual life as our friends.

A difficulty can also arise from the phrase, "to
love others in God," if we mean that we love God
alone and all others somewhat as if contained in God,
in the same way we might love minestrone soup:
we don't care much about the individual ingredients
but we love the whole very much. This is, of course,
an unreal kind of love because it means loving as
if the person were not there. But we must love the
person: "love your neighbor as yourself." And how
else do we love the Blessed Virgin?

St. Paul says (1 Cor. 10:31), "whether you eat
or drink—whatever you do—you should do all for
the glory of God." But in eating and drinking for the
the glory of God, we don't eat God. We do the thing.
Therefore in loving our friends, we must do the thing
also. We do this thing, this delightful thing, because
it is God's will and out of love for him—all our other
reasons are subordinate and are included in this—just
as we do all other things out of love for him. But with
this difference: that this is a better and higher thing
than many other things we do.

Our practical difficulties, however, can be more
serious than the theoretical. These involve the in-
tricacies of human relationships which extend from
the potentially highest to the potentially lowest. Thus
each one of our relationships must be weighed in-
dividually, and our friendships must be able to be
included under the great whole which must be our
all-inclusive love for God.

There are, however, certain specific qualities of
true friendship which can help us in our evaluation.
A true friendship will help us to observe the second
greatest commandment, not with a narrowness by
which we lavish love and service on only one, but

with a love which extends to everyone we meet. True friendship also is not a sponge that absorbs our lifeblood of energy; on the contrary it is something that strengthens us for the observance of our duties. It should increase our ability to bear the tensions of life, especially our frustrations and failures. And finally it should be primarily unselfish. For we do not love the other principally to obtain a safe harbor from the storms of living. We do not love the other to satisfy our need to create, to make someone over for our own satisfaction. We seek to help our friend because of what he is, to be what he is, and by the most delicate exercise of holy prudence we hope to bring this real person to God. This is the ultimate test of friendship, as of all else, that in general, but certainly, it brings both friends always closer to God.

This closeness to God is something which friendship is particularly fitted to help bring about. It is particularly in this that it is a gift of grace. Under the influence of actual grace, it is itself an external grace. Not only does it help by way of mutual prayer, example, and counsel, but the friendship itself provides a natural foundation from which we can more easily go to God. Some of us will find that we respond to love of God only when the barriers of the heart are broken down by human love. We must see ourselves as able to draw forth enduring love before we can come very close to the mysterious and sometimes fearsome love of God. God indeed can bring about his designs without human help but we find that, according to his usual providence, almost indispensable for this is true friendship, one in which we are known and accepted for what we are or despite what we are or were.

In practice, however, the ideal does not always shine so brightly. Each friendship has potentialities, not only to help us to God, but also to draw us away from him. Among the many ways leading away from God there is sometimes that of sexual attraction. The sober fact is that the fascination produced by something so deep in our nature as this attraction can cause us to delay on our way to God if we are not on our guard against the subtle influence of this most beautiful creation.

The externals of the love of friendship, like all things concerned with love of neighbor, must be weighed with more care than we will be inclined to give. For instance, a true love of God and the friend will often require that we say less than the heart yearns to say, lest we turn the friend from God to ourselves. And also, the overzealous desire to do favors for the other requires that less be done than the heart yearns to do, if both are to keep their spiritual equilibrium. The favor must not only be weighed for what it is in itself, but rather for the effect it may have in increasing an already too emotional attachment or dependence.

Finally, despite all the good things about friendship, we must not expect that of itself it will raise us to God. It is an instrument in the hands of God, and therefore our prayer must be for much grace if we are to persevere in his love together...and to persevere not only in love of God. Even the best of friendships will always be relationships between two human beings, and either or both may fail in their potentiality to share the heights and depths of the spirit.

Then too, despite the instinctive optimism to the contrary, we must not expect too much of the friendship even in relation to the friend. Every friendship involves two diverse human beings, and will always contain elements of hostility alongside even the deepest love. As a consequence wisdom, tolerance, and forgiveness must be the companions of love, even the best of human loves. In this way God makes us grow spiritually in ways we would not, except that we must if we would keep the love we value so much.

God and his grace, therefore, are the most important elements in every friendship, making it his gift not only in the beginning but at every precarious step along the way, and above all in the consummation of union of friend with friend in heaven in his all-embracing love.

Chapter 29

The Hidden Pride and
the Elusive Humility

The spiritual life easily puts us on guard against certain of our enemies, for instance the incompatibility of a life of the spirit with a life according to the attitudes of the world. It also does very well in telling us of other enemies that we might not so easily recognize, the chief among these is pride. But pride is not overcome so simply as is an open conflict with the world. It is a major enemy in the beginning of the spiritual life, and it is still major now after we have seen other enemies depart in defeat.

One reason for the persistence of pride is that it rarely fights an open battle; rarely do we meet a temptation in which we confront real pride head on. Rather it fights a guerrilla warfare, weakening our desire to seek grace and diminishing our ability to obtain and use it. It lurks in hidden ambushes and knows innumerable disguises. Our intelligence is inadequate to meet it on all fronts, particularly because it infiltrates our intellect; the beginning of our victory is to recognize that we need God's help and then to ask him.

Perhaps the only aspect of pride to which we are alerted is vanity, the kind of self-admiration which holds our attention beyond the needs of self-knowledge and legitimate self-love. A man or woman may thus over-admire personal physical beauty, mental ability, or the power to achieve. And yet one of the safe things about such temptations is the fact that we are readily on guard concerning them. Even though the influence of vanity is unconsciously present in most people at this stage of the spiritual life, it is rarely given consent with any deliberation. It would be difficult, for instance, to imagine a spiritual person spending long periods in admiration before a mirror.

But the relative ease with which we recognize vanity and put it aside should not deceive us into thinking that the battle with pride is won, beyond a few recurring temptations. In fact the spiritual life in some unavoidable sense brings in a whole new set of occasions to feed hidden pride, and these may never be recognized. A few examples: the amount of time we give to prayer (Our Lord tells us that the Pharisees were deceived by this), or our strictness of life (An echo of "I fast twice in the week"?), or our external works for God ("I give tithes of all that I possess"). Our union with God is not measured by how much torment we inflict on ourselves or even by how much we do for him; it is rather measured by love of God and neighbor.

But the proud man doesn't do very well by his neighbor either. Like the Pharisee who went to the temple to pray (so he thought), there are always the comparisons with those who are not so advanced or so zealous, or who are not so resplendent in liturgical functions as we ourselves. How often, while listening to a sermon or conference, do we not find ourselves silently directing the words to someone else, to someone who "really needs it"? Our minds can become so full of ourselves, and we not be aware of it, that what we think is great love of God is not, and we also fail in authentic love of neighbor or even in duties of justice toward him.

The spiritual life indeed shields us from pride in some areas, but it cannot help being the occasion for failure in others. Obviously a true spiritual life is not the cause of this situation and, equally obviously, it provides the solution through a constant development of the virtue of true humility.

Just as the natural virtues have a connection in the one virtue of prudence and the supernatural virtues in love of God and neighbor, so also is there through pride a connection of all the vices. The most easily observed is the connection of pride with the vices of imprudence and impurity. With dependence upon God removed through pride, our relative blindness leads us into many errors of stupidity, and our lower nature asserts a subtle dominance by which it draws the reason into dangerous rationalizations. But these two effects of pride are only external reminders of an enormous internal denial of grace, and the frustration of its operation when given—this to the extent that we still are proud. Blessedly, however, the failures resulting from pride provide occasions for its cure.

In a man who has made some spiritual advance, pride can be at work especially in providing false attitudes similar to those already mentioned, but they are by no means the only ones. Some of these deserve special mention because they affect more than a few of us, and this in a most basic area. For one, there are various ways of showing our relationship with God, and the higher always must include the lower. Therefore it is no insult to our spirituality to understand that our most fundamental relationship to him is that of creature to creator. Yet it is possible to be so filled

with a somewhat superficial love of God that we
overlook this, that we rather see our soul only as a
child of God, his friend, or his beloved, but fail to
see that we are also servants and, if we will serve no
other way, his slaves.

In our impatient or proud desire for the closest
union, we can fail to emphasize that there are duties
to be performed, steps to be taken, virtues to be carefully and even painfully acquired. Only when we are
filled with the necessity to serve God in practical
details and prudent choices can we allow the servant
relationship to be totally absorbed into the higher
one of friend. "You are my friends if you do what I
command you. I no longer speak of you as slaves"
(Jn. 15:14, 15).

The rejection of false attitudes has everything
to do with humility, which is a virtue of authentic
reality, and much to do with the spiritual life itself,
despite the fact that many of these false attitudes are
very "spiritual." On the contrary, however, they are
a contradiction to it. Whereas the spiritual life is
meant to take away the chains which imprison our
true personality and prevent true spiritual progress,
the adoption of attitudes we may read about or fancy
for ourselves will suffocate our real spiritual vitality
because it suffocates our personal, human, and
psychological vitality. Grace does not destroy nature,
but a false spirituality does.

Thus it is not surprising that much of the pose
that we may unconsciously adopt should center
around humility itself. Here it is easy to mouth certain expressions which one does not authentically
experience, simply because it is very difficult to
experience and live a true humility. But we do not
become saints merely because we talk like them.

There is, however, an aspect of this false kind of
humility which is not acquired by excessive imita-

tion of those we may have read about but comes
darkly from within. This can be the result of self-
hatred brought on by a lack of honest appreciation
of our good qualities, together with the frustration of
trying to live up to a false and impossible image of
ourselves. Or, from another source, it may be the
result of unhealthy feelings of guilt.

As to self-hatred, which is the first of these dark
and unhealthy imitations of humility, we have already said much when speaking in detail of the false
and true image of ourselves. Humility, as one of the
necessary gifts of grace, must necessarily be concerned with the admirable truth about ourselves.
This truth is not contrary to humility if we see it as
a part of a larger truth, that self-knowledge has an
ultimate sense in which I know myself as a creature,
that I am dependent on God entirely. If we understand this deeply and immovably, then our full
knowledge of the true self will not hurt us but help
us. It is really our human dignity, or better, a sense
of our God-given worth.

Self-knowledge and humility are often associated solely with the knowledge of our faults and
limitations, both of natural and spiritual life. This
is, of course, too one-sided for our spiritual and
psychological good. But on the other hand, the value
of knowledge of our good qualities by no means allows us to forget that there is an important spiritual
value in our bad ones. Complete self-knowledge
does not always come down from heaven as a flash
of brilliant insight, nor is humility a gift totally infused by God all at once. Both are hammered out
little by little through contact with an agonizing kind
of reality. And our lives, our gifts, and our pride must
feel the pain of the many blows of the hammer.

But the awareness and appreciation of our good
qualities and our success is an important natural

substratum in acquiring this difficult virtue. In fact we thus find it easier to acquire it. We took refuge in the false image, the pride image, principally because we found so little in ourselves to love and respect. But in the appreciation of ourselves, we are now dealing with insecurity and pride from a position of relative strength. Now, because of a new inner security, we are not afraid to take the kind of look at ourselves which will bring God's supereminence and our own deficiency into practical perspective. We will also love God more freely. For we can sometimes be afraid of loving fully because we are afraid of not being wanted; we are afraid of giving ourselves because we fear not being loved for what we are. As a matter of fact, the deep purification known as the Dark Night of the Spirit can take place only when one has acquired something of this deep inner assurance of God's personal love.

On the other hand, the sentimental, melancholy souls, who are always so aware of sin, ineptitude, and unworthiness, will always find it difficult to come close to God. Often these acquire the public image of saints, but really are languishing in the backwaters of the spiritual life. They cannot come close to God because they continually feel he is displeased with them. The psychological weight is so heavy that it interferes with the giving of the self. For it is hard to split up the person so as to be able to give supernaturally, against a natural repugnance of any giving.

So approved a teacher as St. Thomas Aquinas finds no contradiction between a valid self-esteem and humility. "Humility does not require a man to subject what he has of God to that which may seem to be of God in another" (II,II; 161;3). That is to say, we do not have to deny our own gifts, even in respect to another's, although we may wisely avoid talking

about them. "In like manner, humility does not require a man to subject that which he has of his own
(that is, his own sins and imperfections) to that which
his neighbor has of man (that is, his neighbor's sins
and imperfections); otherwise each one would have
to esteem himself a greater sinner than anyone else"
(ibid.). Even though such expression of abasement
is sometimes found in spiritual books, we can all
see the incongruity of it when we think of some of
the monstrous sinners which the world has produced.
How unreal, then, to hear some delicate nun, for
instance, proclaim that she is the worst of sinners!

If some of the saints have used these expressions,
we must say that they were emotionally overwhelmed
before the great holiness of God or that they saw their
own personal potentiality to great sin or that they
knew very few bad people. Yet since we do not know
the whole of any man, "a man may esteem his neighbor to have some good which he lacks himself; or
himself to have some evil which another has not"
(ibid.).

In the harmony of humility and the true appreciation of the self, we can see a new direction for this
virtue. It does not consist in thinking all possible evil
of oneself, but rather finds ever and ever greater
depths of learning and accepting God's causality in
our lives, the causality of his grace and his universal
providence. More and more does the simple truth become a principle which eventually permeates the
whole man: "Name something you have that you have
not received" (1 Cor. 4:7).

It is true that there is danger of pride in this appreciation for what we have been given. But in this
open acceptance of ourselves we understand that
danger, and understanding it, we can meet it in the
light instead of having a distorted facsimile grow in
the darkness as it would anyway. So we no longer

cringe at the danger, but without minimizing it, we praise God and thank him for what he has given us, as did one of us whose example should give us courage here: "God who is mighty has done great things for me, holy is his name" (Lk. 1:49).

We will now consider briefly the other cause of another unhealthy and false humility, and this is exaggerated guilt. Guilt is an experience common to all of us in various degrees and in various areas of life. In a normal person this remorseful knowledge of weakness or sin is one source of true humility as well as a guide for the future. But in a less balanced person, especially if he has read of some saints as always bewailing their sins, guilt can be a depressant factor in the whole psyche and a barrier to real contact with God. For, only in him can we fully recover our sense of worth, despite the unlovable things we all sometimes have done. In this we stand alongside the rest of humanity, who also have failed; our oneness with them is always a firm basis for reasonable and deep humility. With all men we can look to God as a God of forgiveness and mercy and, therefore, for us a God of hope. But the guilt-ridden man, in a secret pride that avoids all identification with others, will not accept this.

For instance, if I think, because of a false image of myself, that I must never be distracted in prayer or be tempted to impurity, how can I grow close to God when the guilty feelings from distractions or temptation convince me that I am not meant for such union? But if I am convinced that I, like all human beings, am subject to the effects of original sin, I can find God even better by turning to him in the consciousness of my need.

And even in the certain knowledge that I have sinned, or acted less than honorably when perhaps

276 MATURING THE SPIRIT

I have not sinned, or have fallen from perfection and wasted graces he has wanted for me, how I may long for the love he must have had for me before I left his way! But does he not show even more love for me now when he seeks me and finds me and gives me more of his graces? Is not this a greater love for me than I had before I left him?

Perhaps it will now be a surprise, so late in a chapter on humility, to be told that as yet we have not touched the essence of the virtue. Many really proud people hide behind the common assertion that, after all, humility is truth. Yet only an unbeliever would deny that we owe God everything. St. Thomas discerns a fundamental need in human nature which calls for this virtue. He tells us that "it does not follow that humility is essentially concerned with knowledge," but that it is "essentially in the appetite" (*ibid.*, art. 2), and by appetite he here means principally the will.

Although self-knowledge is an important condition for this virtue, the essential purpose of humility is to prevent our fallen nature from exaggerating our idea of our excellence. If the will did not continually keep the mind from concentrating on our excellence too much, to the extent that the will in turn became too enamored of what is there, this would bring on exaggeration and illusion. Humility thus prevents our losing our sense of proportion in regard to the gifts in themselves or in comparison with those of others, or especially in respect to total dependence upon God. All of this is a condition required in the will before he can give us his great love.

Herein then is humility especially a gift of grace. For, which of us could hope to look upon ourselves favorably and still hold back the devouring appetite of self-love in a fallen nature? And now, moving toward God and being filled with more of his gifts, do we not need, with an ever-increasing necessity, this moderating habit of our will? So we should pray for it, and not only a little. The crucial battle of progress or lukewarmness in love may well depend on this.

There are certain virtues closely associated with humility. Prudence or common sense comes easily to mind. By this we regulate the external exercise of humility, using as our example, not some saint with an unusual vocation, but our Lord and among the saints, especially St. Paul. We will find this for ourselves if we read the Scriptures faithfully and carefully. Humility is not the greatest virtue, and so sometimes its exercise must give way to something higher or more important at the moment.

A virtue which flows from humility almost directly is obedience. When our Lord told us that "whoever makes himself lowly, becoming like this little child, is of greatest importance in that heavenly reign" (Mt. 18:4), he could have meant many things by this simplicity of heart, such as faith, trust, purity, and humility, but surely also obedience. Our minds must see not only the necessity for authority in the Church and elsewhere, but also its sacredness. Our wills must submit to it as we do to God, and not only to the principal holders of spiritual authority such as the Holy Father and our bishop, but wherever else we may meet it in the many ways in which it must be delegated in our complex world.

We obey even when we do not see the reason for it, because every man has his blind spot and God wills that our intellect be mortified at times as well as our will and our body. So when we have exhausted those legitimate means of protest which do not harm the Church or public order, when our representations have been rejected or they can be seen to be most probably useless, we must submit our mind at least to this, that we are in contact with God's unfathomable ways.

There is much talk about the charismatic element in the Church, the prophetic mission of certain people chosen by God. But it must be observed that the charismatic element must be subject to legitimate authority. Even St. Paul, a true charismatic, did this. "I went [to Jerusalem] prompted by a revelation, and I laid out for their scrutiny the gospel as I present it to the Gentiles...to make sure that the course I was pursuing, or had pursued, was not useless" (Gal. 2:2).

The spiritual life is a growth in self-control. But self-control comes about best in the peace of self-knowledge and self-acceptance. On one hand we accept the chastening knowledge of our weaknesses and limitations, and we try to cure our weaknesses by the practice of the opposite virtues. On the other hand we keep the appreciation of our strong points under control by the sobering influence of humility. And all this we do out of love.

Humility comes easiest when we love God so much that the love of our own excellence is over-shadowed by our love and appreciation of his, when we want his goodness to be recognized rather than our own.

Chapter 30

Abandonment to God

Our Lord has told us that the greatest in the kingdom of heaven will be those who are most like little children. This does away at one stroke with all the imaginary pictures we may have of sanctity involving miracles, visions, great penances, and long hours of prayer. Our Lord says none of this; instead he says we must become like children. Children love and children trust, and the more they love, the more they trust.

Although this is the ideal toward which we must work, it would be too simple a picture if we did not allow for a great difference between ourselves and the child. The child sees its parents; it calls to them in its needs and they come with visible, tangible love and help. In our situation we are asked to trust a being whom we cannot see or hear, whose help may be a long time in coming and even may never come in the manner we have asked for it.

Furthermore, often it is only with the eye of faith that we can see that it is his help when it does come. We pray for rain, and it rains. Maybe it would have rained anyway. We pray for a successful operation. We get it, but the man who doesn't pray also survives his operation.

This distance and loneliness of our human situation is so unlike the warmth surrounding a loved child that we need a special virtue, a gift from God, to carry us through with comfort and assurance. This gift of grace is hope, which sees with the eye of faith and responds with a heart of love.

It would be easy here, in a book for those somewhat advanced in the spiritual life, to narrow our treatment of this virtue so as to trust only for purely spiritual things; for instance, in finding our personal vocation, how we must be guided among the many voices which urge us along a particular way. But this would not be an adequate spirituality because it would be only partial. The whole of our spiritual life is the entirety of life. God's will for our spirit is reflected in the totality of what we do and what happens to us and around us. Instead of merely speaking to us by inspirations found, for instance, in spiritual books, he often speaks to us through things. Sometimes this is the only way he can reach us in our blindness or stubbornness.

One result of God's inclusion of everything in our spiritual life is that the whole of our life must become the subject matter of our hope when we think in terms of our sanctification. There is an expression which fits this totality better than the word "hope," and this is the term "abandonment" — abandonment, that is, to divine providence. In this way the whole of our life is put into the whole of God's love, wisdom, and care.

It was surely by abandonment to God's providence that so many of the early saints were able to arrive at perfection, and our Lady heads the list. For them there were no learned books on the spiritual life, no complicated system of spirituality, and probably very little in the way of spiritual direction. And yet by this complete trust God was able, through his graces and his wise, careful intervention in details of their lives, to bring them to complete conformity to his will. And this is sanctity.

There is, however, a sense in which conformity to the will of God is an incomplete concept, theologically as well as psychologically, and thus it may not satisfy the whole man; psychologically he may not be able to meet God fully. The reason for this follows from the nature of the will. As we know, it is a blind faculty. It depends on what the intellect proposes to it. Its own nature is to move toward or away through love, desire, or rejection. It is this blind, non-rational aspect of will which we may transfer to God when we speak of the will of God. We may see it, unconsciously it is true, as something capricious, tyrannical, or stubborn, just because we have seen human wills like that (in our parents perhaps) where the will was dominant over every other consideration. And thus we may not fully trust our whole self to such a blind power. It may be especially because of this that the "will of God" is often and erroneously synonymous with the endurance of some evil.

The unconscious fear of a blind force directing our actions does not trouble certain people. They are perhaps those who are led by love more than the rest of us. He whom they love asks this, and it is enough that he asks it. This also applies to those who are led principally by a sense of submission to God simply because he is God.

But others, perhaps those who are accustomed to using their minds more than most of us, are not entirely satisfied by following a force which has any connotation of blindness. These will be helped by considering that, theologically, submission to the will of God, though a handy simplification, is an oversimplification. Not only God's will, but also his mind is an active force in directing our lives. The separation of faculties which is so evident in man is not so with God. His will is one thing with the rest of his nature. It is we who do the dividing of his nature so that we can understand him better. Thus, God is operating, not only by his will, which particularly connotates to us his determination, but also by his intelligence. The inseparable oneness of his nature demands a total oneness when it operates.

By seeing that our lives are the careful and wise thought of God, we can more easily give him the co-operation of our full nature. Our mind is not left languishing, frustrated by continual blind submission. We know, even though we do not understand, that there is Mind working in our lives. To this mind of God we can totally submit, even when we do not know its reasons for acting. We know what mind is; we know also what a superior mind is. And we know that our integrity depends on submission to a superior mind when it is present, to a mind in better possession of the truth.

Our abandonment has a further intellectual aspect; it is abandonment to God's providence. The word "providence," as it is used here, implies a plan. This tells us that he has a particular place and vocation for us on earth and in heaven. It means the ordering of all the details of our lives toward carrying out this plan, without, of course, interfering with our free will. And when it is we who interfere, he is not left helpless but has many alternate plans to bring about his purposes.

There are two difficulties with this idea of abandonment to a plan; one has to do with finding the plan and the other with the meaning of abandonment. The two can, however, be solved simultaneously. Abandonment does not mean that we ourselves cannot act, even though the word might imply that we cast ourselves adrift for the winds to take us as they will. Abandonment means (and thus we find God's plan for us) both accepting and doing. It does not mean only accepting God's will, as when some good or bad fortune comes to us without our having deliberately brought it on. It also implies doing. We may, if we wish, call it passive and active abandonment, but it is conformity to God's mind and will in either case.

People sometimes ask, "How do I know what God's will is for me?" Sometimes (passive abandonment) it is not hard to find, as when we discover that we have broken our leg. At other times (active abandonment) the way is also clear by means of God's commandments, those of his Church, the duties and ideals of our state in life, and so on. Right reason enlightened by faith is the ordinary light that God has given us to guide our lives according to his will.

But there are many cases which are not so simple. One can find reasons on both sides, as when deciding on a vocation or making the choice of a partner in marriage. For these we must sometimes seek counsel from those who are able to help, and in some cases we must seek counsel of God. We have a right to depend on him to know his will. Since he wants us to do it, the pressure is on him, so to speak, to show it to us.

There is an instinct by which we get to know the mind of God and this comes by being close to him. And there is also an insight into his will by getting to know ourselves. By knowing ourselves accurately, we can get a better idea of what he might be asking.

St. Thomas tells us that even a man in good will is not necessarily and always in conformity with the will of God (I,II; 19;10), so that we must not lose courage over the possibility or the fact of honest mistakes. We must act as we see the will of God to be, and be prepared to accept corrections from him through men or through circumstances if we are wrong in assuming our actions to be his will. God does not give us all the guideposts we would always like, nor all at once. Sometimes despite all our searching (and we must search) he gives us only one, and then we must follow this with the same trust in him as if he had given us more and better ones.

Our abandonment, however, is not only to the mind and will of God but, as we have said, also to a particular aspect of his will which is his love. It is perhaps the most impelling of all the motives for giving ourselves over to his action, for he cannot help acting out of love because his love is also one thing with his nature. Even when we cannot see this clearly because of the burden of our cross, it is a simple fact of doctrine following from his indivisible oneness of nature.

Perhaps if we see the figure of the Man on the cross, we will understand that it must always be true. Such love we can trust, even despite the things he will not give us. In our trust we are sure of this one thing: if we do not get what we want, we will get something better; we will get love and we will find a Friend.

On our part abandonment (or our trust, our conformity, and obedience to his will) should be a gift of love. Sometimes it is said that we should consider ourselves as a stick or stone with which God may do as it pleases him. The truth in this is undeniable, and yet there is the danger that, in using such figures of speech, we begin to think that God regards us as sticks and stones. But, of course, he does not. Each one of us is always important, lovingly important, to him. Besides, a stick or stone cannot move, and God sometimes wants us to use our initiative to find his solutions for our problems or to work and battle for his causes. But most of all, a stick or a stone cannot love; it can only stay where it is put. But a human being can love, and our perfection comes about by loving God intensely in all the situations in which we are put or in which we put ourselves.

There is an aspect of abandonment to God's love which is especially important to all of us, and this is abandonment to his mercy, to his wish to give where there is no adequate reason to give. A proud man will not want to accept such gratuitousness because the god he has made of himself does not want to be in such debt to another. A fearful man will hold back from any such gift because he mistrusts, knowing his sins or his abuse of grace. Yet God's intent is clear. Our Lord did not come principally for the just but for the sinners, and from Mary Magdalene to the good thief we can see that he had a good idea of what is meant by sinners.

In some cases, however, God is held off, not because of real sins or infidelities, but by imaginary ones. These are scruples which transform, for their victims, the peace of the Christian life into a torment among angry bees. One root of the difficulty is a certain misunderstanding. The scrupulous man always thinks that the problem is an intellectual problem, trying to decide whether he has sinned, sinned grievously, been honest in telling his sins, and so on, whereas the real problem is fear, an emotional problem.

This is the reason that arguing with oneself is useless, as is much research and endless consultation. Thus these doubts are exceptions to the general advice that we think out our problems before God. On the contrary, it is necessary *not* to think on the matter at all, even when we are (temporarily) winning the argument. The more we do, the more the mind, which works by association of ideas, will make more and more tracks for the tentacles of fear to travel, and the case only becomes worse. This restraint of the compulsion for an immediate and indestructible solution requires courage and self-discipline. Total non-examination and non-confessing of these "sins" is the advice given by wise confessors, and is meant to be permanent. It is not a cure, but a *modus vivendi*, a valid practical way of acting. It gives a breathing space, especially to the young, until the internal balance can be restored.

In chronic cases the psychological causes are not so easy to find or surmount, and with them this non-consideration and non-confessing may be the only permanent solution. The advice or commands given by confessors in such cases is based on heroic trust in God, trust that he is speaking through his Church which in turn is speaking through a man.

Sometimes however, the scrupulous man fears that the priest who gives this advice will be burdened with the guilt of his (to him) very real sins or previous bad confessions. This is not the case, however, and a comparison with another situation will help to see it. If a man were to forget a mortal sin in confession, we all know that the sin is forgiven. He may go to Holy Communion as often as he wishes. The only obligation is that he must tell the sin in the next confession in which he remembers it. But the main fact is that his sin is forgiven, without having been confessed. When he does tell it later, he is only fulfilling the will of Christ who gave this power to men to act in his place.

Similarly, when a priest advises against or forbids the telling of a sin or the repeating of a confession, the sin is forgiven, even though not told now or ever, just as the sin was forgiven in the case of the forgotten sin. All that the priest is really doing is telling the man that he has no obligation ever to tell it. It is completely forgiven by the sacrament but without ever needing to be told. Thus neither the priest nor the penitent must bear the burden of these untold sins, even if they be sins.

Despite the validity of the promises made by God, we (all of us and not only those afflicted by scrupulosity) must not hope for too much from the spiritual life. Our strength will never be such that we become gloriously invulnerable or invincible. Perhaps God sees that our spiritual good is best served if we are left with some weakness of a moral, psycological, or physical nature that will not seem to have improved as we thought it would when we began. This weakness must often be compensated for by greater wisdom in arranging our lives, and by God's arranging them (if we will let him) by his providence. Thus we must always be like children, even when we have arrived at great degrees of grace.

Our hope, therefore, cannot center on an absolute perfection in all things, for even the saints tell us they did not attain this. We can hope only for a perfect result as God sees it, a life mixed with imperfections and failures, all permitted for some greater good as a part of his careful way with those especially who trust him.

In general, again for all of us and not only for the scrupulous, our abandonment should be, in some sense, trustingly blind. There is the human tendency, when we are in a situation that calls for God's intervention rather than our own efforts, to cast about in our imagination to see what solution he may provide. The imagination, involuntarily at least, will live out the possible solutions one after another, with much repetition.

Only a little experience with God, however, should teach us that this is futile, besides spoiling our peace and interfering with the directness of our relationship with him. Many times he shows us our intellectual limitations by providing a solution we had never thought of. He works with us as he works with nature, in a great profusion of his creative power. Many living things, both plants and insects, have the ability to produce millions of descendants in a short time. Even the lowly dandelion can produce hundreds of seeds in one year. Yet relatively few of these possible descendants ever reach maturity. Circumstances are such that they are prevented, as with seed that falls on the highway. It is a choice of God's universal providence as to which ones will survive.

So in our lives we may see several ways that God might take to relieve the pressure of a grim situation, again speaking of those situations in which our initiative is not possible or practical. The solution is solely dependent on his mind and will. He will have a solution; about that we must have no fear. We may pray for any definite one if this does not destroy our intimate contact with him. But we can also, and perhaps better, remain in a prayerful and loving peace, leaving it to him to choose which one it will be.

In this way we fix our eyes where they should be in such circumstances, on God and not on the various events or persons that might bring the solution. If it turns out that we have to act ourselves, we will know it at the proper moment. But until then, we do best by looking at God and remembering that only he can move events and persons to bring about his will. This is a way in which our trials will increase our closeness to him instead of dissipating it.

Besides being based on God's wisdom and love, our trust also rests on his limitless power. The fact that he does not always choose to use this power to bring about what we desire does not change the truth that it is there. When his wisdom, love, mercy, and determination coincide, he will use this power to bring about his purposes infallibly. We become very humble in our knowledge that our plans must always depend on this.

The way of abandonment to divine providence is a simple way through a complicated world. A complicated system of spirituality will not work in busy lives. We sometimes envy those whose lives are leisurely enough to be well regulated, and yet we can also see them often standing still spiritually.

Our hope does not have to be magnificent so as to be without all fear. As with faith it can be as small as a grain of mustard seed and still be hope in the face of all that is against us. Having God; we ought not fear, but we sometimes do. By hope we stand against fear.

To walk on the waters of trust in God does not mean that we renounce all human effort or the prudent use of common sense. But it does mean that we give of ourselves. Our natural instinct is to shrink from so great a giving. We like to rule the ship; we want what we want and we fear what God might ask. But our faith and an honest judgment of our experience will urge us differently.

God desires our perfection and therefore our ultimate happiness much more than we do. We can trust such a desire in such a being. We give ourselves to him with the intense conviction that our profitable aspirations, especially those for closer union, will be safe with him. For every obstacle there will always be a grace. And there will be the needed courage for the asking.

With abandonment there is always gain instead of loss, love instead of stubborn complaint, and growth in the spirit instead of mediocrity. Between the saint and the mediocre man there is only an act of the mind, a continuous act of the mind which says yes to God's will of love.

PART VI:

**Advancing
in Prayer**

Chapter 31

Transition

One of the principal reasons for a book about this period of the spiritual life is the change which is likely to come in the attitude toward prayer and in the prayer itself. The change in attitude may not be what we would expect. With the growing closeness to God in the virtues, we might expect to approach prayer with more eagerness and joy. The truth is that spiritual advancement at times produces just the opposite reactions, but we shall say more about this in the next chapter. Here we are interested in prayer itself and principally in certain clarifications helpful to souls not only burdened with the legitimate difficulties and tensions of this period but overburdened with some that are caused by misunderstanding.

The first of these misconceptions centers around the particular kind of mental prayer called meditation. So ingrained is the word in our everyday spiritual vocabulary that it is often referred to as if it were mental prayer itself, whereas it is really only the lowest form of it. Thus to talk to God in our own words is a higher form of prayer than meditation and perhaps a greatly higher one. For meditation involves thinking out, taking apart, and fitting to our personal lives some lesson from the Scriptures, from a spiritual book, or from some other source. All this has great advantage throughout the spiritual life. It increases the awareness of the implications of Christian teaching, conforms our conduct to that of Christ, and deepens our self-knowledge. But the point to be made here is that by itself meditation is not prayer.

St. Teresa says that prayer consists not in thinking much but in loving much. In other words we are not praying, strictly speaking, while we are reasoning or imagining, beneficial and necessary though this may be. The considerations of the reason and the pictures in the imagination are always meant to bring us to something more, something of the will and heart. Thus if we can pray without involved thinking, or if we can find God without needing to be aroused by various intellectual or imaginative considerations, then we have come at least one step farther in the way of prayer. How futile, then, and how fundamentally frustrating of all spiritual progress, to propose as the spiritual work of a lifetime that at the end one be able to "make a good meditation."

Nor is it even true that we must have succeeded at meditation before leaving it for something better. In fact there are people (and not a few) who have never been very good at it. Their personal bent, even if not their spiritual progress, does not incline them that way. And God in his freedom may not be leading them that way. In any case the authentic movement of progress in prayer is to find meditation generally more and more difficult instead of easier and more spiritually satisfying.

The reason for dwelling at length on this elementary point is that a man may be offered advancement in prayer and not know it. The consequences of this are more disastrous to the spiritual life than we think. Instead of moving on steadily at a slower speed, the man who mistakes the turn in the road may not move forward at all. Instead he will come up against a wall to more intimate contact with God. Mental prayer becomes duller and duller, and he associates this with the God who is surpassing wonder and delight. If he does not take refuge in reading in place of prayer, he is apt to spend the time in discouragement or in endurance of indigestible boredom, and perhaps give up mental prayer entirely. There are other reasons for the abandonment of mental prayer, to be sure, but a true perspective of the road ahead might have prevented some of it.

One might at this point ask, if meditation is to be normally outgrown, what is to follow? But in practice such a question cannot be answered. We are asked to predict what God will do in an individual soul, and this is futile and dangerous because God is free and each man different. Just as one man might suffer by hanging on to meditation too long, another might exhaust himself by trying to force himself into the mold of the "next step." Therefore we can make only a generalization about the progress of prayer. But even here we need not think that we must retrace our steps if God has drawn us ahead without our even knowing that he has passed over certain stages as outlined in books on prayer.

Understanding, then, that God has a personal way with individuals, we may say that in general the way of progress in mental prayer is toward greater simplicity as it is in other aspects of our spiritual life, in our examinations of conscience, for instance. Less and less will we find need of or contentment in considerations of the mind or spiritual situations worked out in our imaginations. The tendency will be to become more and more direct, to move more and more toward what is called affective prayer. By this is meant prayer which is carried on by various acts of the will (or of the heart since these acts may also have an emotional content) rather than by any reasoned procedure. These acts, or affections as they are often called, are not only those of love as the word might imply, but anything of a spiritual nature which we experience at the moment—praise, gratitude, sorrow, trust or abandonment, and need, as only a partial listing of a whole that is as long as the variety of human experience.

These affections will perhaps become more simple themselves. We may say fewer things but say them more often, as is the way of love and lovers. But we do not put ourselves in a mold even here, thinking that we may never go back to something less simple. All our life we will have to talk out things before God in our ever deeper and deeper penetration of the practical details of our relationship with him.

In affective prayer we will meet a difficulty with the counsel that we make a definite resolution each time we pray mentally, this to be fitted into each day. The value of this practice is obvious, but we must not make a fetish of it so that we search for a specific resolution when none is apparent. Resolutions in this stage of the spiritual life will tend to become more and more simple and will often tend to be the same—not a reason for treating them as something merely perfunctory, however. Our free converse with God will bring up many things to be done or eliminated, for we must not forget that the Holy Spirit is an interested, even if silent partner in our prayer. (Not, lest we become deceived, that everything practical that comes to us in prayer is of the Holy Spirit, by any means.)

It is a principle of solid spiritual direction that for those who have reached stability in the spiritual life, a definite resolution is not necessary each time we pray. An increasing love brings generosity in doing God's will whenever it is found, and this can do more to change us for God than searching for resolutions. Any demand that we do search could be as incongruous as if we were to pull at the sleeve of St. Francis of Assisi after he had spent all the night saying "my Lord and my God," and suggest that he do something specific about his attachment to those birds.

All advice which frees the spirit demands sincerity of purpose or it will be used as a subterfuge to avoid the confrontation of our conduct with the practical details of the message of Christ. Similarly the freedom from the constraining bonds of a textbook type of spiritual progress, where one page always follows another, demands the use of common sense. Nor does one launch out into unknown waters after throwing overboard all the directions of those who have sailed through them successfully.

Thus during our mental prayer at this time it is well to keep a book open, not necessarily a book of thought-out meditations, but a book in which a few lines can easily move us to affective prayer. Certain parts of the Scriptures, such as the psalms, can be helpful here. Or if we do not wish to use a book, we can use events of our Lord's life recalled to our memory. And, in an excessive desire for what we think is the way to advancement of the spirit, we should not despise such material things as the crucifix, statues, and pictures. The main idea is to use or to do whatever helps us.

In leaving meditation for other kinds of mental prayer, some people in religious life may find a difficulty because of the prescriptions of certain communities requiring the preparation of the subject of meditation on the night before. Such prescriptions, however, are not to be understood as binding the subject to meditation as a form of prayer. The intention of the legislator (which ultimately is always the Church approving the rule) is never to hold back spiritual progress. However, such a law, where it still exists, can be easily satisfied by a cursory reading of some passage of a book congenial to prayer, or by a determination to bring some problem before God the next day. Thus we will be prepared if our oasis does not contain a fountain as we hoped, but only a well from which we must raise the water laboriously.

When we no longer desire meditation because we want God more directly or because meditation is choking the spirit, we should not hesitate to abandon it. There will be many times when we will return to some form of it because we can never completely give up thinking about ourselves in relation to God and his will for us. However, we must be cautioned not to return to it just because we are now distracted in prayer. We should easily remember that we were distracted during meditation anyway and probably suffocated besides.

Nor should our distractions cause us to change our period of mental prayer into a prolonged period of spiritual reading with the excuse that we will have fewer distractions or will be able to keep awake. This is a surrender in the face of difficulties, unworthy of God or of the love we wish to give him. Only by perseverance in prayer can we win against the difficulties of prayer. We must not forget that God judges our prayer, not by our success in accomplishing what we would like, but by our *intention*. This is not withdrawn by involuntary distractions or sleep, and so prayer even with a prolonged lack of attention can be eminently pleasing to him.

The underlying purpose in this chapter has been to free the spirit so that it can go to God. Understanding, of course, that we keep within the bounds of the Faith and of common sense, we are free in our personal prayer to pray as we are moved to pray, that is, as we want to pray.

Despite all that is true about following the liturgical seasons, our personal, interior prayer knows only one season, the gentle wind of the Holy Spirit. In our freedom we do not forget the universal mediatorship of the Sacred Humanity, especially as it is in the Blessed Sacrament, but this need not always be explicit aknowledgement. Our prayer, as well as all our actions, is directed to the Father through Christ, but this is most often done implicitly, by habitual intention. In our freedom we also do not find any restrictions, other than those of undue emphasis, in praying to Mary or to the saints. Many times we will find that prayer before a plaster statue will bring greater and more permanent graces than our highest flights of the spirit.

Just as we are not bound by external pressures, so also we must not allow our freedom to be curtailed by interior compulsions, as praying in some "more perfect manner," when we would rather pray in another. Nor are we under compulsion to continue added prayers or additional time for prayer that we took up in a season of fervor or when our life was less occupied. We should not feel that we are being unfaithful to grace when we do this, provided that we always keep a reasonable minimum. God is not asking a continuously extraordinary effort under ordinary circumstances. He is like a husband whose wife has prepared an elaborate dinner for his birthday. Although she can do this willingly on various occasions, he would never demand that she do it every day.

Freedom must never be pushed beyond its legitimate limits; it must never become an excuse merely, for doing what one likes in the face of higher obligations. Thus, there are certain people who are concerned with advancement in mental prayer, but who must be cautioned against a disregard, perhaps unconscious contempt, for public worship. We have already written at some length on the reasons for public worship in our book for beginners, and here it is only necessary to emphasize that liturgical worship is important throughout the whole length of our spiritual life. It is the prayer of the whole Church, the whole Mystical Body of Christ, and our spiritual life cannot ever rise disdainfully above that. The same words which we use are used by our fellow members of this Body all over the world, and often are those which were used by Christ, his mother, and the apostles in their own worship (the psalms, for instance). Liturgical worship gives our lives a oneness of direction, and this direction is toward God. The emphasis of liturgical prayer is on him, and this more than any other consideration is the essence of the liturgical spirit. Despite the exaltation that comes from oneness with the group, or despite the tensions because of the group, this oneness with God is the heart of the worship itself and of the various liturgical seasons.

From this essential emphasis on God rather than on ourselves we can easily see that the liturgical life is one aspect of what is called the contemplative life. This contemplative life does not mean only the strictly cloistered life of certain religious communities, nor is it a life of thoughtful meditation, as the words might suggest. It is rather a manner of

living which is practiced in various degrees by all
authentic religious communities as well as by many
people not in such communities. It implies a certain
directness in the approach to God, God for himself,
and it requires that some time be given to him,
again for himself.

Thus it is easy to see that the liturgical life,
especially as it is the adoration and praise of God,
is a part of the contemplative spirit, despite a too
narrow limitation which we may have put on the idea
of contemplation. The presence of God is often found
in the liturgy, sometimes better than anywhere else.
And we must take hold of him where he chooses to
be found.

Yet even in public liturgical worship there is a
limited freedom, limited and perhaps only rarely
present. In public worship we are seriously encour-
aged to participate in the common prayers but we
are not compelled, unless circumstances require it.
Such circumstances easily arise, for instance, for
the priest who ought not to go off into private prayer
when leading the congregation, for religious in their
communities, and for the laity when an individual
voice is needed for the sustaining of the group.
The point here is not to encourage abstention but
to allow room for God to touch our souls if he chooses,
as might happen by some thought inspired by the
service itself, or by God directly. Even though
public worship has rights of its own, we need not on
all occasions distract ourselves from direct attention
to God or to fruitful thoughts inspired by him. His
work in our souls may not always allow us to turn the
next page in the book. Within the group he retains
his freedom over us.

Public worship also provides a means of self-
discipline. It has been wisely said of religious, and
the same is true of the laity, that in public worship

we show what we are. Therefore if we want a good look at ourselves, we may well reflect on our attitudes and our conduct there. All sorts of people are there; the self-assured, the nervous perfectionists, the timid, the slovenly, the lazy, the resentful and the critical, the nosey, the giddy, the irascible, and many others. The chances are that we ourselves will be found among them, for our humiliation, for our blessedly enlightening humiliation, if we will accept the grace to see it.

It should not seem strange to join prayer with self-discipline. For, although we should not out of choice make our prayer uncomfortable, neither should we think it an isolated phenomenon so that it appears to be the whole of the spiritual life. All the virtues affect our prayer, just as our prayer affects our acquiring of the virtues. Our spiritual life is the whole of all the facets of our lives. Prayer is at the heart of it, for this is our direct contact with God. But it is never so narrow as to be prayer alone — or anything else alone either.

Chapter 32

Into Darkness

(a) Living by Faith

The love of God depends on faith, and both love and faith depend on God. They are his gifts and operate from his grace more than by any power of our own. Although we do not ignore the use of our reason to see more deeply into our faith and to see why we should love God, our essential attitudes are determined by our faith and not by our reason.

At the point in the spiritual life with which we are now concerned, this dependence upon faith may mean an excruciating experience in which many of the natural supports of the soul are eliminated and we come to live by faith without their help. We are supported in general by grace alone. This experience is called the Dark Night, and we are concerned in this book with the first part of it which is called the Dark Night of the Senses. The Dark Night is a more or less direct operation of God to purify the soul and thus it is a more immediate hold which we have on him, even if it is not the one we have been accustomed to feel. And unless we understand it as an advance in the spiritual life, it can cause fear of having lost our way.

In this period God may be leading us by a faith which becomes more simple and childlike (childlike in our relations with him, not childish in our thinking or in our conversations with others). Living by faith is a purification of the soul; we live for God because we believe all that he has said simply because he has said it. Despite all the beautiful and ideal things that are said about faith's involving the total giving of the whole man, in the nakedness of the Dark Night basic faith is seen to be not more than the intellect and will, and to be more the determination of the will than clarity of the intellect. In the Dark Night we can expect to deal with little but fundamentals; in fact its purpose is to make us see more clearly and to accept more deeply what is fundamental.

In the Dark Night also we are impelled to live more by hope or trust than by any emotional confidence that may have helped to carry us so far. We trust God for strength we do not have, for understanding love, and for mercy, just because he is what he is, all Goodness, and therefore is trustworthy, and also because he has promised to love and help us and is able to fulfill his promises.

He leads us also by a love which goes to him directly. Increasingly we come to love him for what he is, more principally for what he is than for any other reason. But although it is obvious that this rarefied spiritual atmosphere implies a purification of our previous, more natural motives, this is not the totality of the purification, nor does it indicate the totality of the need for purification.

(b) Purification in Prayer

There is, first of all, a purification even for prayer itself. God does not work in the same manner with everyone in the spiritual life, and it is equally true that not everyone reacts in the same manner to the working of God. But it is a common enough experience that, upon conversion to God in the special way in which most of us seriously enter upon the spiritual life, our whole nature responds. This response is likely to be highly emotional. Our psychological and physical roots tend to become influenced because by a generous infusion of grace we now recognize God as a living person, and we respond to him in a personal manner. Our love, spiritual and emotional, goes out to him much in the same way that it would to a human being toward whom we felt the same kind of personal attraction.

This response of our nature is given the significant name of first fervor. It should never be considered a name of derision, and only fools would ridicule it as such. The newly awakened man is loving in the only way he can love authentically at the moment. If he has any excess or misunderstanding about his state, we must not try to correct too much, or we will drown the love of God in a cloudburst when only a gentle rain was needed. In the providence of God this state of spiritual exaltation has the purpose of showing the newly won man that God is more delightful than all human loves, all other desires and attractions. This is a fundamental lesson; it must be learned and God is kind in allowing it to be done in so delightful a manner.

But the wise way of God with undeveloped souls is usually not to leave them in too much enjoyment, even enjoyment of himself, for too long. The man is not yet perfect; most often he is far from it, and he is not yet able to sustain this delightful relationship with God without spiritual loss. It is strange to think that a feeling of closeness to God can have such a result, and of course this is not because of the delightfulness of God but rather because of an imperfect state of soul.

Indeed in this imperfect state of soul, the emotional effects of God's closeness may be not unlike a sort of intoxication. For one thing such a man may become proud of the very fact that he feels such closeness. He may think that because he feels this way, he is indeed very close. And because it is now easy, in his emotional fervor, to do many hard things he previously could not, he may feel that he has suddenly acquired deep virtues.

He will perhaps petulantly or overzealously wonder why others do not now see things as he does, forgetting that he himself did not see them this way a short time ago. He may also take these graces lightly and lose the awareness that living with God on close terms is a great gift from God. And in his foolish instability he may even become tired of the closeness to God and long for some change, even as the Israelites longed for the flesh pots of Egypt.

And so for various reasons, both natural and supernatural as we shall see, but all under the wise and loving providence of God, there occur periods of dryness in his life of prayer. He no longer can find his former delight in the things of God. Prayer of all kinds becomes a desert, not at all times but in a degree which indicates that his honeymoon with God is ending. Even when he redoubles his efforts, he finds them useless to bring back the sweetness which once flowed without his asking. Even when he makes elaborate plans for his meditation, he finds his mind wandering off in all directions. Even when he can hold it on the subject of his meditation, he finds that he plods ahead with dull steps.

(c) Purification of Life

As he becomes aware of his inability to pray as he would like, this learner in the spiritual life begins to see that he possesses many other limitations and weaknesses as well. His whole spiritual life is being tested, and in the testing is being purified. Now he must continue the kind of life he has begun, despite the absence of the pleasantness which formerly may have been attached to it. He must go on in faith and hope without the emotional support that even before his conversion he may have felt in regard to belief and trust. He must love God without the feelings that he ordinarily associated with love. He must, in short, live on a higher level and rely on grace alone. And instead of thinking that he has fallen back, or that he has done something to cause God to withdraw from his life, he must see in this providential situation a great and increasing love from God for his somewhat bewildered and hurt self.

Faith and hope are often called blind virtues, and here they are manifestly so. In the Dark Night this is also true of love. The soul has nothing to rest on but what is unseen and unfelt, and to the human psyche this is hardly rest. And yet this spiritual life which seems not to be spiritual at all is intensely supernatural. A man in this state can look upon himself as dying to his emotions, but he must understand that life has greater things than the emotions, and that what he will eventually be given in return for them will be enormously greater. Eventually he will know with a certain fullness of response that the new things are enormously greater.

The need for purification in his personal relationship with God through fundamental faith, hope, and love has a counterpart in the other virtues. The glow which changed the color of the landscape has now dimmed, and the spiritual man, if he is not concerned too much with the loss of so much delight, will see in surprise and dismay how much of his life needs drastic improvement.

St. John of the Cross has given us the classic display of the purification which may be needed by a man in this intermediate stage. He does this by showing that the roots of the seven capital sins are still alive and have taken on a new transmutation in their now spiritualized environment (*Dark Night of the Soul*, Bk. I, ch. 2-7). There is no need to repeat here what has been said so well already, especially since not everyone will have to battle with the particular manifestation of each capital sin as described. In the darkness each one will find his own defects by measuring himself against the stature of Christ in attempting to grow in all the virtues.

(d) The Dark Night of the Senses

The Dark Night is intended to purify us of defects which prevent greater union with God. If these are not eliminated on earth, they must be removed in purgatory, and there it is done without any gain in sanctifying grace or love of God. We might wish that on earth we could be purified in a less painful way than the Dark Night, and of course this is not impossible to God.

In discussing the Dark Night, we are, of course, involved in matters of their nature most obscure. But the obscurity is changed into confusion, not only by those who may be much distraught in going through it, but also by those who are supposed to understand it, that is, their spiritual teachers.

Even at the outset we are met with this confusion in respect to the time when it is supposed to occur in the soul, or whether one goes immediately from this first passive purification to one that is deeper, the Dark Night of the Spirit. The truth in practice, however, is that God is free to purify a soul how he wants, when he wants, under what circumstances, and to

what extent. We need never take the textbook de-
scriptions and apply them to ourselves as set down,
in the sense that they are a rigid pattern according to
which God is somehow obliged to act.

The Dark Night of the Senses is particularly a
purification by God of defects which an individual
man cannot reach with the amount of will available.
And so perhaps some of us do not have to experience
the anguish of this darkness because we do not need
such radical purification. There are other ways of
purification besides the Dark Night. For instance, a
man who deeply and generously loves God may get
many insights from grace and follow these perfectly.
As an example of this we can take the spiritual gluttony
of which St. John of the Cross speaks (*ibid.*), which
is an inordinate attachment to the emotional sweetness of prayer. This can quite readily be overcome by
the spiritually sensitive man in the ordinary dryness
which comes to everyone from time to time, without
having to undergo the specific purification of the
Dark Night of the Senses.

Others who do need it and go through it may not
fully experience the pain of it because they understand what is happening, and thus are spared the confusion of thinking they are falling back or are being
punished by God. Indeed it is one of the purposes of
this book to help the soul acquire a balance so as to
be able to cooperate better with this work of God.

Even with knowledge and good will, however,
this relative tranquility cannot be guaranteed. We
may unconsciously hold on to what God wants us to
surrender, and thus the inner conflict can be very
great. As an example, many of us do not pray enough
for deep sorrow for our sins, a wholehearted sorrow
based on love which sees them somewhat as God sees
them or as we ourselves will see them in eternity.
Even when we want this kind of sorrow, there may be

an unconscious part of us which does not regret them. This non-acquiescence can be too deep to be reached by our own effort; it needs to be done by the action of grace alone, and the Dark Night is one way in which grace operates.

And even though these defects are unconscious, and therefore sinless, they are impediments to spiritual growth. How many of us have borne impediments in our early spiritual life that were not obvious to us then, such as exaggerated affections for persons and things, or loyalty to the ideals of the world? And yet our spiritual progress depended on the eventual elimination of these unrecognized obstacles to grace.

We may need purification and not know it or not know the extent of it. We have said that we must become detached from those things which do not lead us to God—do not lead us at least indirectly. But how can we always know if something or someone is not leading us to God in the broad terms of the word "indirectly"? In some cases the judgment required is more delicate than our spiritual sensitivity; even great insights from God can end up in rationalizations which sincerely seem to be inculpable, where we think that the insight was an error. Those who accept these insights eagerly, generously, and permanently may not have to suffer the Dark Night. But for those who need it for one reason or another, or for whom God determines purification in this specific way for their greater spiritual merit and its reparatory value for the Church, the night can be trying and long.

(e) Recognizing the Dark Night of the Senses

In order to co-operate with the work of God in the Dark Night of the Senses, it is helpful to be able to recognize it. Quite obviously not every period of dryness in prayer nor every temptation, however prolonged or severe, indicates that we are passing through this special purification. But, helpful though this knowledge may be, it is not necessary to be continually examining ourselves so as to be able to tabulate our state with absolute accuracy. *Every* trial is purifying to some degree, and that should be enough for us. Moreover, if our faith, hope, and love were strong enough, we would need no other guide than the Holy Spirit and his gifts. But even if not absolutely necessary, this knowledge is still helpful because with our limited vision we can fail to see that it is God at work, or we can impede his action by well-intended but unwise action of our own.

In seeking to understand the Dark Night of the Senses, however, we are not attempting a detailed description. Too often these details as found in spiritual books are personal reactions to the general situation and will mislead us if we try to make comparisons with our own experience. This can be more insidious than it sounds. Sometimes we find it dogmatically stated that the soul must go through this or that trial, detailed with quotations from spiritual sources, before it can advance in prayer. And so, those who have no choice but to believe such respectable writings will hold back, or be held back by their directors, from an evident invitation of God to higher prayer. Thus, we repeat that we must look principally to God in all our trials, and not make undue comparisons with those of others. One person has his trials of purification in this way, another in that, and many times what happens can be described only in terms of causes deep in the psyche rather than in words hallowed by devotional literature.

But whatever it be that must be purified, God does this work not necessarily in a particular cycle or sequence, but when he wills, and how he wills. If, therefore, we continue to seek God in our trials, be they what they may, we will be purified according to his infallible providence for the nuptials of this life and for the eternal ones.

The prevalence of the term "Dark Night" in spiritual literature as a felicitous name for a particular kind of purification comes principally from the influence of St. John of the Cross. It is a purification called "passive" to distinguish it from our own (active) purification, and it has two aspects. The first affects mainly the physical part of man as regards his inner senses, particularly his feelings or emotions. This is therefore called the Dark Night of the Senses. The second goes deeper in the psyche and is called the Dark Night of the Spirit. It is about the first of these nights that we are concerned in this book, although in practice they are not distinguished as sharply as these two names indicate. Hence much that is said about the first applies to the second.[1]

From St. John of the Cross also we have received the three classical signs by which one may know if he is in the Dark Night of the Senses, and thus act so as to move in the direction in which grace is moving him. The three signs are as follows: "The first is whether, when a soul finds no pleasure or comfort in the things of God, it also fails to find it in anything created.... The second sign is that ordinarily the memory is centered upon God, with painful and careful solicitude, thinking that it is not serving God, but going backwards.... The third

1. For an explanation concentrating principally on the Dark Night of the Spirit, see *The Life Within* by the same author. (New York: Sheed and Ward, 1966).

sign is that the soul can no longer meditate or reflect in the imagination, however much it may of itself endeavor to do so" (*Dark Night*, I, 9). There are a few observations to be made on these signs.

(f) The Dryness and Emptiness

In the first place no more must be expected from these signs than they are humanly able to communicate. Despite their wide acceptance, St. John of the Cross himself does not claim for this first sign more than probability, and the same can also be truthfully said for the other two. For we are involved in a complex of effects which can be caused either by nature or by grace, or (what makes it more difficult) sometimes by both together.

The difficulty in ascertaining the presence of this first sign is complicated by a dryness or torpor which can come from other causes than the Dark Night, sometimes from causes which are opposite to the spiritual life. Negligence in the things of God, a lukewarmness in the spiritual life, and a continual enjoyment of the distractions of a worldly life will cause our emotions to react naturally, pouring themselves out on their more natural objects and responding only feebly to things which are above the natural. This is, of course, obvious and if such a person imagines he is going through the Dark Night of the Senses, he is adding self-deception to his other spiritual failings. Thus St. John of the Cross insists that the true dryness is one that finds no consolation in anything created.

But even this requirement does not serve us very well when the pleasing emotions are depressed as a result of poor health or a melancholic temperament. If the poor health is only temporary, we may expect that the emotions will recover their natural vigor when health is restored. But some illnesses are chronic, and a melancholic temperament is inherited. Although this temperament does not by any means rule out the pleasing emotions, it is more subject to depression than any other temperament, and this can become a chronic, disabling, and all-pervading condition similar to poor health, which it really is. These conditions do not rule out the possibility that the Dark Night is present along with them but they make it more difficult to detect, at least from the point of view of the first sign.

It is, of course, not derogatory to the work of God to say that he uses nature as well as grace for this purification. There are psychological processes at work in the life of prayer as well as in every other part of our life. Some of these fit perfectly into this work of purification. One particularly important here is the course usually followed by the emotions, and especially the pleasing emotions. It is our human experience that they become less and less profoundly affected by a given stimulus. This pattern is followed, sadly and sometimes dishearteningly, in such personal relationships as human love and friendship and in our appreciation of such objective things as a beautiful panorama or a work of art when we are in contact with it too long or repeatedly. We have all experienced this, and there are few of our emotions which do not follow this law of diminution.

This lessening of the activity of the emotions can come in the spiritual life as the result of a conditioning, as it is called, from sources external to the pleasing relationship between God and ourselves. Just as in marriage the burdens and responsibilities, the former freedom now under constraint, and the lately discovered faults of the partner can become unconscious ropes holding the emotions close to the ground, so also in the spiritual life. Here, again unconsciously, there can occur a similar conditioning of the emotions from many sources; for instance, from reason and experience, from various recognized, unreasonable dissatisfactions and from others we do do not care to admit even to ourselves, such as a sadness over the loss of so much that we cannot have along with closeness to God. Thus one emotion can bear upon another, and under the tension there is a neutralization of the pleasant emotions.

As a consequence we should not be surprised that an end does come to those pleasing emotions which at the time seemed so permanent a part of the spiritual life but which under the providence of God were given only for our encouragement at the beginning. Now the time has come when there is less need for these consolations, as they are sometimes called, and we are asked to eat the more substantial food of pure faith, hope, and love in order to prepare us for greater union with God, who has shown us how captivating a being he is even when he shows himself to us only a little like what he is.

Characteristic as the diminution of the emotions is, in itself it is not enough to explain the Dark Night of the Senses. The natural tendency of human nature is to move in another emotional direction or toward another emotional stimulus when one way is blocked. Thus if the absence of emotional fervor were the result of any of the moral, physical, or psychological causes already mentioned, the attention would eventually pass to another emotional stimulus, even in the cases of melancholic disposition. Nature abhors this kind of vacuum.

The problem of discovering the existence of the Dark Night of the Senses can also be greatly complicated by the presence of minor emotional disorders. These do not have to be even as serious as deep, obsessive guilt or fear. Milder forms of inhibitions or compulsion can prevent the emotional apparatus from functioning as it should. People with these difficulties are by no means strangers of the spiritual life, just as they are no strangers to any condition of life, including that of great sinners. Some of these people approach the spiritual life with a hope of release from these inner tensions, and this hope can in some substantial degree be realized. But at this intermediate period their spiritual life has had relatively little time to get to the roots of the psychological troubles, and so we must expect that these disorders will be present as a factor which can simulate many of the characteristics by which we are to judge the presence of the Dark Night of the Senses and of other spiritual states as well.

To help us in this forest of uncertainties, we may sometimes distinguish the Dark Night of the Senses from natural emotional states similar to it by our reaction to friendship. Of course there is nothing wrong or surprising that a true spiritual friendship may have an emotional content. But in the Dark Night of the Senses this emotional content will generally tend to become submerged. We will love with an even greater intensity and spiritual purity before God, but we will sometimes wonder what has become of the feelings which we had previously associated with our love. On the contrary, a person of a depressed melancholic disposition, although finding no emotional response in any other facet of life, may quite characteristically find an attraction to another person in what is not a spiritual relationship but rather an emotional one, even though the matters discussed may be almost entirely in spiritual categories.

Such a generalization about emotion in friendship, however, is made less trustworthy by the fact that the Dark Night of the Senses can also have a characteristic which is contrary to its non-emotional nature, and this is temptation against chastity. Although at times sexual feelings may be aroused by mere imagination or by what we see and hear, the more authentic response is toward a living person. And of course, the sexual attraction which can occur even in a good friendship can hardly help having an emotional response also. Indeed, because of the necessity in the spiritual life to sublimate all unwanted sexual feeling, the emotional aspect may be all that is perceivable at the time. Therefore we cannot use the presence of emotion in respect to others as an absolute criterion that one is not in the Dark Night of the Senses. Not only may it exist in this state of soul, but it will tend to increase the internal dullness toward God and the things of the spirit, since under the circumstances the underlying and unconscious sexual attraction is contrary to it.

This does not mean that during this time we must avoid all contacts which are likely to be emotional in nature, because this attraction may occur with people who are good for us. But since we do not have much on the emotional side drawing us to God, we ought to be especially on guard, and we ought not omit many prayers about it. During this trial it is easy to pass unnoticeably from the dullness of the Dark Night to a dullness which is a dissipation of spiritual energies and a loss of the delicate sense of our goal in the spiritual life.

Finally, the dullness toward all things can be a temporary result of the loss of the consolations in prayer. When a principal source of delight or fulfillment is withdrawn, a man tends to become depressed all along the line. At least for a time. Thus the requirement that we feel no emotional interest in anything must stand the test of some rather long period of time.

(g) The Hidden Presence of God

As we can see from these observations, the first sign is hardly one to give much certainty and so "it becomes necessary to apply the second sign and condition" (*ibid.*). This centers more on the constitutive element in the Dark Night of the Senses which is the unseen and unfelt presence of God in the depths of the soul, the dark contemplation so characteristic of the teaching of John of the Cross. This hidden presence of God is not a different one from the kind that can be experienced clearly if God so wills and the soul is able to experience it. This perceivable presence varies in strength from an unavoidable sense of God's presence, to which even the grossest man would have to give his attention, to the slightest breath of his presence which even one who is experienced cannot consciously detect as such, somewhat like people who can predict a change in the weather by the way they feel but cannot specify the atmospheric cause of their feelings.

In the dark contemplation it would seem that we are concerned with the delicate kind of God's presence together with a soul which is as yet incapable of perceiving and enjoying anything but a strong manifestation of his presence. But the presence is there all the same, causing the soul to be unconsciously interested in what it does not even know, in any way that it can know that it knows. This hidden presence, however, is enough to bring on the feeling of quite universal dullness of which we have been speaking. The inner soul unconsciously reaches out to the God within, and this interior interest results in a lack of interest for the things of the senses and for the relatively more indirect manner of perceiving him through the reasoning intellect, or even for feeling him by emotional response.

This dullness and absence of God, in any way that he was formerly considered to be close, brings on the second sign of the Dark Night of the Senses, according to which the soul is "ordinarily centered upon God, with painful and careful solicitude, thinking that it is not serving God, but going backwards."

To make this second sign universal, it is necessary to look for its essential element rather than to expect that everyone will have its more striking characteristics. Thus not everyone will experience the painful care and anguish, and not always will he think that he is going backwards. There are differences in temperament, and St. John of the Cross (*ibid.* no. 3) suggests that the solicitude, care, and grief are increased by melancholy or some other disposition. A more balanced person will recognize that mere dryness in prayer and dullness toward the things of God are not reliable criteria of his spiritual state. He will know that he must judge the tree by its fruits, that is, by his acts and virtues even though he feels no elán in practicing the virtues. He knows that an inevitable dullness affects every phase of human life, and that even great professions such as medicine, law, and writing become hard work after the first bloom has faded.

Furthermore he lives in a post-John of the Cross era. Unlike those for whom the saint was writing, he may well know what to expect in the spiritual life. Indeed the danger today is that, knowing the criteria of the Dark Night too well, some will dramatize themselves into a quasi-experience of them.

The essential element, then, in this second sign seems to be a solicitude and carefulness in practicing the virtues, especially the more fundamental ones of love of neighbor and humility, together with a quiet and persistent attempt to live in the presence of God by faith. We cannot counterfeit such conduct for long, and so we need not fear that we are imagining ourselves in this state of darkness, for the imagination cannot produce these fruits over the long period. Nor need we fear that our state is lukewarmness or a psychological-nervous condition because these not only cause dullness toward God, but also are barriers to practicing the virtues.

And yet we must not degrade the Dark Night of the Senses into a mere normal practice of the Christian life. The presence of God in the depths of the soul, although for the most part hidden, will show itself in a dedication, an earnestness in the pursuit of God and all that leads to him, and will bring on more than ordinary remorse when a true deviation from him is observed. The soul definitely is under tension despite the lack of emotional enthusiasm, the tension arising from the unconscious drawing to God within and from the equally unconscious reluctance to leave its customary and pleasant manner of responding to him and to leave so much else besides.

(h) Difficulties with Prayer

In the third sign or condition we are even closer to the essential element of the Dark Night of the Senses, which is the dim but attracting presence of God. This presence so captivates the inner soul that it no longer has the desire to approach God through the faculties of the reasoning intellect and of the imagination. Thus it becomes very difficult to make a meditation. This repugnance (for it can amount to this) does not come from any temporary disposition since this would mean only a temporary cessation of the power of prayerful thinking. Nor, as we have emphasized, can it come from laziness or lukewarmness, because these would not produce the concern to be one with God in prayer and in the virtues. It is, in a sense, the best of the signs, looked at from the point of view of prayer, but unfortunately this is not obvious to the one going through it.

In this transition in prayer the soul is in a dark night, and it cannot expect to know with clarity of vision what or how much of its condition comes from the hidden action of God and how much may be the result of other processes. A man in this state is too inexperienced in the matter of prayer to be able to arrive at certainty. In fact any investigation will be more apt to confuse him and will turn him away from the central issue which is meeting God in faith. To expect him to know that his prayer is increasingly contemplative in nature would be unrealistic; the most urgent perplexity of such people often comes from the fear that they no longer pray as they used to. Besides, contemplative prayer is elusive; "it is like the air, which escapes if we would close our hand upon it" (*ibid.* no. 6). If there is any personal light on what is happening, it may come by a flash of insight rather than by probing. We will say more about contemplative prayer in the next chapter, but for now it is well to remember that the third sign is not contemplative prayer (although the presence of God is the cause underneath) but a great and persistent inability to meditate. And even though it may seem to be the darkest part of the night, it is really the beginning of the increasing dawn.

(i) Other Difficulties in the Dark Night

In speaking of further difficulties, we must first of all note that they are not essential to the Dark Night of the Senses. Thus they may never occur. In fact some of them are far more characteristic of the Dark Night of the Spirit. To solve this apparent lack of exactness in an all-wise God, St. John of the Cross suggests that some of these storms and trials occur now because God intends to lead these particular souls into the second night (*Dark Night*, I, 14, 4).

Perhaps the better solution is one given by the saint earlier, that there is only one night but that it has various parts (*Ascent of Mt. Carmel*, I, 2, 5). The division into two nights has a basis in the two kinds of purification needed, but this does not demand that all of the first must be completed before the other can begin. In our necessary generalizations, we must not confine the wisdom or the freedom of God, who purifies us in the manner which he sees is needed and according to his design for us.

The Dark Night of the Senses is a deep purification of man in his sensual nature. He is already purified from the grossness connected with sensuality, but it has deep roots. One of these is the human tendency to depend more on the emotions than he should. This need of purification is unlike the cause for the separation, in prayer, of the inner soul from the reasoning intellect. When our reason is under the leadership of faith, we do not ordinarily depend on it too much. Only at the time of contemplative prayer does it impede us; at other times it is likely to be as useful as ever. In this prayer we suffer in the reason only because through it we cannot meet God in the intimate way that he now wants to be met. But with our sensuality, even the good sensuality of the emotions, it is a different matter.

It would be a mistake to suppress the emotions altogether, but this natural-supernatural process of dulling them gives the purely spiritual part of us a chance to emerge. But since there has been this natural dependence on them, the experience of living without them will be painful and will tend to push the soul into fear and uncertainty.

This fear and uncertainty can account for certain temptations which may accompany the Dark Night of the Senses. We can begin at the roots, with faith. Ordinarily our experience of faith has a certain fullness about it, a feeling of security which is both supernatural and natural, spiritual and emotional, as befits the human composite of soul and body. But with our emotional part dulled, we do not experience faith (or hope or love) in the satisfactory manner that we formerly did. And so we may become fearful, and even think that our faith or hope or love is gone.

Contrary to what would result if we had really lost our faith, we now begin more to believe because God has said these various things, rather than because it consoles us in some manner to believe them. And similarly we hope because of what he has promised, and love because of what he is, rather than because of reassuring feelings on our part, and this is an immeasurably higher degree than formerly. Love for neighbor is purified too, not only because we see the relationship of this love to love of God, but also because it now rests less upon what appeals to us and more on real qualities of the spirit. Besides, now seeing our own deficiencies, we become more appreciative of the good we see in others and more willing to overlook their deficiencies. Thus, in the darkness we have been found by humility.

We do not intend to give a list of all the possible effects of the withdrawal of the emotional consolation, but one which we must not be surprised at is that of resentment. This will be involuntary; it is important not to forget this. For, resentment and rebellion even to blasphemy against God may burst forth. But there is no guilt in such thoughts, even though they may arise with much violence. This is an effect we would expect more from the death of self-will in the Dark Night of the Spirit, but insofar as it occurs here, it is reaction against the withdrawal of so much that made the things of God so sweet and delightful. And also, a certain irrational part of us feels that it has been deceived or cheated into bartering much for a handful of dry dust.

When we were happy and joyful, full of the consolations of God, we had indeed to be on our guard against certain spiritual weaknesses. But now the lack of joy surely brings out others. We are perhaps going to find that certain once familiar weaknesses may come back. If this is so, the cause now will be found, not in a falling from grace, but in our temporarily insecure state.

An example may be the reappearance (or the first appearance) of scrupulosity. This, of course, will deepen the darkness. And yet in the process of growth under such trials we will be deepened in our trust for help and in our belief in God's love. Grace for ultimate victory is never lacking.

Again looking at our difficult spiritual state, we will not be thrown into apprehensions about our progress if temptations against chastity are now more severe than we would expect after some time, perhaps years, in successfully overcoming them. Our sexual nature, despite all its essential goodness, is like a deposed tyrant waiting to return in the moment of spiritual, psychological, or emotional weakness. It is in these moments, as we know from our periods of depression, that we are in greatest danger. Now in the Dark Night of the Senses we are in this kind of situation, one where the vibrant part of our nature is not with us. Still we unconsciously desire the fulfillment of our lost feelings, and are insecure in the darkness. But wait. There is within us a powerful source of emotional fullness which promises to compensate for all we are missing, and it will do it with an overwhelming personal involvement and fulfillment. And so the return of disordered sexuality can be very violent, like the return of seven devils instead of the one, as told by our Lord in the parable (Mt. 12:43-45).

And just because we are speaking about something obviously material, the force of our sexuality, we must not think that the reference to devils is only rhetorical. They will return in force, in many ways, to torment us. Our soul has now become a more valuable prize, and our whole emotional nature can be the battleground.

The difficulty is not in fighting just another temptation, but in being asked to accept the weak, tasteless spirituality now thrust upon us and reject the exuberant, inviting, and immediate experience of sexual indulgence. In this stress it is no wonder that a man may easily think that he is going backwards and has been rejected by God.

There may be other trials, even external ones, but since these will be even more of an individual nature, it is best not to discourage ourselves by listing what may never happen. Even many of the trials of which we have just spoken will never happen either, for, as we have said, some of those who go through this night will be troubled relatively little. In any case, however, we must not shrink from generosity to God through fear of them. As a matter of sober fact great trials come to everyone, even to those who are not in the spiritual life or even close to it. And these must go through the trials without the great preparation for grace that we have.

The benefit of those whom God asks to suffer during the Dark Night of the Senses should need no further elaboration. But besides the growth in spiritual life by the many acts of the virtues of trust and love, and besides the assurance that they are on the way to a more intimate relationship with God in prayer, the very pressures of the Dark Night compel them toward perseverance.

The more balanced man who is able to take all this dryness without any disturbance is in one sense not so fortunate. He is not pushed up against God by being made to produce acts of greater intensity just to keep himself afloat. Thus he may not increase so much in sanctifying grace and fundamental love of God. He may even decline spiritually, unlike the man who goes through the Dark Night in some anguish, because he is not aroused to acting heroically out of necessity, and may even fail to see the need to arouse himself to carefulness, earnestness, and fervor—all because of his too easy awareness of what is happening.

There is a further danger for anyone in the emptiness of the Dark Night that, since we are not able to approach God in our usual way of prayer and do not have the support of the emotions, we will become rooted where we are—narrow, sour people who cling to the externals of the spiritual life but without much grace. Or we may give up the spiritual life altogether, like the seed which fell on the shallow soil in the rock. This danger is present not only to those who do not know what is happening, but even to those who do, but who prefer comfort to the hope of further union with God, or who have patience only for a swift and early victory.

The need of the virtue of fortitude or courage should also by now be a dominant observation. Not that all of us have much of it to start with, but it will increase with the progressing trial, especially if we plead for it, as we will if we do not want to lose God or to lose our human integrity either. We should not shrink from purification; rather we should persistently invite God to come to us for this purpose. A true man or woman does not look to the cost—in fact, it is well not to concentrate on any suffering — but rather looks to God and to the increase of union and love both now and farther ahead. Only through love can we abandon ourselves fully to this purifying action which will bring greater love.

Despite all the joy that is written of suffering, we are not asked to go through the Dark Night with a song on our lips. Rather we are asked to attack the enemies we can see and to endure the darkness with whatever forces of grace and nature are available, and these may not seem at the time to be very great. By merely refusing to give up, refusing to stop trusting and loving, we will eventually be purified of many of our deeper obstacles to grace. How much true manhood and womanhood is required in the spiritual life, only those who live it can know.

(j) Practical Counsel for this Dark Night

Several practical suggestions concerning the Dark Night have already been given in this chapter. As regards prayer during this night, more will be said in the next chapter. Thus, there remain only a few things to be said now.

First of all, from the nature of the Dark Night, it should be obvious that no one should be so foolishly ambitious as to try to bring it on by suppressing his emotions. Nor should we try to remove all imperfection from our love so that we become afraid to enjoy God in any kind of love that might possibly be overly emotional. The faculties involved in loving are so delicate that external meddling is apt to inhibit the process of love itself and may end by blighting all love. But even if we could produce all the external phenomena of this night, we could not bring on the essential element of dark contemplation, the hidden but operative presence of God.

Thus we must wait for God who will produce what effects are necessary. He cannot be forced to come.

A similarly unproductive course would be too great a severity with ourselves in order to accelerate the purification. Sometimes we inflict severity on ourselves out of love but often it is a product of fear. When, because of the darkness, we may think we are going backwards or have somehow offended God, the tendency is to decrease or stop anything which does not have a directly spiritual connotation. In extreme cases we can even lose our health or mental balance. Therefore sufficient food, rest, and recreation must be taken — recreation because there are times when we must actually be distracted from the torment, although this relaxation should never exhaust our spiritual energies but rather strengthen them. And the norms here are no different from what was said previously about detachment. Obviously, also, here is an area for careful guidance of a prudent director if one is available.

In giving these cautions, we do not mean to underrate the need for a constant active purification, as opposed to the passive one which comes from God during the Dark Night. Detachment is only one aspect of this; a purification is involved in the acquiring of a more perfect degree of all the virtues. Active purification will furthermore be a result of finding the true self. Indeed we cannot be truly purified for God unless we eliminate all the falsehood and unreality that finding the true self implies.

The plea for balance, however, is particularly directed to those whose reading of St. John of the Cross has not given them a full and rational understanding of his teaching. Like many men dedicated to an ideal, including our Lord in the gospels, he sometimes states his case so forcibly (our Lord told us to pluck out our eye if it was an occasion of sin) that we must seek elsewhere for his full meaning.

Thus we have certain expressions which would seem to indicate a pessimism toward human nature for which the remedy is the total suppression of all desires. What he means, of course, is the suppression of all those desires which lead us from God. Thus he specifies: "he who *sets his heart* upon all the delights and pleasures of the will in all the things of the world" *(Ascent,* I,4,7). He also says that God puts people in the Dark Night *"to reform* their desires" *(Dark Night,* I, 9,9), indicating that desires themselves are not eliminated. And of course God inspires desires: the dark contemplation "gives the soul an inclination and a *desire* to be alone and in quietude" *(ibid.,* no. 6. Italics added in all cases). Nevertheless, despite this explanation, certain people will do well to read this admirable man only when it is possible to consult a prudent director.

Surely there are many areas where desires must be eliminated. These are especially the desires that arise from ourselves as opposed to God, or desires demanding to be fulfilled regardless of God, almost autonomous desires which we vainly try to bring under the will of God, only to find this peace and security eluding us.

While it would seem advantageous to be able to receive counsel for every step, so as to realize all the benefits of the Dark Night, this is not possible because of the diversity of human souls and situations. In a sense it is also not advisable, because too much advice would not bring about so well the principal benefit of the Dark Night which is personal union with God. Although an understanding of what is happening is an enormous help, too much attention

to our state can distract from this principal end.
Throughout we are to fix our attention on God. We
believe because he says it is so. We accept all that
we ought to accept because he wills it. We love because he is there to be loved, without asking ourselves what sort of being this is or seeking any reason
why we should love. In this simple way we prepare
for an easier opening into contemplative prayer.

Thus the many questions of how long the Dark
Night of the Senses will last for us, or whether there
will be an intermittent period of consolation for us
before further purification, or whether we will have
the Dark Night of the Spirit immediately or at all —
these are considerations which depend too much on
the indiscernible plan of God for the individual.

In the loneliness of the Dark Night we find that
God is the one thing necessary. Gone is the proud
delight in what we once imagined ourselves to be.
Gone too is the presumption in our own powers and
in the foolhardy familiarity of a "favored child"
mentality. Instead there is great gratitude for whatever God gives, especially whatever he gives of himself. Along with our increasing love has grown a
respect for him in his absolute transcendency. All
the divergent things we thought to have along with
him (when we thought less of him than we ought)
have failed us. We now love and act more and more
simply, that is, because we see all things in some way
as his will. We are disciplined into seeing life ma-
turely, not emotionally or subjectively or selfishly,
but fundamentally.

We now turn to a further consideration of prayer
during this intermediate period in the spiritual life.
Among other things we will see how to conduct
ourselves in prayer during the darkness and how to
use the moments of light which God will not deny us.

Chapter 33

Toward the Light

(a) Beginnings of Development

Undoubtedly one of the great secrets of prayer is the recognition that we have an inner freedom. This freedom obviously presupposes a balanced person, free from the compulsions of ambition or self-adulation, both of which destroy true freedom. We need only seek God, and if we want him enough and want him sincerely, we will find and be content in the kind of prayer which brings us in contact with him, no matter what kind of prayer it is. This spiritual contact with God is almost the only norm in mental prayer.

We will find much external opposition to this freedom, both theoretical by those who limit certain prayer to "chosen souls," or by others who lack any insight into the spiritual life. Let these see someone reading St. Teresa of Avila, for instance, and immediately there is the accusation of presumption and pride, as if St. Teresa were not the most down-to-earth of all spiritual writers.

And so we have ordinary people whom God wants very close, but who are floundering because of the constraint to make meditations for which they have no natural or supernatural attraction. More than one such person has cried out in desperation: "If I could only pray instead of having to meditate!" Unless the door of the cage is opened, such souls will never find the God who for them must be sought and found in the open skies.

Although we are free of any permanent obligation to pray by the considerations of our reason and the images of our imagination, this does not mean that we may never return to it. But again, our return must be free. We must not return out of fear. This may easily happen in the Dark Night of the Senses when we cannot find God in any kind of prayer. Or it may happen when (or if) we are drawn to another kind of prayer in which we do not seem to be "praying" at all. Nor should we go back to it because of another kind of compulsion, the excessive desire for emotional consolations. These have had their rightful place as natural effects of supernatural graces. We can be helped by them, yet we are not more holy just because we have them. But our becoming more holy may well depend on our advancement in prayer.

Allowing for the fact that God may and sometimes does operate independently of what we might expect, we can trace a general evolution in prayer. There will usually be a tendency toward a more simple kind of prayer. For some time it may be that our prayer will consist predominantly of reflections upon the truths of the Christian life as they apply to our own moral and spiritual situation. Then next we may no longer need to consider at length, analyze, and apply to ourselves what we now grasp immediately without any need for reasoning about it or for portraying it in our imagination. This produces a psychological repugnance toward trying to use what for us is useless in going to God. But even more, prompted by the instinct of grace, we are seeking a way of greater closeness and directness than reasoning provides. And so we do less and less thinking in our prayers, and more and more of direct contact as if we were speaking to someone.

This habit of talking to God in our own words is a not unusual way of moving toward higher prayer. Even if our talking is a mere matter of emotional release from the tensions of a difficult personal problem, we come in contact with God in a direct manner; our will is strengthened by this prayer and not infrequently we find practical guidance for our lives. We are personally better off spiritually than if we had discoursed with ourselves for hours upon rational considerations on a spiritual subject.

(b) Affective Prayer

Again without attempting to give any exact order of the occurrence of any form of prayer in an individual case, we may next come to see that our prayer becomes even more simple than talking to another person — or rather it becomes more like talking to a person whom we love very much. Indeed, although it includes more than love, the name for this kind of prayer is usually the prayer of the affections. It may be quite filled with emotions, as we would expect from the word "affections," but we are making what are, basically, repeated acts of the will such as love, adoration, admiration, trust or abandonment, the choice of God instead of something opposed to him, thanksgiving, prayer of petition, sorrow for sin or infidelity, purpose of amendment, and so on.

These will follow one another naturally, in no prescribed order, for the essential element of this prayer is that it is a spontaneous opening of the heart, and not an organized procedure of the intellect. Not that the intellect is entirely absent, for it may be necessary to direct the affections along certain lines, as when we discover that we have neglected or misused grace, or when we are faced with a trial which requires courage. There is no sharp line between this prayer and what has preceded it; the transition comes when more acts of the affections begin to be mixed in with much free talking to God in our own words.

This, of course, is not the end of our possible development towards simplicity, but before describing what may be the next transition, it is necessary to warn that we should not force these steps. We may tentatively try them and even persevere in any attempt to reach God more simply. But if these changes do not come with a certain naturalness, the mind will become fatigued as much as it would if we held back when everything within was urging us toward the next step. We would discover that we are not ready, by a sense of emptiness, of not being at home in this kind of prayer, of living in an unreality, in a state that is not spiritually or psychologically ours. Any continuance of this prayer would stand in the way of spiritual progress. We would be more ambitious for achievement than for possession of God in the best way we can possess him here and now.

This being said, and perhaps not for the last time, we may well note a further simplification in that we tend to use fewer of these affective sentiments, and that we remain in any one of them for some minutes without needing to go on to anything else. Then we quietly pass on to whatever spontaneously arises between God and ourselves. More and more, however, does God become the center of our prayer, and ourselves and our problems less and less. And the presence of God tends to extend over more of our day than our specific periods of prayer.

We will now have achieved an important step in the spiritual life, the almost habitual living in the presence of God or never far from it. This presence gives a deeper meaning to our lives, and especially to the lives of the many who must spend hours in work which is monotonous, offering no interest or challenge once it is learned, or to lives that have been left in real or psychological loneliness. But it is also a way to find God, not only in more places, but also more intimately, more intimately than if we had much time to read books on him. For in this acquired ability to live in the presence of God we are at the highest extent of human activity in prayer even when aided, as it has been all along, by grace.

(c) Acquired Contemplation and the Prayer of Faith

There are various names for this highest kind of prayer which we can attain by our own efforts. However, we really do not need names, and too much concentration on the kind of prayer we are having can distract from the basic reality of prayer which is contact with God. And this will delay or even stop our progress toward possessing him more fully. But so that the readers of this book will not be isolated from the rest of the literature on this subject, this very simple prayer of short and repeated phrases of our affections is known as the prayer of recollection, the prayer of simplicity, or as acquired contemplation.

Despite whatever name we call it (or better, forget or neglect to call it), it consists in simple acts of the mind and will by which we achieve a union with God, which is consciously or unconsciously built upon our belief in his presence. This presence can be found in any way that we are drawn to it: the special one of his dwelling within us or his presence around about us or the presence of the God-man in the Blessed Sacrament, whether in Holy Communion or in the tabernacle.

Indeed none of the forms of prayer is limited to any particular place in which we must find God. Our freedom is limited only by the will of God as to where and how he chooses to be found by us here and now. All that is necessary for advancement in prayer is that we take God as we find him, without trying to get a clearer representation of him at any time. In the kind of prayer of which we are speaking, we should not bring in our reason to question or analyze. Though the intellect is in contact with God by faith, the will or heart must dominate the meeting.

Throughout this prayer we must keep our freedom to do as we will, provided that we do not force ourselves by great tension. Thus we may pass from one affection of the heart to another as we wish; we may stay on one as long as we wish; we may use words of our own or short phrases from formal prayers or the psalms, or we may pray without words, as we wish. There may often be emotional sweetness, and sometimes there will not be. But always we will have a sense that we are doing what we ought, and we will be in deep peace about it unless we foolishly bring in our own doubts about our prayer.

This prayer of recollection is a spiritual and psychological disposition for another kind of prayer which is not within our power to bring about. In words too technical for this book, acquired contemplation can dispose the soul for infused contemplation but it is essentially different from it and can never be the cause of it. In fact, by God's love and freedom, infused contemplation may be given at times to those who are not at all practiced in any degree of mental prayer.

It is not the purpose of this book to go into details regarding the varieties of infused contemplative prayer.[1] But we have already been particularly concerned with the kind of infused contemplation which begins in the Dark Night of the Senses, the dark contemplation. One may think that the state of dark contemplation differs very little from that of acquired contemplation since the acquired contemplation will have many periods of dryness also. In practice we can do very little to solve this difficulty because the very nature of the dark contemplation is that it is hidden from the soul itself. If the distinction can be recognized by anything, however, it is that there is in the dark contemplation a definite emptiness in our reason and imagination when in prayer. This results from the fact that the inner part of our mind is being unknowingly drawn to God within, thus leaving unsupported its outer faculties of the reasoning intellect, imagination, memory, and emotions. In acquired contemplation these faculties can find God with a certain inner oneness, but can experience little of any feeling of contact in the dark contemplation. We will now discuss the little that can be done.

In the first place we need not return to other forms of prayer such as meditation, although there will be times when we will find meditation helpful in seeking the way that grace is leading us. What we can do more habitually is to seek God by a faith much as we would do in acquired contemplation except that there will be less activity on our part. Our attitude will be more of waiting quietly, in love and adoration, for instance, or in sustained acts of pure faith in his presence within. Never, however, will we seek to create a complete passivity which obliterates all internal attitudes, movements, or affections.

1. Those who wish a fuller discussion of infused contemplation can consult *The Life Within* by this author.

Since this is essentially a prayer of faith, and since God is objectively present even though we have no glimmer of this, we can see how safe a way is this dark night. By faith we cannot be deceived, for although we are in the darkness, faith joins us to the living being, God, who is there also. In this prayer we are seeking God, and how can we be deceived if he is all we seek? How can our prayer not be pleasing to him if he is the one we thus seek in quiet intensity?

We must be content to remain in this arid waiting as long as God determines it. There probably will be times, unexpected and most likely of short duration, when his presence will be more apparent than it is to naked faith. But when it is not, we continuously tell ourselves that he is there, and ask him for an always stronger faith. We accept all manifestations of his presence as flowers from that root. But in the darkness we learn the discipline of love, knowing that even though there is no feeling in our prayer, we are moving closer to the one we love because of the great merit of loving in the darkness. And we are giving great glory to the God we love also, for we are not praying primarily to please ourselves but to please him.

(d) The Beginnings of Perceptible Contemplative Prayer

It is the more apparent manifestations of the presence of God, however, that are among the principal reasons for this book. A man who has made a good start in mental prayer is not likely to seek out books on higher prayer. As a result it can happen that he will be given the beginnings of a call to higher prayer and become frightened by the fact that he cannot pray as he did. Or he may exercise a strong will and determine to continue at all cost the kind of prayer that has served him so well up to now.

In either case he has missed an important step forward in the spiritual life, because truly higher prayer brings forth greater love and a greater intensity in the virtues. If he misses this call or dulls it by his determined will, he will continue his spiritual life only in great confusion, disturbance, or hopelessness. The great promises of the spiritual life, under whose encouragement he started out so hopefully, will seem to him to have been empty and delusive.

To help him understand the call, there is unfortunately no single detailed description to give him as to what to look for or expect. In fact it is better if he looks for nothing of this but continues simply to seek God in prayer. As we have said, if we begin looking for contemplative prayer with any degree of expectancy, we are building a barrier to advancement in prayer itself and of course to love of God. However, the reason for our lack of helpful directives is that no one can predict how God is going to act in an individual soul, nor when, nor where. And it is God who must act in this kind of prayer or we do not have infused contemplative prayer. In some people he will so act that the transition from acquired to given prayer is almost indiscernible. It may be that faint.

Or if it comes in great sweetness, a man will not think it to be very different from prayer in general because the presence of God should be sweet to the spiritual taste. People whom God calls like this are saved many of the problems we will discuss later. They will have arrived without knowing it, and have been protected from the uncertainties and dangers along the way.

With other people God acts in quite complete darkness but there are moments of light when he shows himself somewhat as he is, to the delight of the soul, to the perhaps momentary delight of the soul which is again returned to deep darkness, now wondering if delusion has not been added to its troubles. With still other people God may come with a sense of strong immediateness in which the whole world stops, so to speak, and they cannot but know that it is he. But even so, they are experiencing him in a way entirely different from the familiar love poured out by the emotions.

Or again, he may be known hardly at all except that there is a quiet silence within, and the soul is content to rest in the presence that somehow it knows to be there to draw its attention. And yet so intangible is this presence to any conscious attempt to know it more clearly, that again doubts may easily arise that here is mere idleness and delusion. In any case—and the variety of God's action has not been exhausted—the principal element in the experience is at least a dim awareness of something that is intuitively understood as transcendent, as God, and which was not produced by the faculties or power of the soul but given to it.

This kind of prayer, then, is given. In other words we do not strictly merit it. We cannot be sure of it here and now no matter what our good works, our mortifications, or our perseverance in prayer. We prepare for it indirectly by the virtues, especially love of God and neighbor, humility, and purity of heart and of intention. We also are more likely to put ourselves in the way of receiving it by practicing the kind of recollection which lives with God in simple oneness of heart. But we must not make the mistake of thinking that we must be at prayer in order for it to come to us. There is no situation of our life into which God cannot bring the sense of his presence. It is this sense of his presence which we will learn to recognize and give our attention to. God needs nothing but his presence to tell us that it is he, no voice of his own, no angel, no man. In some way (we know not when nor how) he will be there and we will probably know it.

(e) Practical Counsel for Contemplative Prayer

The practical way to this fuller enjoyment of God is the acceptance of the brief moments of contact he may give. Not only may these be momentary, but they can also be very faint, his presence only being made observable by an indefinable and deep desire for him. But these moments are still a contact with God and should be accepted as great favors, the greatest events in the day from the viewpoint of prayer. We should not try to extend these moments; it cannot be done anyway. Having given ourselves to God in this moment, we then pass on, as God passes on, to other things. By an increasing frequency of these moments (if this is the way we are being led—and how difficult it is to say something that applies at all broadly) we can quietly become more and more able to live with God without being thrown into a self-conscious awareness that we are "hereby praying with contemplative prayer." Thus can the relationship become more and more customary, and God becomes a companion who is gratefully loved for himself and not proudly sought after for the fact that this is higher prayer.

Despite the fact that this prayer—or better *because* this prayer depends solely on the will of God—no one should think himself eliminated because of his state in life, his lack of education, his past (or even present) sins, or the realistic belief that he is not some "chosen soul."

The universality of this possibility for all humanity is illustrated by an incident in the life of St. John Vianney, the curé of Ars. He was accustomed to notice one of his parishioners, an old man, making a visit to church every day, but never using a prayer book or rosary or, seemingly, any kind of prayer that required words. Tactfully he inquired how the man was praying. He replied that he said nothing: "I just look at him and he just looks at me." And there have been others, not numbered among the saints but known to God, who could not finish an Our Father or Hail Mary because of his insistent presence.

It is part of our purpose here to prevent the soul from becoming introspective upon itself praying, and so we shall not attempt to give the various classifications of contemplative prayer. It is enough to know that "God's presence felt" is what it is, and that there are various ways in which we will respond, spontaneously always and not by deliberation. There is an instinct which arises from the prayer itself, which if we learn by experience to follow carefully, will itself teach us how to respond to this presence. Thus at times it will come by imposing a silence upon all activity; at other times it will produce activity such as spontaneous praise, and we will still not lose the presence; and still at other times it will be maintained only along with activity, such as when praying liturgically or writing on the things of God.

Thus it is a mistake to think of this prayer in one narrow framework such as the extreme of swooning or ecstasy, or to think that we must drop to our knees or hasten to a church or chapel. In fact any movement foreign to the particular instinct of this prayer at any given time will quite probably obliterate it. Even some movements which might be considered normal responses, simple movements of the body, can disturb the psychological conditions in which the presence of God has found us, will act as would a distraction, and thereby spoil the delicate ability to concentrate spontaneously, as we must.

Thus we can see that in some varieties of contemplative prayer it is possible to be troubled with distractions. When these occur, they should not be directly set aside but rather should be ignored; our only concern should be to keep in intuitive contact with this presence. Yet even a person who has many distractions in acquired prayer can find himself concentrating beyond his powers when this prayer comes to him. The presence of God usually imposes peace; in fact this is often the way the approach of God is first detected. The silence of God imposes a calmness upon the undulations of our mind and imagination much as the entrance of a teacher should bring quiet to a noisy classroom. And it does it immediately and automatically.

Our real distractions may come from two causes: one, our unconscious effort to see ourselves praying or to examine the prayer itself; and the other, the anguish of doubt that this manner of praying is not really prayer.

As to the first, we speak of contemplative prayer as a contact with God, as a contact with reality. Now, there can be a double response to reality: one is spontaneous and the other is deliberate. In prayer the two ought not to conflict. At the time we are receiving and spontaneously appreciating the objective reality of the presence of God, we should not clog the traffic by trying to impose any deliberate response, by trying to bring forth what we may consider to be the proper kind of response.

We may understand this better if we take as an example our viewing of a piece of art, a painting which has been put on display as a masterpiece. Our aesthetic response will be authentic only if we are able to keep out of our response to it all the things that the critics have told us that we ought to experience. Above all, we must keep out all thought of what

I, the most revered critic of all, feel that I ought to see myself feeling about it. Quite true, the observations of the critics can perhaps educate us as to what to look for. But they cannot substitute for our own response if it is to be authentic, and which must then come from a certain freedom from affectation or even from contrived sincerity.

Now, it is not always easy for some people to do this; it means being able to look at things (in this case, at God) as if we were looking at them for the first time, or looking at them as a child looks at things, without of course telling ourselves this at the time. It requires a certain intuitive and spontaneous power of concentration by which we are able to put aside, not only external distractions, but even more, those which arise from within. Only then can we make a proper response to this reality which is the presence of God.

This constant interjection of the self is a destructive form of pride. We have to be humble to be truly receptive to reality, all the more, again, when this reality is God. The proud man finds difficulty in being receptive; he must show his superiority by admitting reality on his own terms and approval. He is like a stupid person who thinks he is intellectual and who will never really listen to an explanation, but must always interject a comment (usually irrelevant and drawing attention to himself), thus striking a posture whereby he is watching himself listening rather than actually listening. This difficulty with pride underlines the truth that advancement in prayer can come only if there is advancement in the virtues. God does not want to trust his treasures to unteachable blunderers and fools.

The fear which is the second cause of internal distraction is not the same as the fear which all men are likely to feel in the presence of God when they do not

have the instinctive courage to face him as he mani-
fests himself at the moment, with something of his
majesty and transcendence. In certain of our meetings
with him, we may find that we are cowards, and this
not in a derogatory sense but in a human one. At
times, by no means always, it takes courage to meet
God this closely and nakedly. Such fear can exist
along with love.

When the presence is not insistent, this fear can
be the reason that we turn away instinctively from real
invitations from God or succeed unconsciously in
keeping ourselves away from them by our overt concern with even good things other than God. Such fear
is often too deep to be seen, always too deep to be
rooted out by resolution alone. The courage that has
grown in the Dark Night will serve us well here, but
more must be asked for, even as we ask for more love.
Increase in love depends many times on other virtues.

The fear which is the cause of internal distraction
in the more ordinary sense of distraction, however,
is the questioning of the fearful or insecure man concerning prayer itself. Sometimes this questioning
comes, as we have said, because he is not praying as
he did before, but it can also arise from the insecurity of an intellect which fears all that it does not
have under conscious control and observation. In any
case he fears illusion, and perhaps has even thought
up reasons why it could be illusion.

On the contrary, instead of the self-accusation
that this experience is caused by some inner frustration, such as loneliness or a frustrated desire for
fulfillment, which masks itself as a delusion in prayer,
the actual truth, the blessed truth, is quite the opposite. Anyone who has had the experience of contemplative prayer has observed that the presence of
God has its own power to draw the inner soul. No
amount of loneliness or unhappiness can produce this

effect, and no amount of longing or desire for it can do so either. In fact, any grasping at it, pouncing upon it like a hungry animal upon a prey, attempting to make something personally emotional out of it, will destroy it.

Likewise, it is easily observed that when we have deep personal problems that press for a solution, there is the tendency to bring them into contemplative prayer. But again the alien psychological forces brought in by the problem destroy the prayer, even if they are the problems of loneliness, lovelessness, or frustrated ambition which are accused of causing the prayer. The presence of God shows the characteristic we would expect of a God who is love, that he wants to be loved on these more intimate occasions for himself.

Therefore it can be seen that being ourselves in authentic response, by allowing reality to achieve its own response or resonance, has much to do with advancing in prayer. The difficult and necessary way to manage this experience is to allow the receptive processes to work unimpeded. We may get only the faint impression of the divine when we want much more, or we may be flooded with love, wonder, or some equally authentic and spontaneous response. In any case we should accept what is given, and not reflect on whom we are meeting or in what manner. Our spontaneous response may come as we would like it, or it may not. But again we patiently accept our blunders in learning to respond to him.

Even afterwards we must be careful not to analyze the experience. This inner sense of God's presence is not groundlessly compared to the sense of sight, in this case that of a man who has been blind all his life and only now gets occasional, brief use of his eyes. After an experience of seeing is over, he can not possibly recreate or adequately analyze it by means of his sense of hearing, smelling, feeling, or tasting. Similarly the experience of the inner soul cannot be brought out in review before the faculties, even that of our reason, which have been outside the experience. We bring on confusion if we try.

Even when this prayer begins to be given, we will ordinarily be able to pray at times with affective prayer and even with the reflections of meditation, especially when we have to work out the details of some insight into our lives. Never, however, should we place ourselves into a merely passive or completely empty state. St. Teresa is adamant on this (*Life*, 12, 18; *Interior Castle*, IV, 3, 4). It is the trap of those who are ambitious for a thing (contemplation) and not for God, and this is an insult to his love and majesty. It is true that we may desire and even ask for this kind of prayer because of its closeness to the one we love and its spiritual benefit to our souls. But this must be done moderately, and perhaps the less of it the better if one has a proud or overly ambitious nature.

We must also be careful not to try to solve our problems when God is with us in this kind of prayer. When he prepares a love feast by making his presence felt, it is bad manners to insist on bringing up business. After the presence is gone, we may then plead our cause many times over. But in this embrace we must learn to give ourselves to his presence, to have no thoughts or memories except those which arise from the prayer, and really to want only to possess or be possessed by him. We must be convinced that our love itself tells him that we trust him.

This wordless trust breaks through the many fears which come upon us in prayer, whether they are concerned with our spiritual progress, our past infidelities, the effects in our body, or even with our sanity as it was with St. Teresa. Closeness to God in any manner brings many graces just of itself. Without our specifically asking, God himself helps us to avoid many tragic occasions and failures. Even though we should not adopt the attitude of listening in prayer, he will send us many inspirations which will help us, and this not only in spiritual matters.

Especially in the beginnings of contemplative prayer, we may not be able to know with accuracy whether our prayer is brought on by the presence of God or not, and we must avoid trying to find out. We can only observe over long periods of about six months to a year whether our experience is leading us toward or away from God, and this principally by the increase of virtues like humility, fidelity to the duties of our state in life, and love of God and neighbor.

The important point is to keep on in generosity to please God and in determination to have him. From this point of view it should really matter little to us whether we know that we have him in this way or that, in comparison to pleasing him *now*. So, whether a given state of dryness is only a trial or is *the* trial, or whether our oneness with God in prayer is acquired or is a oneness that is given, our course is clear: a simple, sincere trust in his love and a prayerful, peaceful desire to be guided in the way of greater love. Thus prayer itself is one of the deepest of purifications and inner disciplines.

Epilogue

Perseverance in New Life

With this opening into a new life we have come to the end of the book. In these pages we have spoken of many things, but in substance they are only a few. These are that God has a way and a plan for us, that in order better to find this plan we must find ourselves, that the way to God is simple despite any apparent complexity, and that its simplicity is found mostly in faith, trust, and love.

There are ideas in this book which may take roots deeply at once, influencing our way to God permanently. But there are others which may have to become better rooted by repeated reading. Thus the book is not one to be put aside as just another we have successfully read through to the end. Our true spiritual growth implies a certain formation, and to be formation, it must move consistently along certain definite and basic lines. Unless, therefore, we keep meeting the ideas with which we feel an affinity, and which bring us closer to God at the same time, we will grow into a relative formlessness, a distortion of the authentic and beautiful being intended by God when he made us. Or what is perhaps worse, we will not grow at all.

Besides repeated meeting with ideas, there is required persistent effort. Since, blessedly, it is only "God who gives the growth" (1 Cor. 3:7), it is not required of us that we ourselves have all that is necessary for success. In the supernatural life of the virtues there is always a necessary gap between ability and success, and for some of us the gap is wider than for others. Our confidence in ourselves, even the virtues we have acquired or been given, must be a limited confidence and must always be understood as dependent on the actual grace of God given at each moment.

But there may be certain areas where there can be no such limited confidence even in what virtues we have been given. Despite our present determination on great love for God, and on progress in the particular virtue concerned, our past history and our present self-knowledge give us no choice in certain crucial situations but to depend on God totally and on ourselves not at all. But even here, despite proved and repeated weakness, if we do all that we can, if we pray, and then trust for the rest, this is success, this is sanctity, in its very germ.

We would so much like to keep every good resolution, to hold fast to every grace, to bring into actuality every resolution. We would like very much to be able to come to our Lord after reading these pages and say "My Lord, you let me have five thousand. See, I have made five thousand more" (Mt. 25:20). But sanctity grows not only in sunshine and gentle rain, but it also grows in terrifying storms and almost killing droughts.

To grow and persevere in grace, we need an habitual substratum on which our day is built so as to include time for God, if possible through the great channels of his grace which are the Mass and Holy Communion. But we also have need for a virtue which guards the growth we already have and prepares us for more. This is a hidden virtue, often a misunderstood and undervalued virtue in spiritual progress; it is the gift of grace which is at the same time a guardian of love, a companion of love, and a fruit of love. Are we surprised that this virtue is patience?

Patience is a guardian of love. Many of us find it easy, refreshing, to expend effort on some inspiring project. If the spiritual life were such that it could enthusiastically be brought from great success to great success in a short time, it would have many more followers than it does. But there are only a few great successes in the whole of a lifetime, whereas there are many dark nights and slow days. All this time, however, God is moving us. But if we have the patience only for the short, brilliant engagement, we will never get to the victory of his seemingly motionless campaign.

Patience, when we have thought of it, has meant mainly a battle to keep peace with others. A few of us have learned the wisdom to be patient with ourselves, with our limitations and our failures. But the greatest wisdom of all is to be patient with God. He leads us step by step; even when we do find ourselves being led more rapidly, there are always more steps than we want. We must become saints by means of many little things because there are so few big ones. Patience guards our love by not letting us miss the only ways we can grow in love.

As a companion of love, patience makes us more aware of God. We see more and more that it is he who is directing our lives and is immersed in them, and seeing this, we act more out of love for him. With our hand ever in his by means of this virtue, we will overcome our reluctance and find peace and even joy in his particular will for us. Patience gives our love the time to act.

Although patience sometimes means a firm setting of our teeth in the face of hardship or boredom, in the end it brings the peace that is promised to those who follow Christ. This serenity about the ways of God and about those of our neighbor and of ourselves is not a disguise for inactivity. Many times not only must work be done, but battles fought, and wrongs righted by those whose first concern is for union with God. But patience is indispensable in our activity, even in the activity which comes from pressing love.

Patience gives us time to see his way for us. In our active works we are constrained from jumping from the monotony, of which active apostolic or charitable works have their share, into gallant efforts to change the world by an ill-advised enthusiasm which brings exhaustion in the end, if not worse. Instead the patient man, whether building a tower or preparing for battle, considers all things in the sight of God (Lk. 14:28 ff.). In this way he grows into spiritual and human maturity. "Let endurance come to its perfection so that you may be fully mature and lacking in nothing" (Is. 1:4).

Patience is also a fruit of love, just as it is a fruit of our trust. Love makes us want to please, want to accept what our faith tells us is the mind of the other. It makes us take the practical steps of acquiring patience, besides asking for it. It also makes us discipline ourselves. We learn to put other things aside and to act promptly when promptness is a part of God's will. When it is not, we learn to control our impetuosity. We wait. We interpose time, but not so much as to inhibit spontaneity or enthusiasm. We stop to consider, not only to see whether we are acting rightly or wisely, but also to make sure that in our activity we are not losing our hold on God. In this way we will not fail in our life even if we fail in our plans. In an ultimate sense the word "failure" does not exist for the patient man.

Patience is one important guarantee of perseverance in the spiritual life but at this point in the spiritual life we may know without argument that we have need of more than we can bring to it ourselves. Even with all the virtues we still stand alone, our poor and unreliable selves, alone before God. And so God has given us another guarantee of perseverance, not a virtue but a person. This person is the Mother of God.

Now of course it is possible to exaggerate the need for Mary. There are people, not many, whom it is necessary to warn not to stop at Mary. God doesn't want it; she doesn't want it, and she showed this at Lourdes by her gestures when she took the prayers of the thousands of rosaries and with her hands raised them to God. As we get to know God better, we know that we do not have to be afraid of him because of our status as imperfect creatures or because of our past sins. The time comes when we are so certain of his love that, even if there were no Blessed Virgin to plead for us, we would be sure of it despite our poverty and mistakes. But this does not mean that she is now not needed.

For instance, at any point in the spiritual life we ought to have learned lessons. But we forget, we temporize, we rationalize. We need someone who

will ask God for more patience with us, for more
grace, especially when we ourselves are blindly unaware of our crucial need. Many who read this book
will become aware that they have missed graces of
union which were given earlier and which they,
like Jerusalem, did not recognize as the time of
God's visitation. Perhaps only through Mary as the
instrument of his mercy can the lost ground be regained and the tired, tepid soul have the heart now
to press on to victory of which earlier it was too
foolishly confident.

All of us must learn that there are certain persons, things, or situations which ought to be avoided
because they have delayed or halted us on the way
to God before. All of us also know that sometimes
these cannot be avoided and that we must pray very
much not to be harmed by them again. How reassuring to know that in our weakness we have someone
to pray with us, someone who is irresistible to God.
How reassuring to have on our side against the
powers of evil from another world this woman who
is strong and valiant, "Who is this that comes forth
like the dawn, as beautiful as the moon, as resplendent as the sun, as awe-inspiring as bannered troops"
(Sg. 6:10), as the Church assures us that Mary is in
adapting these words to her praise.

All this is even more true of the dangers of which
we are not aware. Ultimately it is God who warns us,
protects us, for he alone is the effective operator in
our souls by his grace. But Mary is someone he has
given because it is his plan that men help men, and
again because it is our nature to be helped by woman,
to have need of woman the mother.

Now, there are various ways of insuring the price-
less help of this woman, and they all require that in
some way we belong to her. Not that we do not belong
already by our baptism. By becoming brothers and sis-

ters of Christ, we share a common Father and we share this mother. But we can make this relationship more explicit by our own choice, by our dedication or consecration of ourselves to her. Some do this under the symbol of being her slaves or her servants. But it would seem even better that we do so by becoming more her children, more than we are hers already.

This dedication or consecration as her children seems to have advantages over the symbol of being her slaves. For one thing, whereas the slave is at a distance, the child is not. A child knows intimacy; a slave does not. Moreover, a slave has set hours for his appearances, but the symbolism of a child allows approach at any time there is desire or need. And a child may say anything to his mother and in his own way. Under the symbol of mother we feel psychologically more certain of her because a mother will do anything for a child, but we do not feel so sure in regard to a slave.

This guarantee of perseverance requires more than a perfunctory devotion to her. She must become *the woman* in our lives. We must give her time for herself, as we would any woman we respect and love. And perhaps, if we are so drawn (decidedly we must be drawn), we can give her something more. It is said of the slave that he can give all things into her hands. As her consecrated children we can do the same; all the good things we do and endure, their value before God is put into her hands for her to use as she wills.

Now this proposal to give all may seem as if we have left nothing for our own souls, for those whom we love or must pray for. But on the contrary there are certain things we cannot alienate from our own souls, as well as certain obligations of duty or love which must be fulfilled. Thus, we cannot give away the increase of sanctifying grace that comes to us, for we cannot change the fact that something we have done or endured has made us more pleasing to God. Similarly when we ask for something for ourselves or others, we cannot obliterate the fact that we have asked, and that God has heard us as a loving Father. All these things we may be sure that we will receive from God, enriched by passing through her hands.

But there are other meritorious aspects of every good thought, word, action, and suffering accomplished in the state of grace: the power to entreat God and the power to make atonement or reparation, just because what we have done is something good in his sight. Even though we do not make these a special prayer for some intention, nothing can change the fact that God is more disposed by them to give us what we want or need, or to remove the debts due for our sins. Our merit under these aspects of petition and reparation we can give to others, just as Christ gave us the merit of his own thoughts, words, actions, and sufferings. And to make them best used for souls and for the world, we can give them into Mary's hands for her to use as she wishes on earth or in purgatory, and ourselves be the richer and more secure for it.

In making such an offering, we do not have to invoke Mary on every occasion, just as we do not have to invoke Christ on all the occasions we address the Father. But we make her a most interested associate in our own spiritual life, as well as in the part of our spiritual life that goes out to others. We can pledge ourselves to work under her direction for the salvation of souls, according to the ability and opportunity given to us.

Not all are called to go to Christ so specifically and totally through Mary as this. But if one is drawn or if one is in doubt, he should not dismiss this special relationship untried. A temporary offering, renewed each day, for six months or a year may turn the doubtful man into a convinced and devoted one. But even if this special consecration, or one like it, is not the way God has chosen for us by indicating our attractions and bents, still everyone who loves God and needs his grace should come always closer to Mary as he grows in spiritual life.

It should not need to be said that none of this giving to Mary takes away from the principal child in the family who is Christ our brother. Nothing that Mary does for us could be done without his redemptive sacrifice. Everything we do through her is also done through him. We are drawn closer to him by loving the mother. In honoring her we honor him who chose her.

This may have seemed a digression, and a long one, from our theme of union with God, and yet it is not so. Only God is always the center of our lives; all other things—the humanity of Christ, the sacraments, worship, prayer, good deeds of all sorts, and our sufferings—and the help of Mary—are only the means to get to him. It is the Lord alone who can fill our hearts, and to him we must personally come if we would find out "how good the Lord is! Taste and see!" (Ps. 34:8)

At this relatively advanced point in the spiritual life it is well once more to recall that tasting the Lord, even in contemplative prayer, is still growth; it is not graduation. What if, instead of tasting, we were to eat and devour? This is the experience, the ultimate joy, of those who have gone onward.

Daughters of St. Paul

In Massachusetts
50 St. Paul's Avenue, *Boston*, Mass. 02130
172 Tremont Street, *Boston*, Mass. 02111
In New York
78 Fort Place, *Staten Island*, N.Y. 10301
625 East 187th Street, *Bronx*, N.Y. 10458
525 Main Street, *Buffalo*, N.Y. 14203
In Connecticut
202 Fairfield Avenue, *Bridgeport*, Conn. 06603
In Ohio
2105 Ontario St. (at Prospect Ave.), *Cleveland*, Ohio 44115
In Pennsylvania
1127 South Broad Street, *Philadelphia*, Pa. 19147
In Florida
2700 Biscayne Blvd., *Miami*, Florida 33137
In Louisiana
4403 Veterans Memorial Blvd., Metairie,
New Orleans, La. 70002
86 Bolton Avenue, *Alexandria*, La. 71301
In Missouri
203 Tenth St. (at Pine), *St. Louis*, Mo. 63101
In Texas
114 East Main Plaza, *San Antonio*, Texas 78205
In California
1570 Fifth Avenue, *San Diego*, Calif. 92101
278 17th Street, *Oakland*, Calif. 94612
46 Geary Street, *San Francisco*, Calif. 94108
In Canada
3022 Dufferin Street, *Toronto* 395, Ontario, Canada
In England
57, Kensington Church Street, *London* W. 8, England
In Australia
58, Abbotsford Rd., Homebush, N.S.W., *Sydney* 2140,
Australia
In Africa
35, Jones Street, P.O. Box 3243, *Lagos*, Nigeria